T209 Information and Communication Technologies:
people and interactions

Security Techniques in Digital Systems

Prepared for the T209 course team by John Monk

This text forms part of an Open University course T209 *Information and Communication Technologies: people and interactions.*

Details of this and other Open University courses can be obtained from the Course Information and Advice Centre, PO Box 724, The Open University, Milton Keynes MK7 6ZS, United Kingdom: tel. +44 (0)1908 653231, e-mail ces-gen@open.ac.uk

Alternatively, you may visit the Open University website at http://www.open.ac.uk where you can learn more about the wide range of courses and packs offered at all levels by The Open University.

To purchase this publication or other components of Open University courses, contact Open University Worldwide Ltd, The Open University, Walton Hall, Milton Keynes MK7 6AA, United Kingdom: tel. +44 (0)1908 858785; fax +44 (0)1908 858787; e-mail ouwenq@open.ac.uk; website http://www.ouw.co.uk

First published 2002. Second edition 2003

Edited, designed and typeset by The Open University.

Printed in the UK by The Alden Group, Oxford.

ISBN 0 7492 5825 X

2.1

Preface

Security techniques in systems around the globe run by governments, organizations, companies and individuals protect data of inestimable value from corruption, error, theft and destruction. A great deal is at stake. It is only possible in an introductory volume to give a flavour of how a measure of security is achieved in digital systems. This book is therefore *not* a practical guide to creating secure systems but an introduction to some of the techniques and vocabulary employed in describing secure systems. No examples in this book should be taken as recipes for achieving security without a great deal more analysis and debate. Indeed, most of the examples in this book are chosen because of their illustrative power and certainly not because they have been analysed for their robustness.

It cannot be stressed too much that the barriers created by secure systems are continually being breached, and that many of these security breaches are a result of carelessness, a lack of imagination about how adversaries might operate and somehow the difficulty of thinking things through. Security technology, therefore, is not enough.

I have described a number of techniques and, for some of them, I have described circumstances under which they will fail to achieve their authors' objectives. In doing so I am not trying to explain how faults are detected. In the field of security, this is still notoriously difficult. The point of revealing failures is that it exposes what the failed technique can and cannot achieve. This helps to establish what needs to be specified when setting out to create new or modified security features. Examination of failures also demonstrates the fallibility of designers – no matter how well-qualified and experienced. Finally, looking at failures often provides a fascinating way of learning about techniques and notations for describing them.

For the serious student of secure systems this book can only be a part of the beginning.[1] Security in digital systems is a broad topic stretching from padlocks to quantum cryptography. The focus in this book is on the outlines of how encryption is performed and on outlines of the protocols that are used in secure communications. The aim is to put the reader in a position to be able to approach specialist articles on security in computers and communication systems and to illustrate some of the computational tasks that have to be performed in providing secure computer and communication systems.

John Monk

10 April 2001

Author's acknowledgements

I would like to thank David Reed, Judith Williams and Nicky Moss for their patient reading of drafts of this book, their helpful suggestions, their attention to detail and the resulting improvements.

Contents

CHAPTER ONE: WHAT IS SECURITY?

CHAPTER TWO: ENCRYPTION

CHAPTER THREE: MORE ENCRYPTION

CHAPTER FOUR: USING ENCRYPTION

CHAPTER FIVE: PROTOCOLS

CHAPTER SIX: AUTHENTICATION

Chapter One

What is security?

Security is a feeling that offers freedom from anxieties that arise from uncertainty. Technology can soothe these anxieties by providing information and tools that help to predict what other people or organizations will do. Technology, though, can also undermine security by hiding information or by presenting convincing but misleading predictions. Security measures and technologies are, therefore, devices that people can use for manipulating their relationships with others.

Just because surprising or disagreeable events do not affect me does not mean that I feel secure. I may not have anticipated my trouble-free future and, therefore, felt vulnerable and insecure although the passage of time may show I had nothing to worry about.

I can divide causes of insecurity into four categories relating to uncertainties about:

- acts of nature
- my own reactions to events
- what other people might do
- what institutions or organizations might arrange to do to me.

Institutions are impersonal bodies. Dealing with an institution often means dealing with personnel who know me only through the records that it maintains. The agents of institutions act towards me in ways governed by those records. Insecurity generated by institutions and organizations therefore arises from worries about how institutional records are kept, maintained, protected, conveyed, publicized and interpreted.

1.1   Military emphasis

Security, as a feeling, is built on confidence, trust and familiarity. Secret codes are only a component of the diffuse activities that promote security, or insecurity.

Early writing about security emphasized military applications where finding out the disposition of an opponent gave an armed force a strategic advantage. Military handbooks have therefore stressed the benefits and techniques for maintaining secrecy and for deceiving the enemy. Cryptography, the study of secret codes, has been a primary ingredient of military science. In diplomacy, secret codes also have a place, but security in diplomacy comes from assurances about the authenticity of diplomatic communications and the credentials of the diplomats.

The expansion of communication networks to a wider public, since the early days of the telegraph, has encouraged the gradual development of commercial uses of communication systems. Commercial transactions whether conducted locally or at a distance require a degree of trust and do not necessarily demand secrecy. Shared secrets, though, can help to provide assurances about the identity of the people I am dealing with and thus contribute to the integrity of a deal.

1.1.1 Insecurity

Because security is about what *might* happen to us and we cannot know that with certainty, our feelings of security are governed by accounts of possibilities. Of course, prior experiences help us see certain prospective situations as being plausible – what has happened to us, or to people close to us, in the past affects what we think might happen to us in the future. Other people's accounts of what has happened to them will also influence our vision of what might happen to us. It is not surprising, therefore, that people show an interest in news and gossip about people like themselves. Perhaps unconsciously, they wonder whether they are likely to find themselves in similar circumstances and, without thinking, assess how closely their own situation resembles the situations of characters in news stories or tales with disagreeable outcomes. Inducing feelings of security in others, therefore, means getting them to pay attention to plausible fictions in which they recognize themselves as a potential character who remains unscathed. Equally, feelings of insecurity can be induced by alternative fictions in which a character, who resonates with the listener, suffers.

In warfare, inflicting casualties on opponents not only weakens by extinguishing them, but also brings a reality to the fears of uninjured survivors, lessening their resolve and feeding them with material for recounting plausible dramas with forbidding outcomes. Of course, the victors as well as the vanquished will see new suffering and cannot remain unaffected. The Cold War demonstrated that insecurity and warfare are less about doing damage and more about the creation of myths that induce fears and move whole populations to direct their activities in ways that the antagonist prefers. The myths of the Cold War, though, affected people and their politics whichever side they believed themselves to be on.

When people are insecure, they become preoccupied by what might happen to them and are distracted from following their own agenda. Methods of inducing insecurity are therefore political devices – they drive people to behave cautiously and alter the priorities they assign to their potential actions. Sources of insecurity are sometimes artfully exploited. This is starkly evident where there are oppressive governments, petty dictators and military actions, but in common domestic, social and business contexts, usually without the same brutality, we similarly induce feelings of security and insecurity in colleagues, partners, relations, friends and acquaintances with the intent of affecting the way they behave towards us.

The legends and histories we construct about our communities influence our feelings of security, and, on a more banal level, advertising often plays on the potential to induce feelings of security or insecurity in our personal relationships. Children are commonly told simple moral tales that they can identify with and which induce in them feelings of security and insecurity. From such examples, it is evident that feelings of security or insecurity can be manipulated by:

- telling certain tales

- encouraging others to tell those tales

- fabricating or collecting real or counterfeit evidence that makes those tales plausible

- generating events that stimulate the creation of accounts which incorporate those tales.

These manipulations can be subverted by:

- discouraging the telling of those tales

- offering credible evidence that makes the tales implausible

- hiding evidence that makes the stories plausible

- altering the circumstances so that a tale ceases to be relevant.

Attempts to directly counter any undesired but effectual tale may well result in confusion, and confusion and its accompanying uncertainty can also increase feelings of insecurity.

1.1.2 Surprise

In the military sphere, Clausewitz, the eighteenth century general, saw '[s]ecrecy and rapidity'[2] as the two factors that cultivate 'the surprise of the enemy' which, in warfare, he claimed 'lies more or less at the foundation of all undertakings'[3] and when a surprise 'is successful in a high degree, confusion and broken courage in the enemy's ranks are the consequences'.[4] Thus, according to Clausewitz, secrecy generates surprises, which disturb an opponent whose insecurity might also be heightened by deceptions. Deception, whether intended or not, is a component of security, and is central to military strategy.

> 'Stratagem implies a concealed intention ... It has therefore ... a great deal to do with deceit ... The deceiver leaves it to the person he is deceiving to commit the errors of understanding ...' [5]

Creating a deception, like creating a surprise, involves hiding things and information about things from an opponent. All participants rely on information, which Clausewitz characterizes as 'all the knowledge which we have of the enemy and his country; therefore, in fact, the foundation of all our ideas and actions'.[6] But through omission, error and deception this information cannot always be relied upon and Clausewitz warns his readers to be wary:

> 'Let us consider the nature of this foundation, its want of trustworthiness, its changefulness, and we shall soon feel what a dangerous edifice War is.' [7]

Thus, Clausewitz points towards the requirements for mechanisms that might offer a military general increased feelings of security. Devices or procedures that might have given him confidence would have:

- kept things secret from his enemy (but not necessarily from his own generals)

- cross-checked to seek out discrepancies and changes in the information that is received

- associated a measure of trustworthiness with the information provided by others

- provided assurances about the timeliness of information

- offered a channel, directed at an opponent, for deceptive propaganda.

1.1.3   Secrecy

The military influence on studies of secure systems is evident in the terminology. For example, in his paper 'Communication Theory of Secrecy Systems', Claude Shannon, the father of Information Theory, in a footnote explains that 'The word "enemy", stemming from military applications, is commonly used in cryptographic work to denote anyone who may intercept a cryptogram'.[8] Similarly, attempts to breach security are often referred to as 'attacks'.

In the 1920s, G.S. Vernam recognized, in 'conversations with officers of the Signal Corps',[9] that secrecy was of prime importance in military operations and he went on to develop a coding scheme that he claimed was 'absolutely unbreakable'. He wrote about

> 'The desirability of obtaining secrecy in telegraphic communications and the … advantages of a system that would be capable of sending messages in such a form as to be entirely secret …' [10]

This deep interest of the military, the diplomats and spies in security has meant that earlier studies of security concentrated on secrecy. Secrecy is also of interest to those who wish to evade the law and who try to hide evidence from the detection and prosecution agencies. The exposure of these incriminating secrets is therefore of interest to the law enforcement bureaux. Because of these vested interests the technology of secrecy systems has seen substantial development both in the methods for keeping things secret and in the methods for cracking codes – known as *cryptanalysis*. The creation of secret codes has also proved to be a fascinating task for mathematicians.

Vernam proposed two different methods for keeping things secret. He wrote,

> 'There appear to be two general methods for securing secrecy in connection with communication, namely, (1) by preventing or at least attempting to prevent access to the messages or to the lines of communication and, in the case of telegraphic communication by rendering the lines incapable of being tapped, and (2) by the use of codes or ciphers with key systems known only to the proper parties.' [11]

His first technique might be called *access control* and includes physical measures or deterrents that prevent or persuade intruders to abandon their attempts to penetrate communication links. Even in present day communication and computer systems, the physical security provided by locked doors, strong walls, fences, alarms and even armed guards still have a role.

Vernam's second approach uses codes to camouflage the data. In a computer or on a digital communication link everything is reduced to a digital alphabet often of strings or arrays of bits – sequences of ones and zeros – that can be interpreted and presented in some meaningful way. These bits can be transformed to make the process of interpretation of the transformed bits more convoluted, less obvious and known only to a few people. A systematic procedure, like Vernam's, that obfuscates data is called an *encryption* process and the corresponding systematic process for recovering data is called *decryption*.

From the times of the Spartans in the fifth century BC, there are records of the use of encryption and devices for encryption. [12] The definitive source on early encryption techniques and security incidents is David Kahn's encyclopaedic work *The Codebreakers*. [13] It is clear from this book that military applications of encryption and their close cousins, diplomatic communications, have been pre-eminent. But there are also many accounts of subversive messages and texts encrypted to avoid challenges by religious or state authorities or even close companions especially when hiding the content of billets-doux exchanged in clandestine affairs. Marie Antoinette is known to have corresponded with her lovers using different codes, and the advertisement columns of *The Times* in the Victorian era commonly carried advertisements containing encrypted messages from one estranged lover to another.[14] There is also evidence of the creation of secret codes and their decryption as an enduring pastime.[15]

Encryption involves encoding a text in a secret convoluted code, which is intended to be intricate enough to allow only those who know the code to recover the text, though there is a long history of successful attempts at cracking codes, often accompanied by consequent dramatic circumstances.[16] To protect the data, potential snoopers must be prevented from finding out how encryption and decryption is done. It is common practice to have a fixed set of procedures for encrypting data that take strings of bits together with an additional secret item – the key. Each possible key will cause data to be obfuscated in a different way, so the procedures for revealing camouflaged data are incomplete without knowledge of the key. The encryption key is the key to completing the encryption of data and the decryption key is the key to the subsequent recovery of the original data.

Auguste Kerckhoffs[17] published, in 1883, an influential book entitled *La Cryptographie Militaire*. In his book Kerckhoffs spelt out a doctrine that still guides security specialists.[18] The doctrine stressed the importance of cryptographic systems with easily remembered procedures. Kerckhoffs also wrote that the people communicating in secret should not be troubled if their systems, or procedures, were discovered. He pointed out that it would be impossible to keep a successful method of encryption secret, since an attractive method would flourish and the sheer number of people involved would ensure that either by accident or deliberately, the procedures would be exposed. It has therefore been common to assume that an adversary knows how encryption is performed but secrets are kept because he or she does not know the keys used to encrypt and decrypt messages.

1.1.4 Commerce

While, no doubt, work continues on developing secure systems for military use, security has become an issue for commerce. It seems that:

> 'Products are becoming digital. Markets are becoming electronic.'[19]

Consequently,

> 'Information has matured into an asset of growing value, with marketable quantities and prices. It is the new digital gold and is one of the most valuable resources at our disposal.'[20]

Such valuable products require protection. Examples of 'information products' include 'financial analyses and news broadcasts' [21] or even 'online museums that can charge "visitors" for reproducing images or even levy an entry fee' [22]. Money itself is stored and transferred less and less in the shape of notes and coins and more and more as recorded digits and '[c]ash and capital … are being replaced by information'.[23] The kinds of things that are now seen as products are the strings of bits that animate '[n]ew kinds of devices … that handle … text, numbers, voice, photos, videos – in digital form'.[24]

Often in commerce, the issue is not whether products should be secret or not but how to ensure that people are operating within their rights. For instance, people can buy musical recordings, and there are no penalties for buying copies from authorized retailers. However, purchases are deals in which the buyer and the seller implicitly stipulate conditions. Most purchases institute a tacit contract that limits the rights of the purchaser, for instance, the sale of recorded music implies that purchasers buy principally the right to play the recording for their own enjoyment. Purchasers are usually requested not to exploit the recording commercially and undermine the profits of the original vendor. For commerce, then, security issues are often about preventing the misappropriation of rights.

1.1.5 Summary

A gradual transition towards the commercial use of digital systems has increased the refinements required of security devices. The emphasis in writing about military systems is on secrecy, but in commercial systems, the partners are assigned rights. Security is then translated into instruments for maintaining rights.

Ultimately, security and insecurity are feelings and they depend not only on security measures, but also how these measures are perceived. Security hinges on how much people trust one another and how much credence they give to documents, messages and notices that they pass between them.

Encryption and *decryption* are therefore useful techniques in achieving a degree of security but they too are only effective if people are confident of their effectiveness. Security is a feeling and is affected by propaganda and emotion as well as the availability of security technologies. Visibly locked doors, muscular guards and thick walls still have a role to play.

1.2 Rights

Breaches of security can be described as the unauthorized exercising of rights. Acts of treason, for example, do not necessarily involve stealing things. Spies often make copies or report on things. They act as agents in transferring a copy or a report to their spymasters while leaving the original material intact. Spies, in terms of rights, exceed their rights by observing things they are not entitled to see or reporting on things to people who they are not at liberty to inform. Breaches of confidentiality, therefore, can be interpreted as a deceitful exploitation of others' rights.

If everyone knew their rights, stayed within the bounds of their rights and their actions did not infringe others' rights then no special mechanisms would be needed. However, people do attempt to exceed the bounds of their rights – out of ignorance, through errors, from some nefarious intent or because they have contradictory rights to draw on and maintain.

1.2.1 Variety

Data has become a commodity and copies of the data and agreements about its use are traded. Laws, too, regulate the uses of certain types of data. The requirements for security can, therefore, emerge as a by-product of entertaining certain agreements or laws. For instance, a European directive 'requires personal data to be protected from, among other things, unauthorised access by hackers'[25] and this, therefore, imposes a duty on the keeper of such data to hold it securely.

Receiving a copy of the data, therefore, makes the recipient a custodian who through trading agreements and the law becomes bound to restrict the uses of copies of data he or she acquires. Data itself does not necessarily provide a record about how it was acquired, what restrictions there are on its use and how it has been used. To demonstrate that they have operated within the law and kept their side of any bargains, custodians will need to show that they have limited people's access to the data and that only authorized users have exploited the data in an authorized manner.

Prudent organizations keep records of the transactions that they engage in and periodically check the recorded actions of individuals against the privileges that they have been assigned. These records help detect unwarranted attempts by unauthorized people to exercise privileges that they are not entitled to. The records also help the guardians of data to mount a defence when they are confronted by false accusations about their negligence.

There is a growing sophistication in the classification of rights and hence in what can be traded and what needs to be protected:

> 'Digital rights fall into several natural categories. Transport rights include permission to copy, transfer or loan. Render rights allow for playing and printing. Derivative work rights include extracting and editing information and embedding it in other publications.'[26]

The situation has changed rapidly as laws and international trading agreements have caught up with technological developments. For instance, 'software development … evolved from being a legally defenseless enterprise to one in which almost every innovation is a candidate for patent protection'.[27] Software writers can, therefore, cite the law to limit the use of copies of their work but, more importantly for commerce, they are also in a position to sell rights for the use of their software. Software, documents, pictures and recordings are valued for one reason or another, and taking copies increases the supply of what were once unique artefacts and sources of information. Taking copies of valuable data might be considered to be a kind of theft because the unbounded creation of new copies devalues extant copies and the original, and reduces the powers of those holding them. Profitable digital commerce, therefore, relies on measures that prevent copying and offer effective policing of tradeable rights.

Deals are struck that give people the right to use strings of bits but their rights may be restricted. They may, for instance, not be authorized to give other people copies. A vendor of rights for a string of bits may feel insecure about this and may wish to deter people from taking further, illicit copies. Politicians, too, may worry about leaked duplicates of sensitive documents and similarly wish to deter the broadcast of copies. Vendors and politicians are likely to base their case for restricting the use or distribution of data on assertions about the need to prevent breaches of rights.

1.2.2 Personal data

Rights, of course, are sometimes infringed so, in practice, claimed rights are expectations. Claims are made, for instance, about rights to privacy and rights of ownership. Bill Gates sums up some contemporary expectations:

> 'You don't want an impostor getting into your government records any more than you'd want an unauthorised person to see your bank account.' [28]

The availability of rights and the knowledge that others will uphold them is one source of security. It has, for example, become the custom to keep medical records confidential. Medical records are collected through interactions with a variety of medical agencies. There are many people involved so the data in a record is not secret, but many people would not want them to be in general circulation. They would rather hope that medical records were made available only to medical personnel who have the skill and the duty to treat an individual. Confidentiality is therefore not the same as secrecy, but implies that readers and writers must be fulfilling specific roles before they have the right to read or modify the data. A breach of confidentiality can put data in the hands of people who might wish to exploit the publication of the data or the threat of its publication.

Disclosures of documents, pictures or recordings that are in preparation and ill-drafted, that make libellous assertions, that report on embarrassing situations or that expose secretive plans of intended actions before they are carried out are potential sources of insecurity. The mechanisms required to avoid such transgressions and maintain confidentiality are not intended to keep the records hidden away but to allow them to circulate and be accessible only to authorized people (that is, people with access rights). This requires methods for keeping the records from some people, making them available to others, and a means of authorizing and identifying individuals and occasionally withdrawing their authorization. Confidentiality, therefore, demands a collection of co-ordinated organizational practices or protocols.

1.2.3 Mechanisms

Security mechanisms that record events and alert authorities to infringements of rights are useful for detecting deceptions, but they may be felt to be intrusive. People feel insecure about records kept about them because they do not know how those records will be used, how they might be correlated with other records, or how mistakes or misinterpretations will be corrected. Those being observed may worry about why they are being treated with suspicion, while the security gained by keeping records of some people's actions may accrue to others who are not recorded and observed or who are not averse to having their actions traced. There is, then, a conflict between those who expect a surveillance system to make them feel more secure and those who are anxious about the uses of the observations. Some may object so strongly that they will do all in their power to subvert the system, and, in spite of the surveillance technology, some will still go about their malevolent business out of desperation, ignorance or the optimistic hope that the security mechanisms will be ineffective.

There is a conflict between those who believe privacy is an inalienable right and those who think that tracing people's movements is an essential and rightful contribution to the security of individuals. Such conflicts of principles arise in debates about security and, in practice, the increased security of one group is likely to diminish the security of another group. The exercising of the rights of one individual or group on occasion prevents another group or individual from asserting their rights. For example, an employer might feel more secure in knowing a great deal about potential employees, but the candidates may be concerned about revealing too much about themselves to employers, not necessarily because they have a shady past, but because handing over some personal details might, at some stage, provide the employer with additional power. Weighing up the gains and losses of security is not a matter of simple arithmetic, and any proposal for a security system is liable to be contested, often with both sides battling under the banner of their notions of fairness.

1.2.4 Trust

Subjects of surveillance and other data collection systems would, in most cases, want the data about them to reflect on them honestly and would want to be assured that alterations could not be made casually. They would also want to be sure that the data was not being treated carelessly or made readily available to snoopers who could use the data to abuse the subject of the data by, for example, targeting junk mail or, worse, stalking their subject. People may not be the victims of explicit abuse but the uncertainty about how the data that is held about them is handled can be enough to make them feel insecure.

People are likely to gain some sense of security, therefore, if they know why the data is being collected and if they feel they can trust the collector to take care of the data and to use it only for the declared purposes. This trust is partly a product of views about the reliability of technology for storing data and partly a product of the reputation and hence the practices of the data collector.

Diplomats conduct international affairs away from their native country. The science of diplomatics originally provided techniques for deciphering diplomas, documents, charters and manuscripts and for establishing their authenticity, date of origin and the identity of signatories. This science was an essential component of discourse amongst states since the forgery of communication was a potentially valuable political tool. Similar practices are now needed to authenticate digital data that is communicated at a distance. Checks are needed on the authenticity of data, the integrity of data, the author of the data and the timeliness of the data.

One way of gaining confidence in an item of data is to call in a trustworthy third party, such as a notary, to inspect and analyse the data and its sources. *Notaries* are people who certify documents and are taken to be trustworthy. Their certification of a document gives guarantees about the source of the document and the time and date of its existence. Sometimes a text will describe an idea that, for example, later becomes the subject of a patent. The patent may be valuable and contested. In settling patent claims, precedence is given to the earliest expression of the idea. Thus a reliable, certifiable date endorsed by a notary adds security to claims about the ownership of the patent, and hence who has the right to exploit the idea.

1.2.5 Summary

Security can be formulated in terms of individual rights and the willingness of others to uphold those rights. Rights encapsulate views on how people should behave towards one another and one another's property. Information technology turns documents and individual identity into data, and commerce turns data into property. The maintenance of rights then becomes a set of practices in handling data. In some instances one practice will come into conflict with another and rights have to be seen as expectations which may not be fulfilled. Insecurity arises where anticipated rights are clearly breached or where the people or technologies that handle the data cannot be relied upon. Security goes hand in hand with trust.

1.3 Threats

Security is an issue where something of value is at stake. Those wanting to grab or destroy the valued commodity have no need to follow rules. This confronts those charged with maintaining security with a difficulty. They cannot generate safeguards or countermeasures when they are unaware of the threats. Analysis of secure systems therefore involves speculating on possible threats to security, appraising the likely effects of such breaches of security and assessing the likelihood of the threats manifesting themselves. Such an analysis, though, can only be tentative and this implies that, even when the analysis is acted on, a contingency plan will be needed when the unexpected occurs.

1.3.1 Intrusion

Parts of information systems are frequently left unattended and this gives intruders the opportunity to interfere. Communication links are installed to allow the transmission of data; these links also provide openings into computers for intruders and they also carry data that may be of value.

Some people may realize that data held in an information system is of use to them, because it helps them to learn something of value, because they can trade it with someone who values the data, because meddling with the data can bring them some advantages or disadvantage others, because disrupting other people's business brings them attention or because they get some satisfaction from upsetting institutions or routines. People who are likely to be disadvantaged by the actions of intruders would, of course, prefer to see mechanisms that deterred or otherwise prevented intrusions. Physical protection can help; for instance, computers can be kept in locked rooms, and mobile computers can be locked in drawers. Obviously, if controlling the access to data involves locking computers away then some care needs to be taken over who has the key, and if the key is lost then some kind of plan for replacing the locks will allow swift remedial action to take place.

1.3.2 Inference

Cunning spies can build up a valuable picture by observing a number of incidental details and then making a deduction. Inadvertently, providing people with data from which they can draw inferences can therefore compromise security.

For instance, computer systems frequently require a user name and a password before they can be used. A total stranger would not only have to find a valid password but would also need to find a valid user name. Now if an invalid user name is entered, the computer can reject the request without needing to check the password. In one particular computer system, the software exploited this. When someone typed in a valid user name then the password was checked but if an invalid user name was typed then the password was not checked and the request for access was immediately rejected. Consequently, a request with a valid user name and an invalid password took half a second longer to process than an invalid user name and an invalid password.[29] A hacker could therefore discover valid user names by noting the response time.

Once the loophole was recognized, the software was changed so that the password was always checked although this was not strictly necessary on some occasions. After the modification, a request with a valid or an invalid name took about the same time to process.

1.3.3   Fallibility

Unexpected gains and losses are created by deliberate, unauthorized acts and also through the careless application of procedures or through the failure of machines to operate as anticipated.

The failure to follow security procedures and the failures of security technology are threats to safekeeping. Failures cut two ways: they can fail to protect a resource but they can also point a finger at the innocent. Security technology, therefore, protects not only valuables but also the reputation and liberty of its authorized users. For example, in a heart-breaking incident, a teenager from Ashton under Lyne in England was convicted of stealing forty pounds from her father although it later transpired that there had not been a theft but a clerical error at the bank.[30]

The reliability of security processes and their vulnerability is entangled with questions of justice and the value of what is protected. Reliability is a central issue for those who wish to maintain secure systems. A comprehensive security policy needs to take account of the reliability of security equipment and procedures and also the measures that promise justice[31] in the event of equipment or procedural failure. Where the evidence of intrusion is dubious or weak (and sometimes where the evidence appears strong) there is a danger of injustice.

Well-publicized injustices are likely to drive people away from the use of secure systems. This highlights a paradox, that excessive enthusiasm for security can make systems unusable and drive people towards easy-to-use insecure systems. Dictators may be able to coerce people into maintaining arduous and costly procedures but for many everyday uses, practical security measures involve balancing the cost of security breaches against convenience. It becomes not a matter of making things secure but of making the security risks and costs acceptable while maintaining a high standard of justice.

1.3.4   Carelessness, mistakes and inertia

Sometimes unwitting errors are mistakenly attributed to security breaches. Such false attributions can undermine confidence in the security procedures that are in place. For instance, in one incident, students were reported to have broken into a computer system and altered their recorded marks. Special security precautions had been taken, for instance the computer system apparently required two passwords. However, a break-in was not needed – the records were altered on a computer that was left unattended after the authorized users had already logged on.[32]

In another incident, a newspaper reported that an unknown intruder had altered the recorded marks of students.[33] In the class of 120, twenty had their marks lowered and two had them raised. The alterations were reported as though there had been a breach of security. The following day the newspaper carried a sequel, which attributed the changes to an administrative error. It was reported that the marks had been altered when a teaching assistant used the computer to sort the list of names in a particular order, but had unwittingly left the marks in the old sequence.[34]

New technologies can demand new and specialized skills that may be awkward to practise or learn, or might interfere with other activities. There is a temptation to reject such technology and, as a result, compromise security simply because old, inadequate security procedures are being followed. Kahn in his book *The Codebreakers* reports that in the First World War at times some Russian soldiers found the use of newly introduced security coding systems too demanding and so resorted to older methods that could easily be decoded by the enemy forces.[35]

1.3.5   Summary

Threats are potential actions that can undermine security and allow an intruder, an impostor or eavesdropper to gain access and meddle with data with significant consequences. There are some technological devices that can provide a defence, but firstly people have to be aware of the threats, secondly they have to install the countermeasures, thirdly the technology has to be operable and finally people have to take security sufficiently seriously so that they carry out the procedures that ensure that the technology is effective.

1.4 Passwords

People impersonate others in order to gain unauthorized access or to conduct unauthorized business with the intent of defrauding others. Credentials and other means of identification guard against impostors. There are a number of variations. Some systems, for example, require a personal card together with a personal identification number (PIN). People are identified by one or more of the following:

- something unique that they have, like an identity card or a key

- something secret that they remember – a password or PIN

- an idiosyncratic skill, like a signature

- some characteristic bodily image, such as a fingerprint.

All these techniques can lose their identifying power. If they are treated carelessly, keys can be lost, passwords can be written down and read by others. Signatures can be forged. The requirement for bodily images can incite desperate people to violent acts. The potential profit from the corrupt use of identification technology will also tempt some insiders responsible for maintaining security to make their identifying tokens available to unauthorized outsiders. In effect, they rent out their identity.

1.4.1 Break-ins

It is hard to get information on how people break-into computer systems. People whose computers have been broken into do not want to reveal to others how hackers have gained access either because they do not wish to reveal weaknesses in their systems or because the incident is embarrassing. But it is clear that to break-into all sorts of systems what is needed is a user or account name or number, and a PIN or password. Finding one of these pieces of data reduces the effort the hacker has to expend.

Sometimes the hacker is given both pieces of information. In one banking system, for instance, customers gained access to cash machines by offering a card that carried the full details of their account number and a PIN. On completion of a transaction, the machine issued a paper record of the transaction with the account number printed on it. Many people carelessly threw away the paper record. A crook was able to pick up the slips and read the account numbers while an accomplice looked over people's shoulders and made a note of the PINs that they entered. The lawbreakers were then able to forge new cards and, with the stolen PINs, withdraw money from people's accounts without their knowledge.[36]

A number of reports on password choice and on break-ins have been published and reveal that carelessness and, occasionally, technology failures are the causes of many security breaches.

1.4.2 Passwords

Passwords – a secret shared by an authority and someone else – are an ancient form of identification; giving the correct password is taken as a sign of the identity of individuals who are authorized by their knowledge of the secret password to conduct business. Stripped to the bare essentials this kind of authentication requires a well-kept secret that is known by both a gatekeeper or sentry and someone who wishes to pass. Of course, if their secret were let out then, to maintain their security, the owners of the password would need to generate a new secret and stop responding to the old one. Indeed, someone who used a withdrawn password might draw suspicion to him or herself and thus aid his or her detection. Records of password use can therefore be helpful in policing a system.

It has become customary for computer operating systems to require users to identify themselves with a user name and a corresponding password before they can use the computing resource. Password systems utilize existing interfaces of information systems and their mechanisms are incorporated in the operating system software. Password systems have, on occasions, been shown to be vulnerable. Many security breaches have occurred because hackers have obtained access to a computer by uncovering unchallenging passwords of users with minimal privileges; they have then exploited any software bugs that give them access to services that should strictly only be available to highly privileged users. Using their illicitly gained privileges, the hackers are then in a position to meddle in the operation of the computer and possibly obtain privileged access to other computers on a network.

1.4.3 A worm

Anyone wanting to break-into a computer can keep trying different passwords until he or she gains access. However, even with a four-digit PIN there are ten thousand possibilities and an intruder might well be discouraged by the time and effort that might be needed to find the right combination of digits. In networked systems, computers are linked to one another and it is sometimes feasible to get one computer to keep trying to log-in to another using a succession of different passwords. The computer will doggedly keep trying and will run through the combinations faster than a person can.

The Internet Worm, an early computer worm, disrupted the Internet. A computer worm is a program that does not damage other programs or files but reproduces itself. It disrupts the operation of a computer by consuming more and more of the computing resources as it reproduces and prevents other programs from running.

> 'After breaking in, the program would replicate itself and the replica would also attempt to infect other systems … [T]he program spread quickly, as did the confusion and consternation … [T]he scope of the breakins came as a great surprise to almost everyone … The most noticeable effect … was that systems became more and more loaded with running processes as they became repeatedly infected. As time went on, some of these machines … were unable to continue any processing; some machines failed completely …'[37]

In order to propagate, the Internet Worm broke into user accounts and did so by trying a range of passwords. First '[t]he worm checked the obvious case of no password'.[38] It then used the account name and some other accessible administrative data. It tried 'the account name, the account name concatenated with itself, the first and last names of the user, the user names with leading capital letters turned to lower case, and the account name reversed'.[39] One study[40] has shown that where no special measures are taken to inform users about the use of passwords then these variations may work for up to 30% of accounts.

If, in its initial attempts, the Internet Worm failed, it had a list of 432 words it would try. Finally, it would use a dictionary of words accessible in the installed copies of the particular operating system it infected and,

> 'For each word … the worm would see if it was the password to any account. In addition, if the word in the dictionary began with an upper case letter, the letter was converted to lower case and that word was also tried.'[41]

In order to infect a string of computers the worm exploited a series of weaknesses, one was a weakness in one of the services that computers were running – this has since been corrected. To gain access to the service the worm relied on what became known as weak passwords – passwords that were relatively easy to guess. In a detailed study[42] of password files, a search for commonly known combinations of characters uncovered almost a quarter of the passwords: 2.7% were found to be variations of an amalgamation of users' names and the names of their accounts; 0.2% were found to be repeated characters. Keyboard patterns and common vulgar phrases contributed 1.8%. 2.2% were male or female names and 7.4% were in a commonly accessible twenty-four thousand word computer-based dictionary.

Trial and error is an approach used by hackers and their job can be made much more difficult by increasing the number of characters in a password. However, in the study, of the passwords that were cracked 2.3% were three characters or less and around 15% were only four or five characters long, about a third were only six characters long.

1.4.4 A hacker

In his thrilling account of his work in tracking down a computer hacker, Clifford Stoll describes how the hacker gained access to a computer and was able to gain significant privileges through a 'subtle bug in an obscure section of a popular program'.[43] Stoll explained that, at the time of the break-in,

> 'on our ... computer, the ... editor lets you forward a mail file from your own directory to anyone else ...'[44]

This proved to be serious because 'It let anyone move a file into protected systems space' and so the hacker was able to plant 'his phoney program where the system expected to find a valid one'[45] and when the system ran the program it gave the hacker super-user privileges. Thus although the hacker entered through an ordinary user's account he was able to masquerade as a highly privileged user because of a software bug. This is a problem that has been widely acknowledged:

> 'if a hacker obtains a login on a machine, there is a good chance he can become root[46] sooner or later. There are many buggy programs that run at high privileged levels that offer opportunities for a cracker. If he gets a login on your computer, you are in trouble.'[47]

Stoll's account shows some ways in which hackers use their pirated privileges on one computer to gain access to other computers. To avoid such incursions, therefore, all users need to be careful about their selection of passwords.

John D. Howard, who studied extensive records of security incidents on the Internet reported in his doctoral thesis that:

> '[t]he most frequently recorded vulnerability involved various problems with passwords (21.8%). Most of the password vulnerabilities were in three categories: *password files*, which indicated that a password file had been copied (13.8%), *password cracking*, generally indicating that passwords had been determined by the operation of a password cracking tool (10.4%), and *weak passwords*, which could easily be guessed (3.6%).'[48]

Howard's view is that

> 'Good passwords have the following characteristics: 1) eight or more characters, 2) both uppercase and lowercase letters, 3) punctuation or other special characters, 4) easily remembered (no need to write down), and 5) can be typed quickly.'[49]

Experiments have been conducted using computer-generated passwords to create sequences that are not commonly found in dictionaries, but the results have not always been encouraging. Stoll reports that:

> 'To keep people from guessing passwords into their supercomputer, Livermore … used random computer-generated passwords, like agnitfom and ngagk. Naturally nobody can remember these passwords. Result? Some people save their passwords in computer files.' [50]

The administrator that Stoll contacted 'saw the problem as ignorant users, not unfriendly systems that forced people to use bizarre passwords'.[51]

One practical suggestion is to make a password out of the initial letters of a phrase. This makes it easy to remember while having an unusual combination of letters. Putting in proper names adds capitals and numbers add digits. So 'It costs 10 pounds to travel to Brighton on Saturday' would give a proposed password of 'Ic1ptttBoS'. Of course, if a user chose a well-known advertising slogan or a line from a popular song, the technique would not be so robust.

1.4.5   Exploiting privileges

Once hackers gain access, they can set about finding further identification data stored in the computer system. Stoll explains that, '… A hacker with super-user privileges would hold the computer hostage … He could … erase his own tracks'.[52] Stoll's hacker, for instance, was able to examine e-mails and, in some cases, the authors of the e-mails had given their names and passwords – one e-mail included the lines:

> 'If you need to get any of my data just log into my account …
> Account name is Wilson, password is Maryanne' [53]

An unfortunate situation can arise when files containing passwords become accessible. In one early incident, passwords were shown to everyone using the computer:

> '… when a system administrator … at MIT was editing the password file and another system administrator was editing the daily message that is printed on everyone's terminal on login. Due to a software design error, the temporary editor files of the two users were interchanged and thus, for a time, the password file was printed on every terminal when it was logged in.' [54]

One precaution is to store, not the passwords, but encrypted versions of the passwords. When anyone then logs in, the operating system can check the validity of the password they type by encrypting it before comparing it with the encrypted version that is stored. If it is particularly difficult to decrypt the stored encrypted versions of passwords then getting a copy of the password file is only a small step towards making a break-in. Although this security measure was described in 1968[55] it has not always been a feature of password systems.

Stoll's hacker with super-user privileges was able to get hold of password files[56] but in the incident reported by him the passwords were encrypted so that 'unless [the hacker] owned a ... supercomputer ... our passwords remained safe'.[57] Although the passwords were encrypted the user names were not and after breaking in the hacker 'knew the names of a few hundred scientists'.[58] Armed with the user names the hacker would have tried common passwords and would have stood a good chance of breaking into at least one account that had a weak password.

1.4.6 Carelessness

Clifford Stoll's tale shows that one major weakness in password systems is the lassitude of the users. When a computer is first delivered, users need to find out from the supplier what the user names and passwords are. One company set up every computer it supplied with the same three accounts using the same three account names and the same three passwords:

> 'There's the SYSTEM account, with the password "MANAGER". An account named FIELD, password "SERVICE". And an account USER with the password "USER".' [59]

Obviously, anyone with some experience of installing one of these computers would be able to gain access to another similar computer unless the passwords and possibly the account names had been altered but, as Stoll reported·

> 'Despite [the company's] best efforts to make the system managers change those passwords, some never do.' [60]

He goes on to describe specific incidents where a hacker was being monitored. In one instance, the hacker

> '[l]ogged right in there as "Field", password "Service" ... The hacker dived right in.' [61]

And the opening of the transcript of an interaction with another computer included the lines:

```
Username: FIELD
Password: SERVICE
WELCOME TO THE AIR FORCE SYSTEM COMMAND ...[62]
```

Stoll comments:

> 'He'd logged in as Field Service. Not just an ordinary user. A completely privileged account.' [63]

Sometimes all that is needed to break-in is an informed guess, as this sheepish confession demonstrates:

'... someone used our old account, SAC. It used to be used for the Strategic Air Command ... it never had much password protection ... The password was SAC.' [64]

Some inside knowledge of a particular computer system can offer clues as the following transcript implies when a hacker attempts, and succeeds, at gaining access to a computer:

```
login: root
password: root
incorrect password, try again.
login: guest
password: guest
incorrect password, try again.
login: uucp
password: uucp
WELCOME TO THE ...    [65]
```

'uucp' is the acronym for a well-known service available in a particular operating system. Someone familiar with the system might therefore expect that an unimaginative administrator might use 'uucp' as a password. In another incident a password was not needed at all:

'He tried fifteen places before he struck pay dirt ... This time, he discovered that the account wasn't protected. No password needed. ... He started listing everyone's mail ... this was stuff that he shouldn't be seeing.' [66]

And in another case entry was straightforward when the hacker made an easy guess:

```
Username: ANONYMOUS
Password: GUEST
Welcome to the Army OPTIMIS database    [67]
```

Once hackers have a user name and a password they can continue to gain access. For this reason it is common practice to ask users to change their passwords periodically, though as Stoll points out, this is not always done:

'The system password hadn't been changed for a couple of years, and outlasted people who had been hired and fired.' [68]

But even when a password is changed people do not always make significant alterations. Computers sometimes force users to change their passwords regularly so once one hacker discovered that the combination 'Field' and

'Service' gave him access to a computer he should have been blocked when the 'Air Force computer ... expired the *Field Service* password'.[69] Alarmingly, Stoll recounts that he

> '... watched him start to log in ... as Field Service, thinking how he would be booted off again. But no! He was welcomed back ... Someone ... had re-enabled the Field Service account with the same old password.'[70]

Once they have gained access to a computer, hackers can make alterations and, for instance, insert a short program which

> '... would prompt a user to enter his name and password ... After he typed his name ... he would naturally type his password. The program then stashes the unlucky user's name and password into a file.'[71]

From Stoll's account, it is clear that people are not always particularly careful when dealing with security measures, and their carelessness makes the systems and the data they hold vulnerable. Obviously, the situation is much worse where staff are disgruntled, threatened, blackmailed or coerced. What can be done carelessly, can also be done deliberately by trusted but alienated or distressed staff. Unfortunately, therefore, measures may be needed to vet staff and to limit the powers of individuals when protecting computer and communication systems.

1.4.7 Summary

Passwords offer a simple technique for restricting the access to confidential data and for restricting the degree of control that a user has over the operation of a computer system. The security provided by passwords depends on how difficult it is to guess the secret. Complicated and difficult-to-guess passwords can also be difficult to remember. It is tempting, therefore, to pick familiar words as passwords or to write down complicated ones.

Studies have shown that people are not always careful about their choice of passwords or about caring for them. Individuals may be slipshod because they believe that there is little at stake and little reason to be vigilant. However, there is evidence that major penetrations of secure computer systems can begin when a hacker gains access to accounts that appear to give their users few privileges. Obscure bugs and a comprehensive knowledge of operating systems have given hackers the opportunity to extend their privileges and compromise security.

The logs of computers commonly record password use and misuse. And passwords are held, encrypted or unencrypted in computer files accessible to administrators. This has made it feasible to conduct research on passwords and password use. The results are worrying and show that security is under threat through the apathy and carelessness of computer users. It is not sufficient to rely solely on the technology. A security policy has to address how people will be convinced and reminded of their roles in sustaining security.

1.5 Technology

Computer technology has advanced and proved suitable for performing particular security operations. In particular computers have made certain encryption and decryption operations convenient. The implied reduction in the cost of encryption has widened the sphere of application and contributed to the development of a digital infrastructure that supports commerce. Security techniques combined with digital communications effectively extend the geographical reach of trusted relationships. This allows organizations to move their operations away from their clients and possibly centralize their business. Or, from another perspective, they permit centralized organizations to deal more reliably with individuals.

The requirement for organizations to reach out to individuals and for individuals to contact organizations in the course of their daily lives implies that communication technologies have become publicly accessible. The open public networks offer opportunities for interference in other people's affairs. So, while digital networks facilitate new patterns of organization, they also make individuals and organizations vulnerable to intrusion. Again, encryption can provide the technological fix that might reduce fears that often come with conducting business in public spaces.

Communication and computer technologies not only simplify encryption but also permit the development of new broadcasting services and present images that can deliberately or accidentally reinforce or destroy trust.

1.5.1 Encryption

Kerckhoffs embraced the technology of his day and thought that the method of encryption should allow cryptograms, the secretly coded messages, to be sent over the telegraph. He also insisted that the system of encryption should be described by a short list of rules and should not induce mental strain.[72] He was perhaps aware that complicated methods of encryption are hard to analyse and therefore make it difficult to identify weaknesses. Additionally, complicated schemes imply that people will make mistakes when following the rules of encryption and that will waste people's time when they come to decrypt messages.

When Vernam proposed his system of encryption he thought that there were difficulties that made it 'unsuitable for general use, unless mechanical methods are used'.[73] But it is likely that the difficulties arose not from the complications of the scheme but from the volume of work that encryption added to the transmission of messages. Vernam solved his problems by mechanizing encryption and thus he heralded the use of information processing machinery and, ultimately, the computer in creating more secure systems of communication.

Part of the point of employing computer systems is to get computers to do automatically what would be time-consuming for the users of the computer. In encrypting data, computers reassign and rearrange arrays of bits that constitute the data to obfuscate what the bits stand for. Since the patterns of bits reflect something of significance, the reorganization of bits that takes place during encryption clouds the connotations once mirrored by the data. At some stage the rearrangement and reassignment of bits needs to be undone, so that the bits can be interpreted and represented in a meaningful way. The computer therefore needs to perform the obfuscation in a systematic way so that a corresponding process can automatically unravel the obfuscated data. Certain mathematical techniques have provided useful and systematic algorithms for encryption, which computers can automate. These mathematical methods and their automation together with the declining costs of computers have made the widespread use of encryption techniques feasible. So, encryption, once mainly a feature of military systems, is now incorporated in consumer goods.

But computers can also help the code cracker.

1.5.2 Access control

In some installations that secure valuables, people entering and leaving must identify themselves and a log is kept of who has entered, when they arrived and when they left. Logs, locks and alarms not only hinder intruders and aid their detection, but they also act as a deterrent to individuals who may be considering breaking in. With computers, however, securing the installation can only be a partial solution since computer systems are often designed to be accessible through communication links that extend beyond physical enclosures.

Computer and communication technologies are especially useful in collecting and maintaining records. Commonly, operating systems integrate software for creating logs of events within the computer system. These logs can be valuable for detecting unauthorized use, or attempts at unauthorized use of computing resources. They can also help in tracking down sources of abuse of systems and their users. Keeping a log on its own, of course, will not reveal anything. In secure computer installations logs are kept, regularly inspected and suspicious events followed up. In his account of a succession of computer break-ins Clifford Stoll notes that a US 75 cent[74] discrepancy in a computer's accounting system proved to be the tip of a security iceberg of international proportions and shows that even small divergences in computer logs and accounts can be revealing. As with financial accounts, users might be reassured if reputable agencies, which are independent of those responsible for running the computer system, carried out the auditing of computer logs. This does not eliminate the possibility of a conspiracy, but it does make it less likely especially where the auditor's reputation is at stake.

The role of these records in aiding detection makes them valuable and a target for theft or modification. As records of activity they might, for instance, provide the raw material for extortion, or attempts might be made to alter the record to cover up a misdemeanour. Activity logs therefore become objects that require protection from theft and alteration, and offer a further application for encryption technology.

1.5.3   Authenticity

The potential for forgery and falsification of documents undermines feelings of security, since it opens opportunities for deception and impersonation. Documents outside the digital domain are certified by attaching the signature of a trustworthy person such as a public notary. The digital equivalent of certification is feasible if a copy, encrypted by the technological equivalent of the notary, accompanies a digital document. If the authenticity of the document is questioned, the notary can decrypt the secured version and, hopefully, show that the result is identical with the accompanying document. Encryption and subsequent decryption identify the document with the notary who holds the secret key. Encryption also makes it impossible for a meddler to alter the encrypted copy of the document and know what the effect would be on the decrypted version. Encryption technology can therefore help prove authenticity and maintain the integrity of documents as well as hiding secrets. Obfuscation not only renders copies of data useless for those who do not hold the key, but it also makes it impossible to tamper with the data in any meaningful way. It does not, of course, prevent full-scale mindless contamination of the data, or recording and fraudulently circulating duplicates of the encrypted data.

1.5.4   Sharing the medium

Changes in communication technology have ensured a more efficient use of communication links but this has meant that individual communications become interleaved when they share communication resources. Labelled fragments of conversations are thrown into the communication pool and emerge at their intended destinations. But since everyone is exploiting the same pool, it makes it easy for anyone who is knowledgeable about the technology to trawl for other people's communications.

Encryption technology can obfuscate communication packets to make them, on the one hand, undistinguished in the pool but, on the other, distinct for those who have the key to the style of obfuscation. This not only hides the significance of what is being transmitted but it also gives the sender and recipient the reassurance that the communications associated with their transactions remain distinct from the transactions of others.

This is reminiscent of the way in which the family of the nineteenth century sailor Richard Collinson attempted to keep in touch with him although they did not know his whereabouts.[75] Figure 1 shows part of the front page of *The Times* of 1 March 1850.

The message starting with a capital 'N' is encrypted and is the first in a series of messages that appeared in successive months. They later proved to be encrypted notes intended for Captain Collinson from his family.[76] Collinson was leading a search for a missing arctic explorer. He and his family presumed that *The Times* would be available across the globe, so they encrypted family news in an idiosyncratic code, to keep it confidential, and published it in the widely available newspaper hoping that wherever his venture took him he would be in touch with his kin. Unfortunately, he was unable to obtain the newspapers until he was on his way home.

Figure 1   One of the encrypted messages from the Collinson family published in *The Times*

Computers, like editions of *The Times*, can be shared by a number of people and, individually, they may want to prevent other people accessing their data. So, operating systems provide security mechanisms that isolate segments of a computer's memory and services from one another. The capability to access computer services and parts of a computer's memory space are referred to as *privileges*. Different users will have different privileges; some will have access only to their allocation of computer memory and services while others, perhaps those responsible for keeping the computer system running, may have access to all the memory and all the services.

1.5.5 Speed

The sheer effort or expense of breaking into a computer can act as a deterrent and frequently the measure of the effectiveness of a security feature is in the number of computer operations that would be needed to defeat it. Security mechanisms that are expected to take an impractical length of time to subvert even using a computer will often be described as being *computationally infeasible*. Conclusions about whether processes are computationally infeasible or not are frequently deduced from mathematical analyses of the process. Mathematics, though, is a developing art and, sometimes, new mathematical discoveries will reveal new techniques or short cuts that reduce the effort needed in a security procedure. Those responsible for the security of systems therefore need to keep abreast of developments in technology and mathematics that might undermine their security procedures.

Improvements in computers and the programs for obfuscating passwords have speeded up the process of logging-in. At one stage, for instance, a new algorithm was introduced on some systems that speeded up the log-in process.[77] This made it quicker for legitimate users, but it also speeded up the rate at which a hacker could try different passwords. The log-in process was, therefore, deliberately slowed down. An alternative, used in some systems, is to allow people a limited number of attempts. Failure after the specified number of attempts causes the computer to block that user's access until its administrators release the account again. Of course, hackers might try to break in again, but they will be continually interrupted and may well be traced after the administrators have been alerted.

1.5.6 Protecting owners' rights

In digital systems, it is easy to make copies of collections of data. In commerce, therefore, owners often sell rights to use data rather than the data itself. The owners, though, probably would make few sales if the data was publicly accessible. Potential purchasers might simply take a copy and assume that their use of the data would go undetected. One possible course of action is to exploit the well-developed technology of encryption to encrypt the documents, pictures or music and to give a secret key only to authorized users. However, untrustworthy purchasers are just as likely to give away the key as they are to give away copies of the data. Another option is to tag the digital data that is subject to restrictions on its use and to keep a separate, secure record of the identity of the rightful users and their rights. When the data and its tag are encountered a check can be made as to whether the use is authorized. If it is not, then punitive action can be taken against those responsible for the unauthorized use. This approach does not prevent unauthorized uses and is only likely to be a deterrent if the systems of detection and punishment are seen to be effective. Tags too might be easily removed or altered, so techniques have been developed to hide tags in the data that is being tagged. If the hidden data is inserted in a complicated but systematic fashion, a casual inspection will not uncover the tag, but someone knowledgeable about the scheme can unravel the message. For instance the message

SEND STALE FROZEN CHIPS

reads differently if the first letter of the first word is joined to the second letter of the second word and so on. The collection of similar, but more elaborate techniques for hiding one message inside another are collectively called *steganography* and can be used to tag data or to hide secrets within innocuous digital records of programs, documents, pictures or sounds. For instance, by imperceptibly modulating the colours in a picture, distorting a sound or microscopically adjusting the position of letters on a page.[78] While the hidden messages might be encrypted, the techniques for hiding the messages are different from methods of encryption. Security technology is therefore not simply the use of secret codes. There is a range of disparate techniques for providing security that sometimes borrow features from one another.

1.5.7   Firewalls

Amongst the collection of differing security techniques are those for restricting communications. Firewalls, for example, are intended to prevent people from outside an organization accessing, entering or altering data within the organization. They also prevent insiders from accessing certain kinds of data on the outside. All the organization's communications are routed through the firewall, which is a service provided by software running on a computer. The firewall software censors messages. It seeks out characteristics in the messages and either routes them towards their destination or ignores them. Firewalls, for example, can check the electronic address in a message to see where it has come from, or where it is going. When the message is from an unauthorized source or is destined for an unauthorized recipient, the firewall will scan the message, discover the address and discard it. In this mode a firewall does not perform any encryption or decryption operations.

1.5.8   Propaganda

To have faith in the effects of technology requires either faith in the statements made by authorities or knowledge of the technology and of the ways in which authorities deploy the technology. Those who wish to generate feelings of security either have to give potential victims a means of learning about the technology and its accompanying organizational processes or they have to create and maintain an aura of authority. So, while security devices are instrumental in securing systems they are not adequate on their own to establish a climate of security.

Technology can provide support for generating and propagating attention-grabbing presentations – for instance, technological effectiveness and an image of strength, certainty and security might be generated by a combination of guided bomb strikes and public television broadcasts. Engineering works can, also, make certain possibilities less plausible – for example, knowledge of the existence of thick-walled bank vaults may make robbery seem unlikely, as once upon a time castle walls made unwanted routine assaults seem improbable. Technology can also generate material for counter-tales that seem to reduce threatening possibilities. For example, the introduction of video surveillance cameras might spawn a conviction that offenders will be detected thus suggesting that potential offenders' insecurities are increased and therefore that it is implausible that an offence will be committed. The potential victim's gain in security is won by promoting the belief that a technology has increased the potential offender's insecurity.

1.5.9 Summary

Digital technologies have evolved to meet common security requirements. They can:

- provide reassurance about who I am communicating with

- provide reassurance about when a statement was made

- restrict who can make sense of my publicly accessible communications

- restrict who can alter records about me

- keep a record of the identity of those who attempt (successfully or unsuccessfully) to access data about me or to alter that data.

Encryption is not an essential feature of all security techniques. It is, nevertheless, a process that recurs in assaults on a variety of threats. A part of the appeal of encryption is that its processes can be automated and integrated into software. Encryption has thus become a valued component of secure systems.

1.6 Conclusion

There are, perhaps, six techniques for protecting valuables of all kinds from intruders covering:

1   the establishment of a moral climate in which non-violence, ownership and privacy are honoured

2   the physical enclosure of valuables, which demands special tools or effort to gain access

3   the concealment, camouflage or obfuscation of things of value

4   active surveillance, detection and detention of intruders

5   record keeping, auditing and recovery

6   publicized, credible and sustainable accounts and demonstrations of the effectiveness of security measures.

All these techniques can be combined in varying degrees. But security is not just a matter of keeping things locked away and guaranteeing their integrity. It is also about establishing trust, maintaining rights, protecting privileges and taking care.

Judgements about trust cannot be automated, but they are an essential part of creating secure systems – systems that make people feel secure. The security of a system, therefore, extends beyond the software and hardware mechanisms of computers and communication links, into the organization charged with the responsibility for operating the information system. Clearly, the allocation of privileges gives individuals different powers and therefore demands different degrees of trust. It is likely that those with universal privileges will be carefully vetted and monitored while those with lesser privileges will be less vigorously assessed.

Security techniques make it difficult for unauthorized people to gain access to things of value. Simultaneously, those who have the right of access to resources should not be unduly inconvenienced when they act within their rights, though they may be willing to accept some inconvenience as the price of the protection that is offered. Where the execution of procedures helps guarantee people's security, their routine undemanding access procedures may dull the senses to what is at stake. Those responsible for security may then be tempted to take short cuts to eliminate the inconvenience imposed by security measures. So security systems can go wrong: people can accidentally intrude, doors can be left unlocked, keys lost and alarms ignored.

Untiring technologies can reduce the drudgery, effort and discomfort in many security procedures. Cameras, communication links, monitors and a viewer in a comfortable room, for instance, can replace a windswept sentry. Swipe cards, electronic locks and computer records can replace signatures, gatekeepers and log books. But these aids introduce a new kind of security threat – the sabotage of security technologies – making the security of, for example, computer systems incorporating security mechanisms a concern.

There is a spectrum of security mechanisms associated with a spectrum of vulnerabilities. Firstly, there are vulnerabilities to what are known as passive threats where a spy simply observes stored or transmitted confidential information. Secondly, there are the active threats where the intruder meddles with the data. In either case intruders need to gain access to the data, and one kind of defence against them is provided by access controls and another through encryption.

The technology of encryption is most obviously useful as a way of obfuscating data and keeping it secure. Nevertheless, the technology of encryption can be exploited to meet some of the other requirements of secure systems. In the remainder of this book I will concentrate on security measures that can be provided by elaborate camouflage of messages, by encryption. Often such messages are a part of extensive transactions. The study of the use of encryption, therefore, must consider the methods of encryption and the sequences of messages, often called *protocols*, that make up common transactions.

Chapter Two

Encryption

The strings of bits that make up digital data can be altered and rearranged in systematic ways that make it hard to extract any sense from them. This kind of obfuscation is central to techniques for providing a degree of security in digital systems. To use the computer to help protect data requires methods for obfuscation that can be reduced to a systematic procedure, which can be written down and converted into a computer program.

Today, encryption is commonly built on mathematical operations that have been widely studied and understood. Data is encoded as a series of numbers and then fed into calculations. The result of the calculation is then treated as the secretly-coded data. To make the business of cracking such a code hard the numbers used are often very large. In this chapter, though, I have deliberately kept the calculations simple to make it easier to illustrate how encryption is done. The techniques outlined here should therefore be treated as an illustration of some principles of encryption rather than as fully-fledged, robust encryption procedures.

2.1   Mathematics

The product of the obfuscation procedure is a confusing stream or block of data, which provides a degree of security because it is unintelligible and difficult to unravel. Unfortunately, not all schemes produce indecipherable data. For some techniques, there are short cuts to finding out what has been hidden in the obfuscated data, but it is not necessarily easy for the creators of code to spot how their codes can be cracked. Methods are therefore needed that provide schemes for obfuscating data and that give some indications as to how difficult it is to uncover the disguised data. These days, code makers are likely to use well-established mathematical results to guide them in creating their codes. The original data is treated as a set of mathematical objects and obfuscation treated as a *mathematical operation*. With this mathematical formulation, a long tradition of thoroughly rehearsed collection of mathematical notations, operations and proofs can be brought to bear on the task. Reassurance about the properties of obfuscation techniques comes partly because mathematicians are involved and through their training they become obsessed with rigour and robustness.

Some methods of obfuscation may therefore be ruled out because they cannot be expressed in a familiar mathematical form. It seems to be tempting to create new or presumed new methods of encryption. As David Kahn wrote:

> 'Few false ideas have more firmly gripped the minds of so many intelligent men than the one that, if they just tried, they could invent a cipher that no one could break. Many have tried and, although only a fraction of their ciphers have been published or patented, the quantity and variety of even this small sample is astounding.' [79]

Yet, in practice, relatively few techniques are in widespread use. Increasingly, the encryption methods that are favoured are those that can be thoroughly analysed by long-established mathematical processes. Mathematicians not only produce results that are useful for code makers they also have ways of identifying mathematical problems that are very hard to do. The task of coding data can then be reformulated to be a way of processing the data so that a potential cracker is faced with a mathematical problem that is very hard to solve.

Numbers are common kinds of mathematical objects. Data can be treated as though it were a string of numbers and the numbers operated on to create an obfuscated object. Ultimately, the authorized recipient will need to undo the operation and then convert the numbers back to the original form of the data.

2.1.1   The Caesar code

One simple code is the *Caesar code* reportedly used by Julius Caesar. To encrypt letters, the alphabet is written out, in alphabetical order, and a copy of the alphabet is written below as shown in Table 1.

Table 1   An encryption table for the Caesar code

A	B	C	D	E	F	G	H	I	J	K	L	M	N	O	P	Q	R	S	T	U	V	W	X	Y	Z
D	E	F	G	H	I	J	K	L	M	N	O	P	Q	R	S	T	U	V	W	X	Y	Z	A	B	C

In Table 1 the alphabet in the bottom row has been moved up three places; the alphabet in the lower row therefore starts with the letter D and continues in alphabetical order until the letter Z is written under the letter W. The letters A, B and C, which have not yet been used in the lower row, can then be used to fill in the three gaps left at the end of the lower row continuing in an alphabetical order. To encrypt a message like the sequence of letters 'CAT', each letter of the message is found in the upper row and then the corresponding letter of the lower row is written down. The C in 'CAT', for instance, corresponds to the letter F in the lower row as highlighted in the copy of the encryption table in Table 2.

Table 2 An encryption table for the Caesar code highlighting the encrypted letters C, A and T

A	B	C	D	E	F	G	H	I	J	K	L	M	N	O	P	Q	R	S	T	U	V	W	X	Y	Z
D	E	F	G	H	I	J	K	L	M	N	O	P	Q	R	S	T	U	V	W	X	Y	Z	A	B	C

The letter A corresponds to the letter D in the lower row, and the letter T corresponds to the letter W. Thus the three letters 'FDW', known as the *ciphertext*, encrypt 'CAT'.

One way of decrypting the message is to have a copy of the encryption table and use it from the bottom upwards. Alternatively, a decryption table can be derived from the encryption table as shown in Table 3. For example, in Table 2 a letter A in the ciphertext is derived from an X. After decryption a ciphertext letter A should therefore generate an X. This is recorded in the first column of Table 3.

Table 3 A decryption table for the Caesar code of Table 2. The letters F, D and W have been picked out.

A	B	C	D	E	F	G	H	I	J	K	L	M	N	O	P	Q	R	S	T	U	V	W	X	Y	Z
X	Y	Z	A	B	C	D	E	F	G	H	I	J	K	L	M	N	O	P	Q	R	S	T	U	V	W

So the upper row of Table 3 consists of letters of the ciphertext and the lower row identifies the letters that the decryption operation delivers. The decryption table is then used in exactly the same way as the encryption table to decrypt an encrypted message. From the table it is clear that the decryption operation generates the three letters 'CAT' from the ciphertext letters 'FDW'.

2.1.2   A numerical version

If an encryption process can be described systematically, then a computer can carry out the encryption. Often encryption operations are systematized by describing them as mathematical operations. I will illustrate this using the Caesar code.

Firstly, the data to be transmitted must be converted into mathematical objects. The letters of the alphabet can, for example, be assigned a number according to their position in the alphabet as shown in Table 4. When dealing with the mathematics of codes and with encodings for computers it is common, as shown in Table 4, to start counting from zero.

Table 4 A possible numerical coding scheme for the alphabet

A	B	C	D	E	F	G	H	I	J	K	L	M	N	O	P	Q	R	S	T	U	V	W	X	Y	Z
0	1	2	3	4	5	6	7	8	9	10	11	12	13	14	15	16	17	18	19	20	21	22	23	24	25

The message 'CAT' would then be coded as the numerical sequence '2 0 19' simply by substituting the numbers that correspond to the letters in Table 4. This original message in its alphabetic or numeric form is often called the *plaintext*. Although this first step is a form of coding, it is not considered to be secure because it is merely a way of expressing a well-known convention that letters are written in an alphabetical order and that, for instance, it is conventional to think of J as the tenth letter of the alphabet which here is coded by the numeral 9. The code is not secure because, as yet, no attempt has been made to confuse the reader. It is an encoding but it would be a particularly easy code to crack because people know about alphabet ordering and which is the first letter of the alphabet. The encoding has not involved an operation similar to the use of the displaced copy of the alphabet in the Caesar code.

Table 5 provides an operation that adds an element of confusion; it is a version of Table 2 but with the letters re-coded as numbers. Table 5 is chosen to generate an unconventional re-coding of the alphabet. It is a re-coding designed to confuse, and is referred to as encryption (or enciphering). If Table 5 is read in conjunction with Table 4, the upper row of numbers corresponds to the alphabet starting with the letter A encoded as 0 and continues in sequence to represent the letters of the alphabet. The lower row of numbers corresponds to a version of the alphabet shifted along by three places, starting with number 3 corresponding to the letter D, and continuing up to the number 25 that represents Z. The last three spaces in the lower row are filled in with the numerical codes 0, 1 and 2 corresponding to the letters A, B and C.

Table 5 An encryption scheme for numerical codes

0	1	2	3	4	5	6	7	8	9	10	11	12	13	14	15	16	17	18	19	20	21	22	23	24	25
3	4	5	6	7	8	9	10	11	12	13	14	15	16	17	18	19	20	21	22	23	24	25	0	1	2

The plaintext word 'CAT' represented by the numerical sequence '2 0 19' is encrypted using Table 5 first by taking the number 2 in the numerical sequence of the message and noting that a 2 in the upper row corresponds to the number 5 in the lower row of the table. Similarly 0 is encrypted by the number 3 in the lower row and the number 19 is encrypted as the number 22. The whole encrypted sequence is '5 3 22'. Table 4 can be used to convert this result back to a sequence of letters. 5 corresponds to F, 3 to D and 22 to W, giving, in a long-winded fashion, the expected result 'FDW'. This encrypted result is the ciphertext, sometimes called the cryptogram. To recover the plaintext from the ciphertext the whole process can be completed in reverse including the use of Table 5 backwards. An alternative method of decryption would be to use Table 5 to construct the decryption table shown in Table 6.

Table 6   A decryption table for the encryption operation shown in Table 5

0	1	2	3	4	5	6	7	8	9	10	11	12	13	14	15	16	17	18	19	20	21	22	23	24	25
23	24	25	0	1	2	3	4	5	6	7	8	9	10	11	12	13	14	15	16	17	18	19	20	21	22

Using Table 6 in exactly the same way as Table 5 was used, the numerical version of the ciphertext '5 3 22' translates to the sequence '2 0 19', which is the numerical version of the original plaintext 'CAT'.

2.1.3   A mathematician's view

It is clear that in Table 5 most of the numbers in the upper and lower rows have a simple relationship with one another. Most of the numbers in the lower row are the corresponding numbers in the upper row with three added: 3 is 0+3, 4 is 1+3, 5 is 2+3 and so on. It would be possible to describe the encryption operation as being the same as performing addition if the last three columns of Table 5 were not included. At the end of the table, ordinary addition does not work: the 24 in the upper row with 3 added is 27, which is clearly not equal to the 1 in the lower row. But a result of 27 would be inconvenient if ultimately we wanted to translate the ciphertext back into letters of the alphabet. There is no letter corresponding to the number 27.

A branch of mathematics does provide a special addition operation, which does exactly what is needed. What is called *Group Theory* works with a fixed number of things, like the letters in the alphabet or a limited collection of numbers. A collection of whole numbers, the integers, that I am working with would be denoted by Z and to indicate that I am dealing with twenty six numbers from 0 to 25 I can use the suffix 26 and write Z_{26}. A *Group*, in Group Theory, has a number of distinctive properties. One of the properties requires that the results of operations that can be performed on a Group always end up being in the Group. These kinds of operations, it is said, guarantee *closure*. The operation described by Table 5, for instance, guarantees closure since it can only be applied to integers taken from Z_{26} and the results are all in Z_{26}. To satisfy the closure property of a Group, mathematicians adopt a special way of performing addition. For the Z_{26} that I am dealing with, numbers are added in the usual way and:

1   If the result is between 0 and 25 then the result stands.

2   If the result is 26 or over then 26 is subtracted.

3   If the result is still 26 or more then 26 is subtracted again and this is repeated until the result is in Z_{26}, in other words the result is a number from 0 to 25.

To distinguish this from the usual kind of addition it is given a special name – 'modulo 26 addition'. A special notation is also necessary. To add 4 and 3 modulo 26 which gives the result 7 I would write:

$$4 + 3 \equiv 7 \bmod 26$$

The phrase 'mod 26' indicates the kind of addition required. Now, if I add 25 and 3 modulo 26, I would write:

$$25 + 3 \equiv 28 \bmod 26$$

However, 28 is larger than 26 so I would need to subtract 26 to complete the operation and the result would be:

$$25 + 3 \equiv 28 \equiv 28 - 26 \equiv 2 \bmod 26$$

Notice that I have not used an equal sign but a sign with an additional horizontal bar. Clearly, 28 is not equal to 2 but in modulo 26 arithmetic I can use 2 in place of 28 and still get the answers people would expect. Where two things can be used in place of one another, mathematicians say that these two things are *congruent*. So I can say that '28 is congruent to 2 modulo 26' and the sign $\equiv$ is therefore read as 'is congruent to', or in less technical terms 'can be used in place of'.

The encryption operation in Table 5 can now be summed up in a formula:

$$c \equiv p + 3 \bmod 26$$

where p is a numerically encoded plaintext letter and c is the corresponding numerically encoded ciphertext. The encrypted version of the plaintext word 'CAT', which is numerically coded as '2 0 19', is:

$$2 + 3 \equiv 5 \bmod 26, \quad 0 + 3 \equiv 3 \bmod 26, \quad 19 + 3 \equiv 22 \bmod 26$$

giving the sequence '5 3 22', which can be interpreted using Table 4 as the cryptogram 'FDW'.

2.1.4 Using a key

In all the examples I have looked at so far I have always shifted the alphabet by three places. Of course, I could shift the alphabet by any amount, but I would need to tell the recipients of the message what the shift is if they are to decrypt it. Specifying the encryption operation in terms of modulo 26 arithmetic makes it unnecessary to construct the encryption table. Using modulo 26 arithmetic encryption involves performing the calculation implied by the formula:

$$c \equiv p + K \bmod 26$$

where, in the examples so far, I have replaced K by 3. Changing the value that I substitute for K is equivalent to shifting the alphabet up by different amounts. Thus shifting the alphabet by nineteen places implies setting K to 19 so encryption operation becomes:

$$c \equiv p + 19 \bmod 26$$

The plaintext word 'CAT' is still represented by the sequence '2 0 19' but its encrypted version is different. Using the rules of modulo 26 addition the encrypted result is given by:

$$2 + 19 \equiv 21 \bmod 26, \qquad 0 + 19 \equiv 19 \bmod 26,$$

$$19 + 19 \equiv 38 \equiv 38 - 26 \equiv 12 \bmod 26$$

The outcome is the sequence '21 19 12', which when translated back into letters using Table 4 gives the ciphertext 'VTM'. Clearly the value of K affects the outcome of the encryption process and provides the key to decryption. Without knowing the value of K, the key, eavesdroppers might find it difficult to work out what the ciphertext said. People interested in obfuscating their messages might use this version of the Caesar code but they would need to keep K secret to make it more difficult for others to interpret their ciphertext.

2.1.5   Decrypting the Caesar code

I have introduced two ways of decrypting the Caesar code: one way is to use the original encryption table but to use it backwards; the other way is to construct a new table and to use it in the same way as the encryption table. There are mathematical equivalents to these two operations. I will take the option that makes the decryption operation the same as the encryption operation.

The formula $c \equiv p + K \bmod 26$ offered an alternative to constructing and using a table for encryption. A similar formula can also be used as an alternative to constructing and using the decryption table. The decryption table, Table 6 for example, is similar to the encryption table of Table 5 except that the numbers on the lower row are shifted by a different amount. This is equivalent to saying that it is derived from the formula using a different key. I will write this decryption key as $\overline{K}$, using the bar over the top of the K to indicate that it is to undo the effect of the encryption key K. Thus, when the ciphertext is c, decryption that gives the plaintext p is described by the expression:

$$c + \overline{K} \bmod 26$$

The encryption and decryption formulae can be combined by substituting the ciphertext c, derived from the encryption formula $c \equiv p + K \bmod 26$, into the expression for the decrypted data and this produces the expression:

$$(p + K) + \overline{K} \bmod 26$$

Rearranging the brackets in this formula to change the order of addition gives:

$$p + (K + \overline{K}) \bmod 26$$

To recover the plaintext, therefore, the decryption key has to be chosen so that adding the combination of $(K + \overline{K}) \bmod 26$ overall has no effect. If K is 3 and the plaintext letter is 'T' say. The numerical code for 'T' is 19 and the expression for first encrypting this data and decrypting the result becomes:

$$(19 + 3) + \overline{K} \equiv 19 + (3 + \overline{K}) \bmod 26$$

By making $\overline{K} = 23$ the result is:

$$19 + (3 + 23) \equiv 19 + 26 \bmod 26$$

Then, because of the rules of modulo 26 addition, the superfluous 26 obtained from the combination $(K + \overline{K})$ can be removed to give the anticipated decrypted message, 19, corresponding to the letter 'T':

$$19 + 26 \equiv 19 + 26 - 26 \equiv 19 \bmod 26$$

If the expression $p + (K + \overline{K}) \bmod 26$ is to reveal the plaintext, the term $(K + \overline{K})$ must always be a multiple of 26. When $(K + \overline{K})$ is 26 then according to the rules of modulo 26 addition:

$$p + (K + \overline{K}) \equiv p + 26 \equiv p \bmod 26$$

Thus, to decrypt using a formula, it is necessary to find the key $\overline{K}$ and this is straightforward knowing that:

$$K + \overline{K} \equiv 26 \bmod 26$$

If, for instance, K was 3 then:

$$3 + \overline{K} \equiv 26 \bmod 26$$

from which it is clear that $\overline{K} \equiv 23 \bmod 26$. Encrypting by using the Caesar code and shifting the alphabet up by 3 is equivalent to using the formula:

$$c \equiv p + 3 \bmod 26$$

Decrypting messages that have been encrypted using the Caesar code and shifting the alphabet three places is equivalent to using the formula:

$$p \equiv c + 23 \bmod 26$$

The word 'CAT' that was encrypted using a key of $K = 3$ produced the ciphertext '5 3 22' and using the decryption key of 23 is decrypted as:

$$5 + 23 \equiv 28 \equiv 2 \bmod 26, \quad 3 + 23 \equiv 26 \equiv 0 \bmod 26,$$

$$22 + 23 \equiv 45 \equiv 19 \bmod 26$$

which gives the result '2 0 19' to spell the original plaintext word 'CAT'.

Decryption of the Caesar code, therefore, can be carried out using the same operation as encryption but using a different key. The decryption key however must be chosen so that it complements the encryption key. In the case of the Caesar code, someone who is expected to decrypt the message either needs to know the decryption key or to know how to perform the decryption operation given the encryption key. Schemes where the sender and the receiver both work from their knowledge of the encryption key are called *symmetric*, and schemes where the sender knows an encryption key and the receiver knows the complementary decryption key are said to be *asymmetric*.

2.1.6   The properties of a Group

In the course of exploring the mathematics of encryption and decryption I have used a number of properties that together characterize mathematical structures known as Groups. Group Theory is widely used in the description and analysis of encryption schemes.

There are five principal characteristics of a Group:

Firstly, a Group consists of a number of elements and an operation that can be performed on those elements. In the previous section, the numbers from 0 to 25, Z_{26}, were the elements of the Group and the operation was modulo 26 addition. For the Caesar code the operation of modulo 26 addition was denoted by + but it is common in the general description of Groups to use the symbol $\circ$ for the operation on the Group. In the case of the Caesar code the symbol $\circ$ is therefore replaced by the addition symbol +.

Secondly, when the operation is performed on a pair of elements in the Group, the result is also an element of the Group. This is called *closure*. Modulo 26 addition ensured that the encryption and decryption operations of the Caesar code gave results that were always in Z_{26}, that is in the range 0 to 25.

Thirdly, one of the elements of a Group, which is called the *identity*, when combined with any other element in the Group leaves them unaltered. In general terms, if the identity is symbolized by e and an element of the Group is a and the operation is denoted by $\circ$ then $a \circ e \equiv a$ and $e \circ a \equiv a$. In the earlier examples of encryption 0 plays the role of the identity e since for instance $0 + 12 \equiv 12 \bmod 26$ and $12 + 0 \equiv 12 \bmod 26$. For the Group used in the previous sections this characteristic translates into the basic property of modulo 26 addition where for any number denoted by a in the range 0 to 25, $a + 0 \equiv a \bmod 26$ and $0 + a \equiv a \bmod 26$. From these results the congruences $a + 26 \equiv a \bmod 26$ and $26 + a \equiv a \bmod 26$ can be derived because, using modulo 26 addition, 26 can be used in place of zero.

Fourthly, for every element in the Group, a for instance, there is one other corresponding element, denoted by $\overline{a}$ and called the inverse of a, which can be combined using the operation to give the identity. If the operation is denoted by $\circ$ then $a \circ \overline{a} \equiv e$ and $\overline{a} \circ a \equiv e$. For the Group used earlier this means that any number in Z_{26} denoted by a has a unique partner denoted by $\overline{a}$ that ensures that $a + \overline{a} \equiv 0 \bmod 26$ and $\overline{a} + a \equiv 0 \bmod 26$. The key 3 for example has an inverse of 23, and $3 + 23 \equiv 26 \equiv 0 \bmod 26$.

Fifthly, if the operation is denoted by $\circ$ and a, b and c are elements of the Group then $(a \circ b) \circ c \equiv a \circ (b \circ c)$. That is, it does not matter which of the two instances of the operation is carried out first. This property is so common in ordinary arithmetic that it is often taken for granted.[80] This particular property has a technical name – it is called the *associative* property and was used in the previous section to say $(p + K) + \overline{K} \bmod 26$ is the same as $p + (K + \overline{K}) \bmod 26$.

2.1.7 Summary

The Caesar code encrypts by substituting letters of the alphabet. Because the substitution is done systematically the encryption operation can be described mathematically. In this case encryption and decryption involve modular addition with an encryption or a decryption key. Given the encryption key it is possible to work out the decryption key. If someone is to decrypt an encrypted message, therefore, they either need the decryption key or they need the encryption key and the means to work out the decryption key. When the person encrypting and the person decrypting use the encryption key as their starting point they are said to have symmetric keys. When the person encrypting the plaintext sends the decryption key to the person who is to decrypt the ciphertext, they work with different keys, which are said to be asymmetric.

Modular addition has well-known properties which makes it analogous to the operation in a mathematical 'Group'. For the mathematical operation to be applied the plaintext has to be expressed as a sequence of numbers, the addition performed and the resulting numbers can be re-coded as letters to form the ciphertext. Encoding data in the form of numbers is therefore a crucial step in the encryption process.

2.2 Working with codes

An encryption system that is intended to obfuscate a plaintext should not be easy to crack. To assess how good a system is requires us to have an idea about how the code might be cracked and an assessment of the effort or the amount of computing equipment a cracker would need to break the code. A judgement then has to be made about the value of what would be gained by the code breakers and whether it is worth their while to set about breaking the code.

It can be advantageous to use an encryption method with a well-known cracking procedure, if it is also known that that procedure requires an inordinate amount of effort. It can be disadvantageous to use an encryption procedure that does not have a known method for breaking it since it is then impossible to estimate the effort involved on the part of crackers and impossible to weigh up the costs they face in attempting to break the code.

Because of the value of knowing how hard it is to crack a code, it has become commonplace to publish the methods of encryption and to encourage their investigation. It is also hoped that by making methods of encryption public that early and public warnings might be forthcoming when new mathematical discoveries provide new attacks on codes. This doctrine is perhaps less relevant for military applications, but is significant for encryption schemes for pervasive, publicly accessible systems.

2.2.1 Cracking a code

Crackers may know the encryption methods, but initially do not know the key that decrypts or encrypts messages and they do not know what the messages are. Without any additional knowledge a cracker would have to try a succession of keys until he or she found a plausible message. For the Caesar code, there are 26 possible keys. One key, however, leaves the message unaltered so there are 25 usable keys. Sometimes, the first key tried might, by chance, decrypt the message, but on other occasions it would be necessary to try all 25 possible keys in turn before the message was revealed. On average, therefore, it would take 12.5 attempts to find the key. Another way of putting this is to say that the probability of cracking the code with one attempt is one in twenty-five or $1/25 = 0.04$.

It may, however, be possible to shorten the odds by finding out something about the messages. For instance, something may be known about the language used and this might help in uncovering messages. It is well known, for example, that in English that the most common letter is the letter E. Figure 2 shows as an illustration the distribution of letters in Mary Shelley's novel *Frankenstein*[81] where E is clearly the most common letter and T is the next most common letter.

Figure 2   Letter distribution in the novel *Frankenstein*

A message enciphered using the Caesar code will always replace the letter E with the same letter. If, for example, the key is 10 then E, the fifth letter in the alphabet, will always be replaced by the fifteenth letter of the alphabet, that is O, and if the message has the characteristics of English then the 'O's replacing the 'E's will be the most common letter in the ciphertext. Take for instance the ciphertext of a message:

COXNWYBOMROOCO

This ciphertext has five 'O's out of a total of fourteen letters so it is likely that O is replacing E. Assuming the encryption key was 10, this ciphertext decrypts to give:

SENDMORECHEESE

which is a plausible message. The following text though does not have an immediately obvious choice for the letter E:

DPCZVLKVEREKWFIZEJKRETVZJRDREFWNFEUVIWLCTFL
IRXVREUVEKVIGIZJV

It is possible to use a computer to analyse messages and to work out how frequently a letter occurs. Table 7 shows the letter frequencies for this ciphertext, and if it is known that the message is in English then it can be compared with the expected frequencies of letters. The letter V and the letter E occur the same number of times. Now if in the original message an E translated to an E in the ciphertext there would have been no encryption, but if E, coded as 4, translated to a V, the twenty-second letter of the alphabet, coded as 21, then the key would have been 21 − 4 or 17.

Table 7   The upper row shows the letters in order of the frequency of their occurrence in the encrypted message. The lower row indicates how often the letter above was repeated.

V	E	R	I	Z	K	F	W	L	J	U	T	D	C	X	P	N	G	Y	S	Q	O	M	H	B	A
8	8	6	5	4	4	4	3	3	3	2	2	2	2	1	1	1	1	0	0	0	0	0	0	0	0

If the encryption key was 17 the asymmetric decryption key would satisfy the congruence $17 + \overline{K} \equiv 26 \bmod 26$. Because $17 + 9 \equiv 26 \bmod 26$, the decryption key is 9 and the decrypted message is:

MYLIEUTENANTFORINSTANCEISAMANOFWONDERFULCO
URAGEANDENTERPRISE

which is plausible.

Knowledge of the statistics of the plaintext messages can therefore help in cracking codes by reducing the number of possible keys that need to be considered. Methods of encryption that do not offer a direct substitution for individual letters can make it harder to use these statistics.

2.2.2 Examples

The Times of London carried, for many years, advertisements and announcements on the front page. They make fascinating reading and often tell heart-rending stories. In some cases the advertisements were encrypted.

Figure 3 is an extract from the front page of the London *Times*. The message to Cenerentola (better known in English as Cinderella) includes the following text:

'N bnxm yt ywd nk dtz hfs wjfi ymnx tsi tr rtxy tscntzx yt mjfw ymf
esi, bmjs dtz wjyzws fsi mtb qtsldtz wjrfns mjwj. It bwnyf f kjb
qnsjx jfwqnsl uqjfxj. N mfaj gjjs ajwd kfw kwtr mfuud xnshj dtz
bjsy fbfd'

Unfortunately for the sender there are a few mistakes, possibly introduced by the typesetters. The code is particularly easy to crack because the letter N stands on its own once or twice. So, if the message is in English, either N stands for A or for I.

Figure 3   The personal advertisement for Cenerentola is written in a Caesar code

Figure 4 shows the frequency analysis for the message to Cenerentola. The most frequent letters in the ciphertext are 'j' and 'f' which would be encoded as a 9 or a 5. Since 'e', encoded as a 4, is likely to be the most frequent letter in the plaintext then the decryption key is likely to be either 5 or 1.

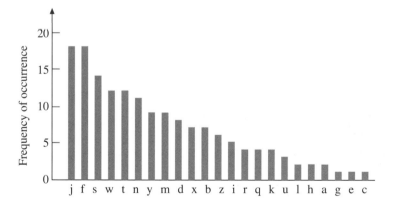

Figure 4   Frequency analysis of the message to Cenerentola

When 'j' is taken to stand for 'e', 'N' stands for 'I', the decryption key is 21 and the messages sadly reads:

> 'I wish to try if you can read this and am most anxious to hear tha
> znd when you return and how longyou remain here. Do writa a few
> lines earling please. I have been very far from happy since you went
> away'

The apparent errors in the message are understandable when the ciphertext is examined. Without the usual patterns of letters, it would be difficult for the typesetters to tell whether the message was correct or not. The implications are that once plaintext is turned into ciphertext many of the checks that are taken for granted, but depend on the comprehension of parts of the message, may fail. With more elaborate encryption schemes small, undetectable errors in the ciphertext can render the plaintext incomprehensible.

Figure 5 shows the personal advertisements from another edition of *The Times*. At the head of a column there is an encrypted message addressed to Robert:

> 'Zkb gr brx frw frph ru zulwh iru ph? Vxfk julhi dqg dgalhub! – Rk! Oryh Oryh.'

You may like to crack this for yourself. It is encrypted in the Caesar code and there are a few typographical errors. Figure 6 is the frequency analysis for the message to Robert. The decrypted version is given in the notes.[82]

Figure 5   A extract from the front page of *The Times*, 13 May 1859

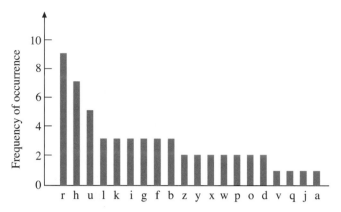

Figure 6   Frequency analysis of the letters in the message for Robert

2.2.3 Digraphs

There are three sources of weakness in the Caesar code:

1   The calculations involved in all the encryption, decryption and cracking processes are fairly simple and easily performed, especially with a computer on hand.

2   The number of possible keys is small so it would be straightforward to try each of the usable 25 keys until a recognizable message emerged.

3   The statistics of the original message are not camouflaged. Therefore, knowledge of the kind of message and its language helps a potential cracker.

An encryption system that had more potential keys would discourage a cracker from using the brute force approach of trying all the conceivable keys.

The Caesar code can be extended to provide more keys by using a similar approach to encrypt groups of letters. A simple extension would be to encrypt pairs of letters, which are known as *digraphs*. First, as with the Caesar code, letter pairs have to be turned into mathematical objects. There are 26 possible first letters in the pair and for each of these there are 26 possible second letters giving a total of 26×26, which is often written as 26^2, combinations and which turns out to be 676. One way of coding pairs of letters is to start with the pair 'AA' and code it as 0, then code 'AB' as 1 and to continue up to 'AZ' as 25. After that, assume 'BA' is 26 and so on until the combination 'ZZ' is encoded as 675. This scheme can be expressed in a formula. First, find the position in the alphabet of each letter in the pair. For example, in the pair 'DO', the first letter is the fourth letter of the alphabet and the second letter is the fifteenth letter of the alphabet. These are coded as before as 3 and 14. Next, multiply the first number by 26 and add the result to the code of the second of the two letters in the original pair:

$$3 \times 26 + 14 = 92$$

and the result is taken to stand for the letter pair 'DO'.

To perform the reverse operation to find the letter pair given the number 92 notice that the first part of the earlier calculation involved multiplication by 26. So, the number of times that 26 will divide into 92 gives a clue to the code for the first letter of the pair and the remainder after dividing by 26 gives the code for the second letter of the pair. Using a calculator, 92 divided by 26 is 3.53846. Considering the whole number part of this result, 26 divides 92 three times. The first of the encoded pair of letters has the code 3, which stands for the letter D. Again using the calculator, $26 \times 3 = 78$ so the multiplication of 26 by 3 accounts for 78 of the original 92 and the remainder is $92 - 78 = 14$. The second letter was, indeed, O, which is coded by the number 14. The coding from a pair of numbers to a single larger number and its decoding are not, strictly, encryption and decryption. No attempt has been made to deliberately obscure the data.

Now to encrypt a pair of letters with 676 combinations it is possible to work modulo 676 and to draw the codes from Z_{676}. As with modulo 26 addition, modulo 676 addition means adding numbers together as usual, but if the result is 676 or greater, repeatedly subtracting 676 until the result is less than 676. The key is, therefore, a number between 0 and 675, say 637, then encrypting the coded letters 'DO' involves adding, using modulo 676 addition, the key to the code for the letter pair, which was calculated to be 92. The ciphertext is given by:

$$c \equiv p + K \bmod 676$$
$$\equiv 92 + 637 \bmod 676$$
$$\equiv 729 \bmod 676$$

Then, using the properties of modulo 676 addition,

$$c \equiv 729 \bmod 676$$
$$\equiv 729 - 676 \equiv 53 \bmod 676$$

To convert the result to a letter pair, divide it by 26:

$$53 / 26 = 2.03846$$

The whole number part is 2. According to the coding scheme devised in this section, the first letter of the pair is given by 2, which encodes the letter C. The 2 accounts for $2 \times 26 = 52$ of the original code of 53. The remainder is therefore $53 - 52 = 1$. This gives the second letter of the pair as the second letter of the alphabet, B. The encrypted pair is then 'CB'.

To decrypt the message the pair 'CB' is first encoded again which gives, as expected,

$$2 \times 26 + 1 = 53$$

The decryption key added to the encrypted message should restore the original plaintext message. For the Caesar code and in this case, the decryption key, $\overline{K}$, is given by the expression:

$$K + \overline{K} \equiv 676 \bmod 676$$

For a key of 637:

$$637 + \overline{K} \equiv 676 \bmod 676$$

Therefore, $\overline{K} = 39$, since

$$637 + 39 \equiv 676 \bmod 676$$

The decrypted message is then given by adding the decryption key to the encrypted message modulo 676:

$$p \equiv c + \overline{K} \bmod 676$$
$$\equiv 53 + 39 \bmod 676$$
$$\equiv 92 \bmod 676$$

92 is the encoded version of the original plaintext 'DO'.

An advantage of using digraphs is that there are a larger number of keys to try. The arithmetic too is becoming a little more involved, though not daunting, especially if a computer is available. It is also more difficult to use the statistics since there are many more combinations of letters to deal with and the probabilities of pairs are less easily discriminated, though Figure 7 shows there are some distinct differences that would aid a cracker in finding the encryption key.

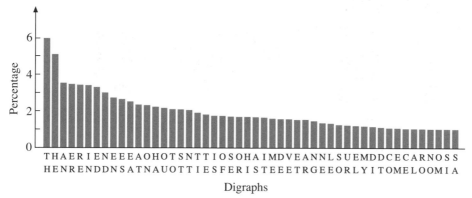

Figure 7 The probability of the most frequently occurring digraphs in Mary Shelley's *Frankenstein*

Using two letters as a key, it would take 26×26 attempts to try all possible keys. One or some of these combinations might not adequately conceal the message but between one and around $26 \times 26 = 676$ attempts would be needed to find the key giving an average of about 338 attempts, or a probability of cracking the code in one attempt of $1 / 676 = 0.00148$. Clearly, cracking the system with two letter keys is likely to need substantially more attempts than with the key based on a single letter. For the cracker, the lower probability of cracking the code in one attempt implies that more time and effort might be needed. This makes it less likely that the cracker will succeed, or if the probability were sufficiently small they might be deterred from attempting to break the code.

Encryption and decryption can be made more secure by increasing the number of letters that are encrypted in a block; however, there are other operations that can also be used.

2.2.4 Encoding

So far I have looked at encrypting one or two letters, but in practice, objects more extensive than a few letters need to be protected by encryption – long texts, tracks of commercial music, for example, and pictures. Long texts can be treated as a succession of characters and each character can be encrypted separately. Or characters can be grouped together in digraphs or much larger blocks and encrypted in these larger blocks using potentially larger keys. Musical recordings represent the pressure variations that cause a microphone to vibrate. The microphone effectively measures the pressure variations and samples of these measurements are taken. The succession of numbers that represent these samples, on their own or in combination can form the blocks that are treated as mathematical objects and encrypted.

Figure 8   A picture of a key sampled for use in a computer

Pictures can also be encrypted if a suitable encoding can be found. Figure 8 is a black and white picture of a key. If black is denoted by a one and white by a zero I can draw out the key on a grid with the numbers highlighting the different areas as shown in Figure 9.

```
000000000000011111111000000000000000000000000000000000000000000000000000000
000000000000011111111000000000000000000000000000000000000000000000000000000
000000000001111111111110000000000000000000000000000000000000000000000000000
000000000011111111111111100000000000000000000000000000000000000000000000000
000000000111111111111111110000000000000000000000000000000000000000000000000
000000000111111111111111110000000000000000000000000000000000000000000000000
000000111111111111111111110000000000000000000000000000000000000000000000000
000001111111111111111111111100000000000000000000000000000000000000000000000
000011111111111111111111111111000000000000000000000000000000000000000000000
000111111111111111111111111111111111111111111111111111111111111111110000
001111111111111111111111111111111111111111111111111111111111111111111000
011111011111111111111111111111111111111111111111111111111111111111111100
111110001111111111111111111111111111111111111111111111111111111111111110
111100001111111111111111111111111111111111111111111111111111111111111111
111100001111111111111111111111111111111111111111111111111111111111111110
111100001111111111111111111111111111111111111111111111111111111111111100
111100001111111111111111111111111111111111111111111111111111111111111000
111100001111111111111111111111111111111111111110011111111111110000
111110001111111111111111111111110111001111110011001100111110000
111100011111111111111111111111110110011001100111001100110011001111000000
111110011111111111111111111111110110011001100111001100110011001110000000
011111111111111111111111111111000000000000000000000000000000000000000000000
001111111111111111111111111111000000000000000000000000000000000000000000000
000111111111111111111111111111000000000000000000000000000000000000000000000
000011111111111111111111111110000000000000000000000000000000000000000000000
000000111111111111111111111100000000000000000000000000000000000000000000000
000000011111111111111111111000000000000000000000000000000000000000000000000
000000001111111111111111111000000000000000000000000000000000000000000000000
000000001111111111111111111000000000000000000000000000000000000000000000000
000000000001111111111111111000000000000000000000000000000000000000000000000
000000000001111111111111110000000000000000000000000000000000000000000000000
000000000000011111110000000000000000000000000000000000000000000000000000000
```

Figure 9   The picture of the key encoded in 0s and 1s

The picture is not yet in a form that can be encrypted using the Caesar code. A convention is needed to sweep up the 1s and 0s into groups. There are 75 characters in each row so one possible convention is to start at the top left of the picture, work along the top row and group the bits into groups of 5. Doing this for the first row gives the successive groups:

00000, 00000, 00011, 11111, 10000, 00000, 00000, 00000, 00000, 00000, 00000, 00000, 00000, 00000, 00000

These individual groups can be treated as numbers using the convention that any noughts stand for 0 (zero), but a one in the rightmost position of the group of five stands for 1. A one in the second position stands for an additional 2; a one in the third position from the left stands for an additional 4; a one in the fourth position stands for twice as much, an additional 8; and, finally, a one in the leftmost position stands for an additional 16. For the first row all the groups containing all zeros 00000 stand simply for 0. The others that include ones need further interpretation. 00011 for instance has a one in the rightmost position and this counts for 1 and a one in the next position which counts for an additional 2 – a total of 3. The group 11111 is interpreted as $16+8+4+2+1$, which adds up to 31, while the group beginning with a one, 10000, is represented by 16 alone. The first row can therefore be encoded by the sequence:

$$0, 0, 3, 31, 16, 0, 0, 0, 0, 0, 0, 0, 0, 0, 0$$

The result of repeating this operation for each row is shown in Figure 10.

0	0	3	31	16	0	0	0	0	0	0	0	0	0	0
0	0	7	31	24	0	0	0	0	0	0	0	0	0	0
0	0	31	31	30	0	0	0	0	0	0	0	0	0	0
0	1	31	31	31	0	0	0	0	0	0	0	0	0	0
0	3	31	31	31	16	0	0	0	0	0	0	0	0	0
0	3	31	31	31	16	0	0	0	0	0	0	0	0	0
0	15	31	31	31	24	0	0	0	0	0	0	0	0	0
1	31	31	31	31	31	16	0	0	0	0	0	0	0	0
3	31	31	31	31	31	16	0	0	0	0	0	0	0	0
7	31	31	31	31	31	31	31	31	31	31	31	31	31	16
15	23	31	31	31	31	31	31	31	31	31	31	31	31	24
31	3	31	31	31	31	31	31	31	31	31	31	31	31	28
30	3	31	31	31	31	31	31	31	31	31	31	31	31	30
30	3	31	31	31	31	31	31	31	31	31	31	31	31	31
30	3	31	31	31	31	31	31	31	31	31	31	31	31	30
30	3	31	31	31	31	31	31	31	31	31	31	31	31	28
31	3	31	31	31	31	31	31	29	25	31	25	31	31	24
31	3	31	31	31	31	31	31	29	25	31	25	31	31	16
31	23	31	31	31	31	31	31	29	25	25	25	25	25	0
15	31	31	31	31	31	31	31	29	29	25	25	25	30	0
7	31	31	31	31	31	16	16	0	0	0	0	0	28	0
3	31	31	31	31	31	16	16	0	0	0	0	0	0	0
1	7	31	31	31	31	24	0	0	0	0	0	0	0	0
0	7	31	31	31	31	16	0	0	0	0	0	0	0	0
0	3	31	31	31	31	16	0	0	0	0	0	0	0	0
0	1	31	31	31	30	0	0	0	0	0	0	0	0	0
0	0	31	31	30	0	0	0	0	0	0	0	0	0	0
0	0	15	31	24	0	0	0	0	0	0	0	0	0	0
0	0	3	31	0	0	0	0	0	0	0	0	0	0	0

Figure 10 Black and white data grouped into five bit groups and encoded

Each number corresponding to a group of five bits can be encrypted separately and the entire picture encrypted as the string of numbers taken row after row. Provided the recipients know how to reassemble the numbers after decryption they can reconstruct the original picture. Notice that there are a large number of repeats in the data and encrypting each number with the same key will not hide this repetition. Figure 11 shows how the data encrypted using modulo 32 addition would appear if the encrypted data were treated as a picture when the key is 22 and is the same for each block of data.[83]

Figure 11 The encrypted image reproduced as a picture

The image is obfuscated but the original image still shows through. There are three courses of action to try to make the obfuscation more thorough; the first is to group larger numbers of bits together before encrypting them, the second is to change the key from block to block, possibly copying Vernam's method of encryption for telegraphed text[9] in which he used a different key for each letter. The succession of keys might be chosen purely at random or a series of keys might be repeated.

Figure 12 The image encrypted using a random succession of keys

Figure 12 shows the image encrypted in blocks of five bits using modulo 32 addition with a key selected at random for each successive block. The encryption appears to be very successful since the original image has been obscured completely. Of course, to decrypt the encrypted image, the corresponding random sequence of decryption keys must also be sent to the recipient, presumably in secret.

2.2.5 Summary

Encryption using addition can be made more robust by increasing the amount of data that is encrypted at a time. This means increasing the modulus in the modular addition. For text this means encrypting several letters at a time and that requires a scheme for encoding strings of letters as numbers. Pictures can also be encoded and more robust encryption can be achieved by grouping together more picture elements.

When short blocks of data are encrypted with the same key, any repetition in the plaintext appears as a repetition in the ciphertext. This can be detected by examining the statistics of messages, which can provide clues for cracking the code.

Changing the key frequently can reduce the repetition, but that brings to the fore the problem of distributing keys in secret.

2.3   Conclusion

The Caesar code can be described in mathematical terms. Both encryption and decryption can be treated as mathematical operations using modular addition. For encryption the plaintext is transformed into a number and the key is added using a suitable modulus. For decryption the same operation is performed by adding a complementary decryption key to the ciphertext.

The characteristics required for encryption are also the characteristics of mathematical 'Groups'. A Group has to have a set of elements, like the set of coded characters to be encrypted. There has to be an operation, such as modular addition, and the result of performing the operation has to ensure closure. For every element in the Group there has to be a corresponding element that effectively undoes the operation. In terms of encryption, every encryption key must have a corresponding decryption key. Finally, a Group is associative so it does not matter in which order a sequence of operations is performed. Associativity ensures that encryption followed by decryption recreates the plaintext. Because the properties of a Group meet a set of requirements for an encryption scheme, it is worthwhile looking for other Groups, especially other operations that have similar properties. They are candidates for different forms of encryption.

Once data is encoded as a number, modular addition can provide a method of encryption. There are conventions for recording pictures, moving images and sounds as strings of bits, which can then be re-coded as numbers. Modular addition, therefore, offers one way of encrypting text, music, films and documents.

Because encryption protects valued data, code crackers will find it worthwhile to try and break a code. In the case of the Caesar code this means finding out the key. Statistical analysis of ciphertext can help the cracker but also shows those who want to protect data what the threats are to their encryption schemes and how they might thwart attempts to crack the code. At a first glance it looks as though changing the key frequently will help.

Chapter Three

More encryption

Besides modular addition, other mathematical operations can form a Group. Two operations that have characteristics that make them suitable for encryption are *modular multiplication* and *modular exponentiation*. The techniques using modular exponentiation also go under the name of *discrete logarithms*.

There are some restrictions on the keys and ranges of numbers that can be used for multiplication and further restrictions when using exponentiation. Identifying the restrictions requires a look at the mathematics surrounding the operations. It is a price that has to be paid for encryption operations that can provide protection against a wide range of threats and which have some useful properties.

Associated with the operations of multiplication and exponentiation are a number of procedures that make it feasible to perform operations on very large numbers. Using very large numbers and hence large aggregates of data in cryptograms makes it more difficult for people who try to crack the encryption.

3.1 Multiplication

Multiplication has some similarities with addition and with appropriate restrictions can be made to have the properties of a Group. The properties of a Group provide many of the characteristics that are required of an operation used for encryption. The restrictions on multiplication can be reduced by working with prime numbers. The calculations involved can still be daunting but special procedures can reduce the size of the numbers generated in the course of the calculation. Calculations can then be preformed using a calculator. Also, with the special procedures and the use of a computer, much larger numbers can be used in the encryption process, and this makes the results of encryption difficult to crack.

3.1.1 Encryption using multiplication

Instead of using modulo 26 addition it is possible to use modulo 26 multiplication. At first sight this would appear to be straightforward. By treating encryption using multiplication as an analogue of encryption using addition, then with plaintext p and a key K the ciphertext c would be given by the expression:

$$c \equiv p \times K \bmod 26$$

For instance if the key K is 15 and the letter of the plaintext message being encrypted is 'R', which is encoded by the number 17, then the ciphertext is given by the calculation

$$17 \times 15 \equiv 255 \bmod 26$$

The result, 255, is larger than 26. Working modulo 26, means that 26 can be subtracted repeatedly until the result is in the range 0 to 25. Thus:

$$255 \equiv 255 - 26 \equiv 229 \bmod 26$$

Subtracting another 26 gives:

$$229 \equiv 229 - 26 \equiv 203 \bmod 26$$

This process can be continued until the result is less than 26. After subtracting 26 nine times the final result is 21, which corresponds to the letter 'V'. With a key of 15, therefore, the letter 'R' is encrypted as the letter 'V'. A complete table can be drawn up which shows how the alphabet could be encrypted using multiplication modulo 26 and a key of 15.

Table 8 An encryption table for the multiplication process with a key of 15 working modulo 26

A	B	C	D	E	F	G	H	I	J	K	L	M	N	O	P	Q	R	S	T	U	V	W	X	Y	Z
0	1	2	3	4	5	6	7	8	9	10	11	12	13	14	15	16	17	18	19	20	21	22	23	24	25
0	15	4	19	8	23	12	1	16	5	20	9	24	13	2	17	6	21	10	25	14	3	18	7	22	11
A	P	E	T	I	X	M	B	Q	F	U	J	Y	N	C	R	G	V	K	Z	O	D	S	H	W	L

The first row of Table 8 gives the alphabet, the second row is a numerical coding of each letter, the third row is the result of the encryption using modular multiplication and the last row shows the encrypted numerical code translated back into letters. So, for example 'CAT' would be encoded as '2 0 19', encrypted as '4 0 25' and the ciphertext would be 'EAZ'.

A defect of this particular encryption table that will be attended to later is that the encryption process does not modify the letter 'A' or the letter 'N'.

3.1.2 Using a calculator

Multiplying whole numbers gives larger results than adding them. When working with modular multiplication it is, therefore, helpful to be able to use a calculator. Some calculators will perform modular arithmetic directly, but an elementary calculator can also be of assistance. Suppose, for instance, the plaintext letter 'V' corresponding to a code of 21 is to be encrypted using a key of 15. Multiplying the two together using a calculator gives the result 315.

To work out the result using modulo 26, the modulus has to be repeatedly subtracted until the result is less than the modulus. There are several methods for doing this with the aid of a calculator.

Suppose 315 was divided by 26, using the calculator the result would be 12.115385. Of course, the exact number of digits in the result depends on the model of the calculator. The result implies that $315 = 12.115385 \times 26$. I can split the result into two parts and write it as $12 + 0.115385$ and when it is multiplied by 26 I get

$$315 = 12.115385 \times 26$$
$$= (12 + 0.115385) \times 26$$
$$= 12 \times 26 + 0.115385 \times 26$$

According to the rules of modulo 26 arithmetic, I can simplify the last expression by subtracting 26 twelve times. This is the same as subtracting 12×26.

$$315 \equiv 12 \times 26 + 0.115385 \times 26 \bmod 26$$
$$\equiv 12 \times 26 + 0.115385 \times 26 - 12 \times 26 \bmod 26$$
$$\equiv 0.115385 \times 26 \bmod 26$$

Using the calculator to work out 0.115385×26, I get 3.000010. I would hope to get a whole number, but because calculators have a limited precision the result is not exact and will depend again on the model and make of the calculator, however the result is very close to 3.

Alternatively, I could have subtracted 12×26 from 315 using the calculator and I would have got

$$315 - 12 \times 26 = 315 - 312 = 3$$

In summary, using a calculator, the calculation to find 315 mod 26 can be performed by:

1   dividing the number by the modulus

$$315 \div 26 = 12.115385$$

2   take the whole number part and multiply by the modulus

$$12 \times 26 = 312$$

3   subtract the result from the original number to find the remainder, which is the required result

$$315 - 312 \equiv 3 \bmod 26$$

3.1.3 Decryption

Decryption of ciphertext can be performed by using Table 8 backwards, or by deriving a decryption table from Table 8. Table 9 is a decryption table for text encrypted using a key of 15.

Table 9 A decryption table for the multiplication process assuming encryption was performed using multiplication modulo 26 and a key of 15

A	B	C	D	E	F	G	H	I	J	K	L	M	N	O	P	Q	R	S	T	U	V	W	X	Y	Z
0	1	2	3	4	5	6	7	8	9	10	11	12	13	14	15	16	17	18	19	20	21	22	23	24	25
0	7	14	21	2	9	16	23	4	11	18	25	6	13	20	1	8	15	22	3	10	17	24	5	12	19
A	H	O	V	C	J	Q	X	E	L	S	Z	G	N	U	B	I	P	W	D	K	R	Y	F	M	T

The '4 0 25' is the encoding for the ciphertext 'EAZ'. The third row of Table 9 shows that when decrypted this becomes '2 0 19' which corresponds to the plaintext 'CAT'.

Following the analogy of modulo 26 addition it is to be expected that decryption can also be performed by doing a simple calculation. If the asymmetric decryption key is $\overline{K}$ then the decryption operation would be expected to be of the form:

$$p \equiv c \times \overline{K} \bmod 26$$

This works for encryption with a key of 15. The decryption key is 7. Taking the encoded ciphertext to be '4 0 25', corresponding to the ciphertect 'EAZ' and performing modulo 26 multiplication with the decryption key gives the following results:

$$4 \times 7 \equiv 28 \equiv 2 \bmod 26$$

$$0 \times 7 \equiv 0 \bmod 26$$

$$25 \times 7 \equiv 175 \equiv 19 \bmod 26$$

The result is as anticipated '2 0 19', which corresponds to the plaintext 'CAT'.

The plaintext is derived from the ciphertext by multiplication with the decryption key and this decryption operation is summarized in the formula:

$$p \equiv c \times \overline{K} \bmod 26$$

The ciphertext in this formula can be replaced by $p \times K$ and the result describes the encryption operation followed by the decryption operation, which should reconstitute the plaintext:

$$p \equiv (p \times K) \times \overline{K} \bmod 26$$

Because multiplication is associative, the composite formula can be rearranged to give:

$$p \equiv p \times (K \times \overline{K}) \bmod 26$$

Because multiplication by one does not alter a number, then, provided $K \times \overline{K} \equiv 1 \bmod 26$, the result of encryption and then decryption will give the original plaintext. For the key $K \equiv 15$ the decryption key was $\overline{K} \equiv 7$ and, as required, their product is:

$$K \times \overline{K} \equiv 15 \times 7 \equiv 105 \equiv 26 \times 4 + 1 \equiv 1 \bmod 26$$

The decryption key is, therefore, the number that when multiplied, modulo 26, by the encryption key gives the answer 1.

3.1.4 Some problems

Unfortunately, encryption using multiplication has some peculiarities. Most obviously, encryption with a key of 1 leaves the plaintext unaltered, and, perhaps worse, encryption with a key of 0 (zero) produces a ciphertext code of 0 for any plaintext. A key of 0 therefore obliterates the plaintext.

A second deficiency arises by encoding a letter, the letter 'A' in Table 8 with 0. Any key when multiplied by the code for a plaintext 'A' will generate 0 and any letter 'A's in the plaintext appear as 'A's in the ciphertext. This could be of assistance to a cryptanalyst.

However, there is a more subtle problem with multiplication which arises with certain choices of keys and can be illustrated when the key is 8 working with modulo 26 multiplication. Table 10 is an encryption table derived using a key of 8.

Table 10 An encryption table for the multiplication process with a key of 8 working modulo 26

A	B	C	D	E	F	G	H	I	J	K	L	M	N	O	P	Q	R	S	T	U	V	W	X	Y	Z
0	1	2	3	4	5	6	7	8	9	10	11	12	13	14	15	16	17	18	19	20	21	22	23	24	25
0	8	16	24	6	14	22	4	12	20	2	10	18	0	8	16	24	6	14	22	4	12	20	2	10	18
A	I	Q	Y	G	O	W	E	M	U	C	K	S	A	I	Q	Y	G	O	W	E	M	U	C	K	S

Encrypting the plaintext 'CAT' would generate the ciphertext 'QAW'. The recipient of the message might try to use Table 10 backwards to decrypt the ciphertext, but would be immediately confronted with a problem because in the last line of the table 'Q' appears twice. The person decoding the message would not know whether the 'Q' in the ciphertext corresponded to a 'C' in the plaintext or a 'P'. Similarly, for the second letter they would not know if an 'A' or an 'N' was intended and the last letter, 'W' in the ciphertext, might have been a 'G' or a 'T'. 'CAT', 'PAT', 'CNT', 'PNT', 'CAG', 'PAG', 'PNG' or 'PNT' are all possibilities.

The possibility of introducing such ambiguities during encryption restricts the choice of key and makes it necessary to choose the modulus and the key carefully.

It turns out that when working with a modulus of 26, ambiguities also arise for a key of value 13. This perhaps gives a clue to the restrictions that have to be imposed since 13 is a factor of 26. Two is the other factor. Saying 26 has the factors 13 and 2 means that when 13 and 2 are multiplied together they give the result of 26. Or, in other words, 2 or 13 can divide 26 and there will be no remainder. Two is a factor of 26 and a factor of all the even numbers. Like 13, even-numbered keys such as 8 generate encryption tables containing ambiguities when working with modulo 26 multiplication.

3.1.5   Coprime numbers

There is a theorem, a mathematical finding, that says:

> 'If you take a set of distinct numbers and multiply, using modular multiplication, each of them by a particular number then the collection of results will contain no repeats provided the particular number that was used in the multiplication was either 1 or has no factors in common with the modulus.'

Two numbers that have no factors in common are said to be *coprime*. The even numbers are *not* coprime with 26 because the even numbers and 26 can both be divided by 2. And 13 and 26 are not coprime because they both have the factor 13 and can therefore be divided exactly by 13. It should, therefore, be expected, from a knowledge of the theorem, that even numbered keys or the key of 13 will create ambiguities when encrypting using multiplication modulo 26.

For any number it is straightforward, but often tedious, to work out how many smaller numbers have no factors in common with the original choice. If the number is 26 then only the odd numbers below 26 except 13 are coprime with it. This gives 1, 3, 5, 7, 9, 11, 15, 17, 19, 21, 23 and 25 or a total of 12 smaller numbers which are coprime with 26. This characteristic of a number has been given a special status by being associated with the oddly named *Euler Totient Function*. The Euler Totient Function is usually denoted by the Greek letter ϕ (called 'phi'). For 26, I have discovered that $\phi(26) = 12$. This means that there are twelve numbers smaller than 26 which are coprime with it and implies, in the encryption scheme using modulo 26 multiplication, there are twelve keys that will not generate ambiguous results.

3.1.6 Working with a prime number

One way to ensure that multiplication can be used as an encryption operation for any key is to choose the modulus of the operation as a *prime number*. This works because prime numbers have no factors other than one and themselves. This is to say, all the numbers smaller than a prime number are *coprime* with that prime number. Because given a prime number q there are $q - 1$ smaller numbers that are all coprime with q, the Euler Totient Function for a prime number is $\phi(q) = q - 1$.

To enable the encryption of letters using modular multiplication and to avoid restrictions on the keys that might be used, a modulus other than 26 has to be used. The nearest prime numbers to 26 are 23 and 29. With 23 it would not be possible to encode all the letters of the alphabet but 29 would do. Table 11 shows, in the first row, the alphabet and an extra two symbols to exploit the additional codes (a left and a right angled bracket). The coding of the letters has also been altered by adding one to the earlier code of Table 10 so that the code of zero is no longer used. This avoids some of the problems identified in subsection 3.1.4.

Table 11   An encryption table for a multiplication operation modulo 29 using a key of 8

	A	B	C	D	E	F	G	H	I	J	K	L	M	N	O	P	Q	R	S	T	U	V	W	X	Y	Z	<	>
0	1	2	3	4	5	6	7	8	9	10	11	12	13	14	15	16	17	18	19	20	21	22	23	24	25	26	27	28
0	8	16	24	3	11	19	27	6	14	22	1	9	17	25	4	12	20	28	7	15	23	2	10	18	26	5	13	21
	H	P	X	C	K	S	<	F	N	V	A	I	Q	Y	D	L	T	>	G	O	W	B	J	R	Z	E	M	U

The coding convention for the alphabet in this scheme is therefore different from the convention used before where 'A' was encoded as 0. 'A' is now encoded as 1. The second row is the numerical code assigned to the letters and brackets; the third row is the result of performing the encryption operation by multiplying by a key of 8 and working modulo 29. For instance if the plaintext was the letter 'C' then it would be coded as a 3 and encrypted as $3 \times 8 \equiv 24 \bmod 29$. The final row of Table 11 gives the interpretation of the encrypted data as symbols of the alphabet and the two added brackets. The letter 'C' is therefore encrypted as an 'X'.

Using Table 11 the plaintext 'CAT' is encoded as '3 1 20' and using modulo 29 multiplication and a key of 8 the encrypted numerical codes are:

$$3 \times 8 \equiv 24 \bmod 29$$

$$1 \times 8 \equiv 8 \bmod 29$$

$$20 \times 8 \equiv 160 \equiv 5 \times 29 + 15 \equiv 15 \bmod 29$$

The resulting numerical sequence '24 8 15' becomes the ciphertext 'XHO', which is confirmed by the entries in Table 11.

3.1.7 Finding the decryption key

Individual letters can be decrypted using an *asymmetric decryption key*. Encryption with a key of 8 modulo 29 is the operation:

$$p \times 8 \bmod 29$$

If the asymmetric decryption key is $\overline{K}$ then the decryption operation would be expected to be of the form:

$$p \equiv c \times \overline{K} \bmod 29$$

Substituting the ciphertext derived from encryption in this formula produces the result

$$p \equiv p \times \left(8 \times \overline{K}\right) \bmod 29$$

Provided $8 \times \overline{K} \bmod 29 \equiv 1$ then the result of the decryption operation will be the plaintext. Finding $K \times \overline{K} \equiv 1 \bmod n$ is not so easy. One way is to search systematically through the possible keys until one is found that satisfies the congruence. Multiplications can be simplified a little when the operation is broken down into a number of steps and it is recognized that working modulo 29 means that numbers generated in the calculation can be reduced to less than 29. First, a set of multiplications by 1, 2, 4, 8, 16 and so on are performed:

$$1 \times 8 \equiv 8 \bmod 29$$
$$2 \times 8 \equiv 2 \times \left(1 \times 8\right) \equiv 2 \times 8 \equiv 16 \bmod 29$$
$$4 \times 8 \equiv 2 \times \left(2 \times 8\right) \equiv 2 \times 16 \equiv 32 \equiv 3 \bmod 29$$
$$8 \times 8 \equiv 2 \times \left(4 \times 8\right) \equiv 2 \times 3 \equiv 6 \bmod 29$$
$$16 \times 8 \equiv 2 \times \left(8 \times 8\right) \equiv 2 \times 6 \equiv 12 \bmod 29$$

And then the multiplication of interest is decomposed to exploit the calculated results, for instance, because 23 is $16 + 4 + 2 + 1$:

$$23 \times 8 \equiv \left(16 + 4 + 2 + 1\right) \times 8 \bmod 29$$
$$\equiv \left(16 \times 8\right) + \left(4 \times 8\right) + \left(2 \times 8\right) + \left(1 \times 8\right) \bmod 29$$

Once the calculation has been decomposed the calculated results can be substituted, added and the calculation completed.

$$23 \times 8 \equiv (16 \times 8) + (4 \times 8) + (2 \times 8) + (1 \times 8) \bmod 29$$
$$\equiv 12 + 3 + 16 + 8 \bmod 29$$
$$\equiv 15 + 16 + 8 \equiv 31 + 8 \bmod 29$$
$$\equiv 2 + 8 \equiv 10 \bmod 29$$

With a simplified process for multiplication in place, a search for the decryption key can be carried out to find out the value that when multiplied by the encryption key of 8 gives the result of 1. The outlines of successive calculations are shown in Table 12 and the number that when multiplied by 8 modulo 29 gives 1, proves to be 11.

Table 12   A search for the decryption key

n	$8 \times n \bmod 29$		
1	$1 \times 8 \equiv$		8 mod 29
2	$2 \times 8 \equiv$		16 mod 29
3	$(2 + 1) \times 8 \equiv$	$16 + 8 \equiv$	24 mod 29
4	$4 \times 8 \equiv$		3 mod 29
5	$(4 + 1) \times 8 \equiv$	$3 + 8 \equiv$	11 mod 29
6	$(4 + 2) \times 8 \equiv$	$3 + 16 \equiv$	19 mod 29
7	$(4 + 2 + 1) \times 8 \equiv$	$3 + 16 + 8 \equiv$	27 mod 29
8	$8 \times 8 \equiv$		6 mod 29
9	$(8 + 1) \times 8 \equiv$	$6 + 8 \equiv$	14 mod 29
10	$(8 + 2) \times 8 \equiv$	$6 + 16 \equiv$	22 mod 29
11	$(8 + 2 + 1) \times 8 \equiv$	$6 + 16 + 8 \equiv$	1 mod 29

The ciphertext 'XHO' encoded as '24 8 15' decrypted with a decryption key of 11 gives a series of results:

$$24 \times 11 \equiv 264 \equiv 9 \times 29 + 3 \equiv 3 \bmod 29$$
$$8 \times 11 \equiv 88 \bmod 29 \equiv 3 \times 29 + 1 \equiv 1 \bmod 29$$
$$15 \times 11 \equiv 165 \bmod 29 \equiv 5 \times 29 + 20 \equiv 20 \bmod 29$$

These results form the sequence '3 1 20' which once again corresponds to the plaintext 'CAT'.

3.1.8 Groups and multiplication

The properties of the Caesar code that made it useful as an encryption scheme were the same as the generalized properties of a Group. Encryption using multiplication with a modulus given by a prime number has similar properties. Firstly, a Group consists of a number of elements and an operation that can be performed on those elements. For modulo 29 multiplication the numbers from 1 to 28 are the elements of the Group. Zero (0) causes complications and is omitted. The operation modulo 29 multiplication was denoted by $\times$, which can be put in place of the symbol $\circ$ used in the general description of a Group.

Secondly, when the operation is performed on a pair of elements in the Group, the result is also an element of the Group. Modulo 29 multiplication ensures that the encryption and decryption operations give results in the range 1 to 28 and that there is, therefore, closure.

Thirdly, there is an element of the Group that is called the identity, symbolized by e, which ensures that for any element of the Group a, $a \circ e \equiv a$ and $e \circ a \equiv a$. For encryption using modulo 29 multiplication the identity is 1 since for any number denoted by a in the range 1 to 28, $a \times 1 \equiv a$ mod 29 and $1 \times a \equiv a$ mod 29.

Fourthly, if the operation is denoted by $\circ$ and a, b and c are elements of the Group then $(a \circ b) \circ c \equiv a \circ (b \circ c)$. This associative property is required to prove that encryption followed by decryption regenerates the plaintext. Multiplication is associative and, for example, $(p \times K) \times \overline{K}$ mod 29 is the same as $p \times (K \times \overline{K})$ mod 29.

Fifthly, for any element, a for instance, in the Group there is one other corresponding element, denoted by $\overline{a}$, which can be combined using the operation to give the identity. If the operation is denoted by $\circ$ then $a \circ \overline{a} \equiv e$ and $\overline{a} \circ a \equiv e$. For the Group used above this means that any number in the range 1 to 29 denoted by a has a unique partner denoted by $\overline{a}$ that ensures that $a \times \overline{a} \equiv 1$ mod 29 and $\overline{a} \times a \equiv 1$ mod 29. Strictly speaking it is not possible to find a number that when multiplied by zero gives the result 1. With 0 included Z_{29} and multiplication do not constitute a Group. A Group can only be formed if 0 is omitted. The symbol Z_{29}^* refers to the integers up to 28 with zero omitted and thus Z_{29}^* with modulo 29 multiplication forms a Group.

The ambiguity found when dealing with modulo 26 reveals that working with a modulus that is not a prime number means that the number a does not always have a unique partner for $\overline{a}$. A Group cannot, therefore, be formed using modulo 26 multiplication, even with 0 omitted from the calculations.

Sometimes, the suffix p is used to indicate that a prime modulus is required. Thus Z_p^* with modulo p multiplication constitutes a Group.

3.1.9   Digraphs

As with addition, strings of letters can be combined before encryption is performed. Digraphs, for example can be formed and then encrypted. There are 676 pairs of letters from 'AA' to 'ZZ' and by a fortunate coincidence 677 is a prime number. After omitting 0, encryption using multiplication modulo 677 could, therefore, neatly accommodate the 676 combinations of letter pairs.

A system is then required for coding the pairs of letters. For example, reverting to the earlier convention single letters are encoded using the number sequence 0 to 25. Then the code for the first letter is multiplied by 26 and added to the code for the second letter. Encoding the letter pair 'GO', containing the seventh and the fifteenth letters of the alphabet, generated

$$6 \times 26 + 14 = 170$$

This is not satisfactory for encryption using multiplication because 'AA' would be coded as 0. To avoid this, 1 can be added to the result. Now, 'GO' is encoded as:

$$(6 \times 26 + 14) + 1 = 171$$

This is not a standard form of encoding, but it is convenient in this example. Suppose the key is 143, then encryption of the digraph 'GO' using multiplication modulo 677 is:

$$171 \times 143 \equiv 24453 \bmod 677$$

Using a calculator to divide 24 453 by 677 gives 36.119645 so 24 453 is given by 677×36 plus a little more. In fact,

$$24453 - 677 \times 36 = 24453 - 24372$$
$$= 81$$

The encrypted digraph is therefore given by:

$$171 \times 143 \equiv 24453 \bmod 677$$
$$\equiv 36 \times 677 + 81 \bmod 677$$
$$\equiv 81 \bmod 677$$

Turning this into letters again requires a calculation. First subtract the 1 used to avoid the code of 0 to get $81 - 1 = 80 \bmod 677$. This encodes a letter pair. The first letter is given by how many times 81 can be divided by 26, which is 3 times. The first letter is therefore the letter 'D'. The second letter is given by what remains after subtracting $3 \times 26 = 78$. This is $80 - 78 = 2$, and 2 encodes the letter 'C'. The ciphertext is therefore 'DC'.

The decryption key is 303. To perform the decryption operation the coded ciphertext is multiplied by the decryption key:

$$81 \times 303 \equiv 24543 \bmod 677$$
$$\equiv 24543 - 36 \times 677 \bmod 677$$
$$\equiv 24543 - 24372 \bmod 677$$
$$\equiv 171 \bmod 677$$

which corresponds with the original encoded plaintext.

3.1.10 Summary

Multiplication can be used as a method of encryption, but there are restrictions. The restrictions are minimized when multiplication is performed using a modulus given by a prime number. Provided 0 is left out of possible encodings of plaintext, encryption using multiplication with a prime modulus forms a Group that has certain desirable properties, which allow a full range of ciphertexts and keys to be encrypted and decrypted. When the modulus is not a prime number, the number of keys that can be used is restricted. The Euler Totient Function gives an indication of how many numbers smaller than a given number are coprime with that number. This, too, is the number of valid keys.

There are various shortcuts for performing modular arithmetic and some allow calculations to be done on elementary calculators.

3.2   Using exponentiation

Exponentiation effectively involves repeated multiplication. It gives rise to greater computational difficulties than multiplication but has the useful property that it is computationally infeasible, with a suitably large modulus, to work out the key given a sample of ciphertext and the corresponding plaintext.

Encryption using exponentiation is also a feature of a number of specialist protocols including the RSA protocols that allow secure communications to take place even when the encryption key is made public.

3.2.1   Encryption

Exponentiation is a shorthand way of indicating that a number is multiplied by itself several times. For example $2 \times 2 \times 2$ is abbreviated by writing 2^3. The normal-sized 2 indicates the number that is to be multiplied and the small raised 3, called the exponent or index, denotes how many twos are involved in the multiplication. Thus $2^3 \equiv 2 \times 2 \times 2 \equiv 8$. Sometimes people will describe the operation using different words and say, for the example, that '8 is the result of raising 2 to the power of 3'.

This exponentiation operation can be combined with modular arithmetic to provide a method of encryption. The plaintext encoded as a number p is encrypted by the operation:

$$p^K \bmod n$$

where K is the key. So, for example, if I work modulo 26 and use a key of 11 and I wish to send the letter 'T' (standing for 'true') then first I encode 'T', the twentieth letter of the alphabet, as 19. With $p = 19$ the encrypted message, which I will denote with a c, is,

$$c \equiv p^K \bmod n$$
$$\equiv 19^{11} \bmod 26$$

Aside from the problem of raising nineteen to the power of eleven – multiplying eleven copies of nineteen together – there are some pitfalls with this method of encryption. Firstly, if I were to encode the letter 'A' as a 0 then the encrypted result would be 0 whatever the key. Similarly, if 'A' were coded as a 1 and then encrypted by raising 1 to some power (that is, 1 multiplied by itself a number of times) the result would always be 1 so 'A' would, whatever key was used, always be encrypted as a 1. Similarly, for a modulus n, $n - 1$ raised to any power gives either 1 or $n - 1$. Encoding 'A' as a 1 is easily avoided by coding the letters using numbers starting at 2 and ending at 27. Working modulo 29 would then avoid the use of the problematic numbers. The new coding table for the letters is given in Table 13.

Table 13   A coding table for the alphabet avoiding problematic encodings

		A	B	C	D	E	F	G	H	I	J	K	L	M	N	O	P	Q	R	S	T	U	V	W	X	Y	Z	
0	1	2	3	4	5	6	7	8	9	10	11	12	13	14	15	16	17	18	19	20	21	22	23	24	25	26	27	28

A second drawback is that for certain combinations of plaintext, key and modulus the encoding is ambiguous. For example when I use a key of 8, the new coding and a modulus of 29, I get the ciphertexts shown in Table 14.

Table 14   An encryption table for exponentiation process with a key of 8 working modulo 29

		A	B	C	D	E	F	G	H	I	J	K	L	M	N	O	P	Q	R	S	T	U	V	W	X	Y	Z	
0	1	2	3	4	5	6	7	8	9	10	11	12	13	14	15	16	17	18	19	20	21	22	23	24	25	26	27	28
0	1	24	7	25	24	23	7	20	20	25	16	1	16	23	23	16	1	16	25	20	20	7	23	24	25	7	24	1
		W	F	X	W	V	F	S	S	X	O		O	V	V	O		O	X	S	S	F	V	W	X	F	W	

There are several problems arising from the data in Table 14. Perhaps the most serious is that different letters in the upper row are encrypted using the same letters in the lower row. This duplication in encoding leads to ambiguity in the decryption as for example an 'X' in the ciphertext might stand for 'C', 'I', 'R' or 'X' in the plaintext.

These ambiguities can only be avoided by avoiding certain keys. A part of making exponentiation a practical method for encryption involves finding simple rules for the choice of suitable keys.

Encryption through exponentiation is described by the expression:

$$c \equiv p^K \bmod n$$

Someone trying to crack the code would want to find K, the secret key, so they could decrypt subsequent cryptograms. They might think themselves lucky if they managed to get a plaintext message and its cryptogram; they would hope that with the plaintext and the corresponding ciphertext they could work out the secret key. There is an operation that, given the ciphertext c and plaintext p, enables me to find K. The operation is the inverse of exponentiation and is called the logarithm. With modular arithmetic, finding logarithms is surprisingly hard and time-consuming and this helps to add another layer of security to this method of encryption. With a suitably large modulus it becomes totally impracticable to work out the logarithm in a reasonable time.

Logarithms sometimes lend their name to encryption using exponentiation so, sometimes, encryption using exponentiation is referred to under the heading of the discrete logarithm.

3.2.2 Finding powers

The letter 'T' for 'true', the twentieth letter in the alphabet, would now be encoded as 21 according to Table 13. Suppose the modulus is the prime number 29 and the key is 11 (this key does not produce ambiguous results), then the encrypted message is:

$$p^K = 21^{11} \bmod 29$$

Raising 21 to the power 11, multiplying 11 copies of 21 together, looks like a lengthy and error prone task which will result in calculations involving numbers with many digits (in fact $21^{11} = 350\ 277\ 500\ 542\ 221$). However, to work out the result I can take advantage of two things:

1   I only need to work with numbers up to 29.

2   I can break down the operation of raising 21 to the power of 11 into a number of stages.

The approach is similar to that used in subsection 3.1.7 for multiplication.

21^{11} means multiplying eleven copies of twenty-one together. A clue as to how this calculation might be broken down is given by writing the exponent of 11 as a sum of, for instance, three components $8 + 2 + 1$ then

$$21^{11} \equiv 21^{8+2+1}$$

This shows that multiplying 11 copies of 21 together is the same as first multiplying eight copies of 21 together and then multiplying the result by the product of a further two copies of 21, giving a total of 10 copies. Next, to make the total number of copies 11 the result would need to be multiplied by another copy of 21. 21^{11} can therefore be written as $21^{8} \times 21^{2} \times 21^{1}$.

A second observation can also be valuable. It is that, for instance,

$$21^{8} = 21^{4+4} = 21^{4} \times 21^{4}$$

That is, 21^{8} is the same as multiplying two copies of 21^{4} together. This can be summarized in the notation of exponentiation as $\left(21^{4}\right)^{2}$. Note also that 21^{4} can be found by multiplying two copies of 21^{2} together so that

$$21^{4} = 21^{2} \times 21^{2} = \left(21^{2}\right)^{2} \text{ and } 21^{8} = \left(21^{4}\right)^{2}$$

Now, exploiting the advantage of working modulo 29:

$$21^{2} \equiv 441 \bmod 29$$
$$\equiv 441 - 15 \times 29 \equiv 6 \bmod 29$$

Using the result for 21^{2} and taking a further step gives 21^{4} as:

$$21^{4} \equiv \left(21^{2}\right)^{2} \equiv 6^{2} \equiv 36 \bmod 29$$
$$\equiv 36 - 1 \times 29 \equiv 7 \bmod 29$$

and then utilizing the result for 21^{4} to obtain 21^{8} gives:

$$21^{8} \equiv \left(21^{4}\right)^{2} \equiv 7^{2} \equiv 49 \bmod 29$$
$$\equiv 1 \times 29 + 20 \equiv 20 \bmod 29$$

With these results the encryption calculation can be completed without the need to perform arithmetic on very large numbers:

$$21^{11} \bmod 29 = 21^{8+2+1} = 21^{8} \times 21^{2} \times 21 \equiv 20 \times 6 \times 21 \bmod 29$$
$$\equiv 120 \times 21 \equiv \left(4 \times 29 + 4\right) \times 21 \bmod 29$$
$$\equiv 4 \times 21 \equiv 84 \equiv 2 \times 29 + 26 \bmod 29$$
$$\equiv 26 \bmod 29$$

Thus by exploiting the properties of exponents the calculation is reduced to a series of simple calculations to obtain the result of encryption, which is 26, and which, using Table 13, is equivalent to the letter 'Y'.

Although the calculation is reduced to a series of simple steps there is still a lot of work involved. However, this form of staged calculation makes it ideal for incorporating into a computer program. Exponentiation is therefore a practical form of encryption when computers are available to perform the calculations.

3.2.3 Decryption

Of course, to be useful in communicating messages it must be possible to decrypt the results of encryption. The decryption procedure for exponentiation is similar to the encryption procedure. If the decryption key is $\overline{K}$ and the encrypted message is c then I would expect the decrypted message to be:

$$c^{\overline{K}} \bmod n$$

The person decrypting then needs to know the modulus n and a suitable value for the decryption key $\overline{K}$ that uncovers the original plaintext p. Writing out the whole encryption and decryption process I get:

$$c^{\overline{K}} \bmod n \equiv \left(p^{K} \bmod n\right)^{\overline{K}} \bmod n$$
$$\equiv \left(p^{K}\right)^{\overline{K}} \bmod n$$
$$= p^{K \times \overline{K}} \bmod n$$

If the decryption is successful then the result must be the original plaintext p and therefore it is to be expected that:

$$p^{K \times \overline{K}} \equiv p \bmod n$$

Unfortunately, given the encryption key K it is not immediately obvious what the value of $\overline{K}$ should be to regenerate the plaintext message.

There is a well-known and useful mathematical finding, a theorem, that offers a clue as to how the decryption key can be found. The result of using the *Euler–Fermat Theorem*, a theorem of *Number Theory* named after two mathematicians, implies that:

$$p^{K \times \overline{K}} \equiv p \bmod n$$

works as a decryption operation[84] provided

$$K \times \overline{K} \equiv 1 \bmod \phi(n)$$

where $\phi(n)$ is the Euler Totient Function that was described in subsection 3.1.5. For a prime number n, the Euler Totient Function $\phi(n)$ is $n - 1$.

For an encryption operation using exponentiation with a modulus of 29, decryption keys can be derived from the congruence:

$$K \times \overline{K} \equiv 1 \bmod \phi(29)$$

For a key of 11 and knowing that, because 29 is a prime number, $\phi(29) = 29 - 1 = 28$, the decryption key is found using the congruence:

$$11 \times \overline{K} \equiv 1 \bmod 28$$

Without a computer this task is not straightforward, but the successive multiplications recorded in Table 15 reveal that:

$$11 \times 23 \equiv 1 \bmod 28$$

Table 15   Multiplication table for 11 mod 28

n	1	2	3	4	5	6	7	8	9	10	11	12	13	14	15	16	17	18	19	20	21	22	23	24	25	26	27
$11 \times n \bmod 28$	11	22	5	16	27	10	21	4	15	26	9	20	3	14	25	8	19	2	13	24	7	18	1	12	23	6	17

Using exponentiation, a key of 11, a modulus of 29, the letter 'T' as plaintext and the character encodings in Table 13 the ciphertext 'Y' was derived from the encoding and encryption using the expression:

$$21^{11} \equiv 26 \bmod 29$$

The decryption key has been found to be 23 so the decryption operation can be described by the expression:

$$26^{23} \bmod 29$$

Now $23 = 16 + 4 + 2 + 1$, so the decryption operation can be broken down to give

$$p \equiv 26^{16+4+2+1} \equiv 26^{16} \times 26^4 \times 26^2 \times 26^1 \bmod 29$$

Table 16 contains some powers of 26 modulo 29 which can be substituted in this expression of the plaintext:

$$p \equiv 26^{16} \times 26^4 \times 26^2 \times 26^1$$
$$\equiv 20 \times 23 \times 9 \times 26 \equiv 460 \times 9 \times 26 \equiv (460 - 15 \times 29) \times 9 \times 26 \bmod 29$$
$$\equiv 25 \times 9 \times 26 \equiv 225 \times 26 \equiv (225 - 7 \times 29) \times 26 \bmod 29$$
$$\equiv 22 \times 26 \equiv 572 \equiv (225 - 19 \times 29) \bmod 29$$
$$\equiv 21 \bmod 29$$

The outcome, 21, is the result of the decryption operation. Using Table 13 this result is the code for the letter 'T', which was the original plaintext.

Table 16   Selected powers of 26 modulo 29

$$26^2 \equiv 676 \equiv 23 \times 29 + 9 \equiv 9 \bmod 29$$
$$26^4 \equiv (26^2)^2 \equiv 9^2 \equiv 81 \equiv 2 \times 29 + 23 \equiv 23 \bmod 29$$
$$26^8 \equiv (26^4)^2 \equiv 23^2 \equiv 529 \equiv 18 \times 29 + 7 \equiv 7 \bmod 29$$
$$26^{16} \equiv (26^8)^2 \equiv 7^2 \equiv 49 \equiv 1 \times 29 + 20 \equiv 20 \bmod 29$$

3.2.4   Conditions

The mathematical operations that were needed to find the decryption key impose conditions on the encryption and decryption process. The Euler–Fermat Theorem, for instance, is only valid if a particular relationship exists between the plaintext and the modulus. However, the condition is automatically satisfied if the number corresponding to the plaintext is less than the modulus n, and n is a prime number. Using a prime modulus of 29, for example, satisfies these conditions.

A second condition is imposed when trying to find $\overline{K}$ from the congruence

$$K \times \overline{K} \equiv 1 \bmod \phi(n)$$

Results in Number Theory tell us that we can only find values of $\overline{K}$ using this congruence when K has no factors in common with the modulus, which in this case is $\phi(n)$. In other words K is coprime with $\phi(n)$. If n is 29 then $\phi(n) = n - 1$ = 28. The keys that have complementary decryption keys are only those that are coprime with 28. 28 can be written as $2 \times 2 \times 7$ so numbers with a factor of two, that is all the even numbers, share a factor with 28 and cannot be used as keys, and the numbers 7, 14, 21 and 28 are ruled out because they share a factor of 7 with 28. The remaining numbers 1, 3, 5, 9, 11, 13, 15, 17, 19, 23, 25 and 27 can all be used as keys, though a key of 1 makes the ciphertext the same as the plaintext and is therefore not useful for encryption. The total number of valid keys is the number of numbers less than $\phi(n)$, which are coprime with $\phi(n)$.

Now, strangely, the Euler Totient Function tells us how many lesser numbers are coprime to a given number. So the number of numbers coprime with $\phi(n)$, the number of valid keys for a modulus n, is $\phi(\phi(n))$ less 1 if a key of 1 is to be discounted. For a prime number $\phi(n) = n - 1$ therefore, because all prime numbers are odd except 2, $n - 1$ must be even and must, therefore, have a factor of 2. Because the keys must be coprime with $\phi(n)$ they cannot have 2 as a factor. For a prime modulus, therefore, a key cannot be even and this rules out around half of the keys. With a prime modulus n there cannot be more than $n/2$ keys.

The number of keys available for a particular encryption scheme is a useful measure, because it indicates how many keys a cracker has to search through when trying to find out what an encrypted message says. The upper row of Table 17 lists a series of prime numbers and the lower row indicates the number of valid keys that would be available when using the prime number as a modulus. Clearly there is a general trend that shows there are more keys for larger numbers, but it also shows, as is common with the results of Number Theory, that there are substantial variations from this trend. For greater security, there needs to be a large choice for keys so larger moduli appear to offer advantages.

Table 17 The numbers of valid keys working with different prime moduli and using the exponentiation operation

n	13	17	19	23	29	31	37	41	43	47	53	59	61	67	71	73	79	83	89	97	101	103	107	109	113
$\phi(\phi(n)) - 1$	3	7	5	9	11	7	11	15	11	21	23	27	15	19	23	23	23	39	39	31	39	31	51	35	47

3.2.5 Summary

Encryption using exponentiation is equivalent to multiplying the code for the plaintext by itself a number of times. The key determines how many times. As with multiplication there are a number of ways of reducing the calculations involved and thus encryption using exponentiation is feasible. It is infeasible, however, given a sufficiently large modulus to crack the encryption and discover the key.

There are restrictions on the keys that can be used but they are eased when exponentiation is performed using a prime modulus.

3.3 RSA algorithm

Encryption using exponentiation is significant partly because it is the encryption method employed in the *RSA algorithm*. The RSA algorithm is a very widely used procedure that uses a special and valuable way of selecting keys. The letters in the name of this algorithm are the initials of the surnames of

Ron Rivest, Adi Shamir and Leonard Adelman, the trio that invented this particular process of encryption and selecting encryption keys. Similar work was conducted by British codemakers at an earlier date but because of the secrecy surrounding their work it was not revealed until quite recently. In the meantime the names of Rivest, Shamir and Adelman had become indelibly attached to the techniques.[85] The RSA technique derives the encryption and decryption keys from secret data using a difficult but tractable process. However, without the secret data, even if given one of the keys it has proven to be computationally infeasible to work out what the other one is. The effect of this is that even if the encryption key is made public, deliberately or by accident, it is impossible with a suitable large key and present-day computing resources to work out the decryption keys and, hence, decrypt the messages.

This has had far reaching consequences for secure systems. For instance, it makes it possible to publicly circulate the encryption key. Anything encrypted with that publicly accessible encryption key can only be decrypted by the holder of the decryption key, which is usually kept private. Systems exploiting these properties are often referred to as public key/private key systems.

3.3.1 The algorithm

The RSA technique uses exponentiation as the method of encryption and the problem it attempts to solve is 'How can I choose a pair of complementary encryption and decryption keys so that knowledge of one does not help me find the other?'. Inevitably, such a solution uses a calculation that is easy to do but difficult to undo. The centrepiece of the RSA calculations is simply the multiplication of two very large prime numbers. It seems that given the result of the multiplication, it is very difficult to work out what the two original numbers were.

The first step in the RSA procedure is therefore to choose two large prime numbers and keep them secret. I will denote them by the letters a and b. The numbers are multiplied together and their product is taken to be the modulus used in the encryption calculations. If the modulus is n then:

$$n = a \times b$$

The original numbers were large and the algorithm works using the modulus that is their product, which will, therefore, be huge. The plaintext too is anticipated to be taken from a set of potentially large numbers and hence long strings of bits, digits or encoded letters.

A key is chosen and encryption, as before, is done using exponentiation but with the modulus n which is not prime, but the product of two primes $a \times b$:

$$c \equiv p^K \bmod ab$$

Next, the decryption key is calculated. When the modulus for encryption was a prime number the decryption key was found by finding the decryption key $\overline{K}$, that satisfied the congruence $K \times \overline{K} \equiv 1 \bmod \phi(n)$. $\phi(n)$ is easy to calculate if a and b are known because as prime numbers a and b are coprime and if they are coprime it is known that:

$$\phi(n) = \phi(a \times b) = \phi(a) \times \phi(b)$$

and also because a and b are prime numbers,

$$\phi(a) = (a - 1) \text{ and } \phi(b) = (b - 1)$$

However, because the modulus for encryption is now the product of two numbers it cannot be prime and the result is that different encryption keys can have exactly the same effects. To obtain keys that have unique effects a different modulus closely related to $\phi(n)$ can be used to first select the encryption key and then to calculate the decryption key. Suppose this modulus is m. Then the task of finding the decryption key is to find $\overline{K}$ given the encryption key K and the relationship

$$K \times \overline{K} \equiv 1 \bmod m$$

With large numbers, this computation is not simple, but it is feasible and only needs to be done after a new encryption key is chosen and the new corresponding decryption key is being created. However, as noted in subsection 3.2.4, this congruence does not permit the calculation of $\overline{K}$ unless K is coprime with the modulus. So, a large number of potential encryption keys cannot be used.

Once a valid encryption key is found, the congruence can be solved to give the decryption key, $\overline{K}$, and decryption is performed, as might be expected, using the operation

$$p \equiv c^{\overline{K}} \bmod n$$

where n is the same modulus as used for encryption and is given by $a \times b$. To encrypt a plaintext someone would need the key K and the modulus n. To decrypt the message they need $\overline{K}$ and the modulus n. Often in this scheme the encryption key is said to be the pair (K,n) because both the key and the modulus are selected in the key generation process and both are needed to perform the encryption. Similarly the pair of numbers $(\overline{K}, n)$ is often called the decryption key.

Now, the crucial point about this scheme is that given K, a and b it is feasible to work out $(a - 1)(b - 1)$ and then the decryption key. Although $n = a \times b$, knowing the modulus n does not make it easy to find a and b. So it is not practicable, given n, to work out a and b and hence $(a - 1)(b - 1)$, and therefore without knowing a and b it is not feasible to work out the decryption key, even if the original encryption key K and the modulus n are known. As computers get faster and more capable it may become possible to find prime factors more speedily, but this algorithm can always be made more difficult by choosing larger prime numbers as its starting point.

3.3.2   An example

To illustrate the algorithm and to avoid too much arithmetic complexity, I have chosen small prime numbers. I have chosen a to be 11 and b to be 7. The modulus for encryption is therefore $n = a \times b = 11 \times 7 = 77$ and the encryption operation described by:

$$c \equiv p^K \bmod 77$$

Before an encryption key can be chosen it is necessary to look at the process of deriving the decryption key. The RSA algorithm does not encrypt using a modulus that is a prime number. The mathematical theorems behind RSA therefore enforce new conditions on the derivation of the decryption key because encryption relies on a product of two primes. The way to work out the modulus for selecting the encryption key and then for calculating the decryption key is to factorize $(a-1)$ and $(b-1)$ individually and make a note of the factors they have in common. $\phi(n)$ is divided by these common factors and the result used as the new modulus.

For example with $a = 11$ and $b = 7$, $a - 1$ is 10 and its factors are 5×2. $b - 1$ is 6 and its factors are 2×3. They have a 2 in common so the new modulus is $\phi(n) \div 2$ or $\frac{1}{2}\phi(n)$, which for the example is $\frac{1}{2}(a-1)(b-1) = \frac{1}{2}(10 \times 6) = 30$. Both the encryption and decryption keys should be less than this number and the decryption keys are worked out using the congruence

$$K \times \overline{K} \equiv 1 \bmod 30$$

As before, this congruence is only applicable when the values of K are coprime with the modulus. Omitting 1 as a valid encryption key and discarding any above 30 restricts the choice to the numbers that are coprime with 30, and those are 7, 11, 13, 17, 19, 23 or 29. I will use 13 as an encryption key. Suppose the plaintext is the letter 'R' for RSA and encoded according to Table 13 as 19, the encryption operation is:

$$19^{13} \equiv 19^{8+4+1} \bmod 77$$

It is immediately apparent from this daunting expression that this method of encryption with large prime numbers is only practicable with the aid of a computer. Calculating the powers of 19 modulo 77 gives:

$$19^2 \equiv 361 \equiv (361 - 4 \times 77) \equiv 53 \bmod 77$$

then:

$$19^4 \equiv \left(19^2\right)^2 \equiv 53^2 \equiv 2809 \equiv (2809 - 36 \times 77) \equiv 37 \bmod 77$$

and similarly:

$$19^8 \equiv \left(19^4\right)^2 \equiv 37^2 \equiv 1369 \equiv (1369 - 17 \times 77) \equiv 60 \bmod 77$$

The ciphertext is then given by:

$$19^{13} \equiv 9^{8+4+1} \bmod 77$$
$$\equiv 60 \times 37 \times 19 \equiv 2220 \times 19 \equiv (2220 - 28 \times 77) \times 19 \bmod 77$$
$$\equiv 64 \times 19 \equiv 1216 \equiv (1216 - 15 \times 77) \bmod 77$$
$$\equiv 61 \bmod 77$$

The encrypted data is the number 61, which I will leave simply as a number. Decryption requires a decryption key and a decryption key can be derived by solving the congruence:

$$K \times \overline{K} \equiv 1 \bmod 30$$

For an encryption key of 13 this becomes:

$$13 \times \overline{K} \equiv 1 \bmod 30$$

Table 18 is a multiplication table for 13 with a modulus of 30 and it can be seen that 13 multiplied by 7 produces the result 1 when working with a modulus of 30. In this case, therefore, the decryption key is 7.

Table 18   A multiplication table for 13 using a modulus of 30

1	2	3	4	5	6	7	8	9	10	11	12	13	14	15	16	17	18	19	20	21	22	23	24	25	26	27	28	29
13	26	9	22	5	18	1	14	27	10	23	6	19	2	15	28	11	24	7	20	3	16	29	12	25	8	21	4	17

Decryption of the ciphertext, which was the number 61, is carried out by the operation:

$$61^7 \bmod 77$$

Going through the familiar procedure and using the results in Table 19,

Table 19 Selected powers of 61 modulo 77

$$61^2 \equiv 3721 \equiv \left(3721 - 48 \times 77\right) \equiv 25 \bmod 77$$

$$61^4 \equiv \left(61^2\right)^2 \equiv 25^2 \equiv 625 \equiv \left(625 - 8 \times 77\right) \equiv 9 \bmod 77$$

$$61^8 \equiv \left(61^4\right)^2 \equiv 9^2 \equiv 81 \equiv \left(81 - 1 \times 77\right) \equiv 4 \bmod 77$$

$$61^{16} \equiv \left(61^8\right)^2 \equiv 4^2 \equiv 16 \bmod 77$$

the plaintext is revealed through the calculation

$$61^7 \equiv 61^{4+2+1} \equiv 61^4 \times 61^2 \times 61 \bmod 77$$
$$\equiv 9 \times 25 \times 61 \equiv 225 \times 61 \equiv \left(225 - 2 \times 77\right) \times 61 \bmod 77$$
$$\equiv 71 \times 61 \equiv 4331 \equiv \left(4331 - 56 \times 77\right) \bmod 77$$
$$\equiv 19 \bmod 77$$

This plaintext code of 19 corresponds to the letter 'R' that began this lengthy encryption and decryption calculation.

3.3.3 Picking primes

The RSA algorithm starts with the selection of two very large prime numbers. The security of the ensuing encryption and decryption depends on the two prime numbers being known to the person who creates the keys but to no one else. Now, it is possible that a potential cracker does not know which prime numbers are being used but does know how the prime numbers are chosen. The cracker could then have a go at working out which prime numbers have been used. Some attention, therefore, needs to be paid to the methods that are used to select prime numbers for RSA-encrypted ciphertext. Indeed, for any encryption scheme it is important, if it is to remain secure, that the method of choosing a key is kept secret or at least has an element of unpredictability about it. One area of development and research in the application of encryption algorithms is therefore looking at ways of generating random numbers and keys, and any assessment of the security provided by encryption schemes needs to look at the ways in which keys are created and communicated.

There is no known way of generating large prime numbers using a computer. What happens is that numbers are picked and then tested to see if they have factors. If they do then they are ruled out as candidates and another large number is tried. Speedy tests for prime numbers are therefore required. Although there are ways of testing to see if numbers are not prime, people are always looking for faster methods. In an encryption scheme such as RSA the encryption process can be straightforward, but methods for selecting keys can be complicated and are under development.

Certain combinations of keys, plaintext and prime numbers constituting the modulus make RSA easier to crack than other combinations. Research continues to try to find simple rules that will help people to find the most secure options.

3.3.4 Summary

The RSA encryption process encrypts using exponentiation. The modulus is the product of two large primes. A suitable key can be chosen once the two primes are known. The encryption key and the two primes also allow the formulation of a congruence which allows the decryption key to be calculated. Anyone not knowing the two large primes would find it infeasible to work out one key, even if they knew the other and the modulus. The procedure for selecting a key and finding a decryption key is slightly complicated, because encryption does not use a prime modulus.

3.4 Finding decryption keys

One outstanding problem with encryption using multiplication and encryption using exponentiation is the derivation of the decryption keys. In the examples so far the decryption keys have been found by searching systematically through the possibilities. There is, however, a way of explicitly calculating the keys using the *Euler–Fermat Theorem*.

3.4.1 Using the Euler–Fermat Theorem

Both encryption using multiplication and encryption using exponentiation require the solution of congruences of the form:

$$K \times K \equiv 1 \bmod n$$

The Euler–Fermat Theorem provides a clue as to how the decryption key can be derived from this congruence. For any number x the theorem says that:

$$x^{\phi(n)} \equiv 1 \bmod n$$

provided x and n are coprime. Of course, if n is a prime number all the numbers below n are coprime with n and the Euler Totient Function $\phi(n)$ is $n - 1$. I can put K in place of x, and for a prime modulus therefore rewrite the Euler–Fermat Theorem to read:

$$K^{n-1} \equiv 1 \bmod n$$

Now, I can rewrite this congruence as:

$$K \times K^{n-2} \equiv 1 \bmod n$$

Thus, when working with a prime modulus, choosing the decryption key to be $K^{n-2} \bmod n$ ensures that the condition $K \times \overline{K} \equiv 1 \bmod n$ is met. For example, suppose encryption is to be carried out using multiplication, a modulus of 29 and a key of 8, then the decryption key should be:

$$\overline{K} \equiv K^{n-2} \equiv 8^{29-2} \bmod 29$$

This decryption key is $8^{27} \bmod 29$ and can be calculated by breaking it into a sequence of multiplications:

$$8^{27} \equiv 8^{16+8+2+1} \equiv 8^{16} \times 8^8 \times 8^2 \times 8^1 \bmod 29$$

To help complete the result a table of powers of 8 has been constructed and is shown in Table 20.

Table 20   Selected powers of 8 modulo 29

$$8^2 \equiv 64 \equiv (64 - 2 \times 29) \equiv 6 \bmod 29$$

$$8^4 \equiv \left(8^2\right)^2 \equiv 6^2 \equiv 36 \equiv (36 - 1 \times 29) \equiv 7 \bmod 29$$

$$8^8 \equiv \left(8^4\right)^2 \equiv 7^2 \equiv 49 \equiv (49 - 1 \times 29) \equiv 20 \bmod 29$$

$$8^{16} \equiv \left(8^8\right)^2 \equiv 20^2 \equiv 400 \equiv (400 - 13 \times 29) \equiv 23 \bmod 29$$

Now,

$$\overline{K} \equiv 8^{16} \times 8^8 \times 8^2 \times 8^1 \bmod 29$$
$$\equiv 23 \times 20 \times 6 \times 8 \bmod 29$$
$$\equiv 460 \times 6 \times 8 \equiv (460 - 15 \times 29) \times 6 \times 8 \bmod 29$$
$$\equiv 25 \times 6 \times 8 \equiv 150 \times 8 \equiv (150 - 5 \times 29) \times 8 \bmod 29$$
$$\equiv 5 \times 8 \equiv 40 \equiv (40 - 1 \times 29) \bmod 29$$
$$\equiv 11 \bmod 29$$

The combination $K \times \overline{K} \bmod 29$ is therefore $8 \times 11 \bmod 29$, which is $88 \equiv 1 \bmod 29$ as expected.

3.4.2   Working with non-prime numbers

If x and n are not coprime then the Euler–Fermat Theorem is not satisfied and a decryption key cannot be found. But if, for instance as in the example in subsection 3.3.2, if x were 13 and n were 30 the theorem is applicable although 30 is not a prime number because 13 and 30 have no factors in common and are therefore coprime. For these numbers, the Euler–Fermat Theorem gives:

$$13^{\phi(30)} \equiv 1 \bmod 30$$

Since 30 is not a prime the Euler Totient Function is *not* 30 − 1. 30 has the factors $2 \times 3 \times 5$ and the numbers below 30 that do not have these factors are 1, 7, 11, 13, 17, 19, 23 and 29 − a total of eight numbers less than 30 are coprime with 30. The Euler Totient Function for 30, $\phi(30)$, is 8 and the Euler–Fermat Theorem gives us the, apparently arcane, result:

$$13^8 \equiv 1 \bmod 30$$

Now, I can rewrite this congruence as:

$$13 \times 13^7 \equiv 1 \bmod 30$$

And supposing I had an encryption key of 13 and I had to find the decryption key $\overline{K}$ from the congruence

$$13 \times \overline{K} \equiv 1 \bmod 30$$

it would become clear by comparing the last two congruences that the decryption key was given by $13^7 \bmod 30$ which is 7. Thus, as required,

$$13 \times 7 \equiv 91 \equiv 1 \bmod 30$$

This result is identical to the result obtained in subsection 3.3.2. The process illustrated in this section is therefore useful in calculating decryption keys when encrypting using multiplication or exponentiation.

3.4.3 Summary

The Euler–Fermat Theorem, together with a technique for working out powers of numbers, can provide a method for solving the congruences that arise when trying to work out decryption keys. The method is straightforward when the congruence has a prime modulus, but when the modulus is not prime the procedure only works when the encryption key is coprime with the modulus. With exponentiation that modulus is the value of the Euler Totient Function of the modulus used for encryption.

3.5 Conclusion

Encryption can be carried out using the multiplication and exponentiation operations of *modular arithmetic*. With both operations there are restrictions on the keys that can be used. These restrictions are eliminated for multiplication when working with a modulus that is a prime number. To undo the exponentiation operation involves another operation called the discrete logarithm. This name is sometimes given to procedures surrounding encryption using exponentiation. Finding the discrete logarithm is known to be a difficult task and consequently the task of finding a key given both the ciphertext and the plaintext of a message is infeasible when working with a sufficiently large modulus. Because exponentiation provides a defence against this threat, it is often preferred as an encryption method.

Encryption using exponentiation is used in the RSA algorithm. In addition to the benefits of encrypting using exponentiation, the procedure for choosing the key in the RSA algorithms makes it infeasible to calculate the decryption key given the key for encryption.

The numbers involved in performing encryption using a very large modulus can be huge and the exponentiation and multiplication operations aggravate the computational problem. Special arithmetic procedures that exploit the properties of modular arithmetic are available for calculating, for instance, large powers of large numbers with a realistic allocation of resources.

Chapter Four

Using encryption

Feelings of insecurity are aroused when it is easy for other people to find out something that could be exploited to a victim's disadvantage. Keeping things hidden from others is, therefore, one way of gaining a greater sense of security, but insecurity is not always induced by a fear of giving something away. Sometimes it is fuelled by the possibility of a deception by an embarrassing or obstructive fraud. Those wanting to undermine the security of others might counterfeit documents, messages or records, or impersonate trusted individuals. Such meddling is easier when communications travel across the airwaves or public networks, where impostors and fraudsters can interfere more readily in IT systems assisted by the lack of intimacy and the remoteness of communicating partners and the impermanence of digital media.

Ideally, comprehensive security measures for digital communication systems ensure confidentiality, guarantee the integrity of communicated messages and the authenticity of relationships they describe. Encryption, as it happens, can provide mechanisms that help with these requirements. However, ingenious and determined antagonists can usually, with some effort, find ways of subverting such security schemes. The analysis of a security mechanism, therefore, includes thinking of conceivable threats to security and then seeing whether they can be countered by the proposed security mechanisms.

4.1   Confidentiality

People have long felt vulnerable when messages are sent over publicly accessible communication links. In 1854, for instance, an anonymous writer wrote:

> 'Means should ... be taken to obviate one great objection, at present felt with respect to sending private communications by telegraph – the violation of all secrecy ... The clerks ... are sworn to secrecy, but we often write things that would be intolerable to see strangers read before our eyes. This is a grievous fault in the telegraph, and it *must* be remedied by some means or another. ... [S]ome simple yet secure cipher, easily acquired and easily read should be introduced, by which messages might to all intents and purposes be 'sealed' to any person except the recipient.' [86]

A common response to the desire for greater security has been to make things secret and thus an obvious application for encryption is in obfuscating data and documents so that unauthorized people cannot fathom out the content. If two people, Bob and Alice perhaps, share a key that they do not disclose to anyone else then Alice can send Bob an encrypted message, which Bob can decrypt and read but which will be unintelligible to anyone without the key.

4.1.1   Notation, custom and analogy

It is customary, in the security field, to give two people involved in secure communications the names Alice and Bob. Alice and Bob are known as the *principals*. Of course, there may be other people involved including someone who may be attempting to uncover secrets or subvert the principals' communications. Eve, perhaps, might eavesdrop and intercept Alice and Bob's exchanges.

It is also common to describe the interactions between communicating partners using a notation that has a mathematical style. The notation is not standardized[87] and you would see variations if you were to study published papers and books on security. In the notation, which helps to describe the interactions that take place between Alice and Bob, an arrow indicates that a message has been sent. Alice sending Bob a message would be denoted using the initials of their names by the expression

$$A \rightarrow B$$

The message can also be signified by a letter, for instance M. Using a colon to separate the message from the correspondents, I can denote the transaction between Alice and Bob by the expression

$$A \rightarrow B : M$$

Suppose Alice recognizes that there is a security threat. She may, for instance, realize that Eve can intercept her message as it travels on the public network and can, therefore, read the contents. Alice circumvents the threat by encrypting the message so that Eve will not be able to make sense of it. To show that Alice's message is encrypted, in my description of the transaction, I can enclose the letter denoting the message M, in braces (curly brackets) with the key added as a subscript to give $\{M\}_K$. The letter K is often used for keys. What the notation does *not* show is the method of encryption. This has to be described separately. $\{M\}_K$ then is the ciphertext for the plaintext M.

If Alice sends a message M to Bob and encrypts it using the key K then the whole transaction is denoted by joining two pieces of the notation with a colon to give:

$$A \rightarrow B : \{M\}_K$$

There are few obvious or common ways of manipulating this notation to give answers or solutions to security questions. Some elementary manipulations, though, are possible. For instance, if the decryption key $\overline{K}$ is known then decryption can be expressed in the same form as encryption. If C is the ciphertext then the decrypted message is $\{C\}_{\overline{K}}$. Now when the ciphertext C is the encrypted message $\{M\}_K$, then this expression can be written in place of C and when the result of decryption is $\{\{M\}_K\}_{\overline{K}}$, then this must be the original message M and therefore:

$$\{\{M\}_K\}_{\overline{K}} \equiv M$$

This result can be read as saying simply that after a message has been encrypted and then decrypted with a complementary key then the original message will emerge. Although the result has a mathematical flavour, it is not particularly illuminating. The implication is that the notation is not particularly helpful for making deductions about secure systems. It primarily offers ways of writing down terse descriptions of messages that act as compact reminders of how messages are composed, what messages are sent and who is involved.

4.1.2 Distributing keys

If Alice wishes to send Bob a message that is to be kept secret from other people, such as Eve, then she can encrypt the data with an encryption key and send it to Bob.

$A \rightarrow B : \{M\}_K$	Alice sends a confidential message M to Bob

If Bob has the *decryption* key $\overline{K}$ and the ciphertext $\{M\}_K$, then the decrypted message is denoted by $\{\{M\}_K\}_{\overline{K}}$ and implies that the ciphertext $\{M\}_K$ is decrypted using the decryption key K.

Alice can either work out the decryption key and send it, cautiously, in some secure fashion to Bob or she can, with care, send him the encryption key and leave him to work out how to decrypt the message. This might simply involve, for instance, Bob working out the decryption key and then using that to decrypt the ciphertext, or there might be a more direct way of decrypting given the encryption key. When Alice sends Bob the encryption key, he must perform a different operation on the key and the ciphertext. A superscript of -1 is added to the notation. Thus the expression $\{\{M\}_K\}_K^{-1}$ means decrypt the ciphertext $\{M\}_K$ assuming you have the encryption key K. The result of decryption is again the original message M.

4.1.3 What Bob needs

For Bob to make any sense of the message he needs to have three things:

1   knowledge of the decryption method

2   computing resources to perform the decryption

3   an encryption or a decryption key.

It is common to make the encryption and decryption methods widely known. Alice and the people she deals with will probably have agreed on the encryption method for all their future transactions. In practice, they will want to do this so that they can acquire and install compatible encryption and decryption software. The decryption method is unlikely to be kept secret.

The plaintext of Alice's messages can only be hidden from Eve, the eavesdropper, if Eve either does not have adequate computing resources or if she does not know the key for decrypting Alice's ciphertext. At the same time, Bob will not be able to make sense of Alice's message unless he knows the key. Alice, therefore, has to get the decryption key to Bob without revealing it to Eve. She also has to trust Bob to take care of the key.

4.1.4 Threats

Analysing systems that are supposed to be secure is a Machiavellian business. Making assumptions about conceivable threats is the only way to assess the efficacy of security arrangements, and this often involves picturing people as adversaries who are acting malevolently, or as collaborators who act carelessly.

When Alice sent her encrypted confidential message, for instance, she assumed that Bob had a key that would enable him to decrypt the message while her adversaries did not have a copy of the key and could not decrypt the message. Eve, the eavesdropper who was spying on Alice, may have tried and succeeded in intercepting and copying the key Alice sent to Bob. Eve's plot could have been thwarted if the key to decrypt the message had not been distributed.

The RSA algorithm makes it practicable to create an encryption key and its complementary decryption key, in such a way that it is infeasible to work out one key given the other. Because of the symmetry in the algorithms, it does not matter which of the two keys is used for encryption, the remaining key will decrypt the ciphertext. It is common to make one of the keys public, and to keep the other a complete secret and known only to one principal. The key that is kept secret is called the *private key* and the key that is made public is called, inevitably, the *public key*.

Bob for instance can create, in one process, a public key K_B, and a complementary private key $\overline{K}_B$. He circulates the public key, but keeps the private key to himself. For Alice to send Bob a message in confidence, using a system of public and private keys, she encrypts the message with Bob's public key K_B and sends it to him:

$A \rightarrow B : \{M\}_{K_B}$	Alice sends a confidential message M to Bob

Eve cannot decrypt this confidential message. Although she has access to Bob's public key, she cannot work out the decryption key because of the properties of the RSA algorithm. Only Bob has the private key and since he does not need to distribute it across communication networks, Eve cannot intercept it by eavesdropping. Bob then decrypts Alice's message using his private key $\overline{K_B}$. Anyone can therefore send Bob a message in confidence by encrypting their message with Bob's public key. Charlie, for instance, can send a confidential message to Bob:

$C \rightarrow B : \{M\}_{K_B}$	Charlie sends a confidential message M to Bob

Again, only Bob can decrypt the message with his private key.

4.1.5 Digital envelopes

A common criticism of the RSA algorithm is that the encryption process for long messages can demand excessive computer resources. This is exacerbated when a message is to be sent in confidence to a group of people. For instance, suppose Diane, who is a doctor, wants to pass on her concern about a patient to a number of medical staff but wants to make sure that the data is kept confidential. Using the public/private key method, she would have to encrypt the message differently for each recipient. To send it to Bob she would encrypt it with his public key, and to send it to Alice she would encrypt it with Alice's dissimilar public key, and so on for the whole team. Alternatively, Diane could encrypt the message once and make sure that everyone in the team had the decryption key, but that raises the problem of how to distribute the decryption key securely.

There is a further worry, and that is for each patient Diane may deal with different teams of medical staff. She will want to be reassured that each message is accessible only to the relevant addressees. One solution to her difficulties is to encrypt each message with a different key and to distribute the key only to those who are entitled to read that message. This, of course, magnifies the problem of key distribution and makes it more likely that a determined infiltrator will intercept one or more of the keys.

Digital envelopes use a combination of schemes. Each new message is encrypted using a fresh key, and the key, which should be shorter than the messages, is encrypted using the public keys of the authorized recipients and distributed with the message. So, for instance, Diane encrypts a message M

with a new key K, which she chooses, and creates the ciphertext $\{M\}_K$. She then works out the corresponding decryption key $\overline{K}$, and encrypts that with Bob's public key K_B, to get $\{\overline{K}\}_{K_B}$ before appending it to the encrypted message. In the shorthand notation, this could be shown by putting $\{M\}_K$ next to $\{\overline{K}\}_{K_B}$ to give $\{M\}_K\{\overline{K}\}_{K_B}$, but sometimes, though perhaps not on this occasion, it can be hard to distinguish the two separate components. In the symbolic notation, a comma is added to avoid running the two components together and the result is $\{M\}_K, \{\overline{K}\}_{K_B}$. In the actual transmission, something other than a comma might to be used to distinguish the two parts. Diane sends the composite message to Bob.

$D \rightarrow B : \{M\}_K, \{\overline{K}\}_{K_B}$	Diane puts a message in a digital envelope and sends it to Bob

On receipt of the message Bob can find out the decryption key $\overline{K}$ by decrypting it using his private key $\overline{K}_B$ and then, using this newfound decryption key, he can decrypt the message.

Eve, who is not authorized to read the message, might intercept the encrypted message but cannot uncover the key to decrypt the message because she does not have Bob's private key.

Digital envelopes can be addressed to a group of people. Diane can encrypt the medical data M with the fresh key K, and append a number of copies of the encrypted key. Each copy of the encrypted key would be encrypted by the public key of a different member of the medical team comprised of, perhaps, besides Diane herself, Alice, George and Charlie.

$D \rightarrow A, G, C : \{M\}_K, \{\overline{K}\}_{K_A}, \{\overline{K}\}_{K_G}, \{\overline{K}\}_{K_C}$	Diane sends a confidential message to the team

Any of the three in the team who issued the public keys, K_A, K_G and K_C and can find out the decryption key $\overline{K}$ using their private keys. Once they have exposed $\overline{K}$ they can each decrypt the confidential message. People who are not part of the team would be unable to do so.

4.1.6 Summary

Encryption hides the content of messages from spies. A weakness of the simplest schemes is that an authorized recipient has to have a suitable key to decrypt the message, and this key has to complement the key that was used to encrypt the message. The security problem shifts from keeping messages secret to one of keeping keys secret when they are distributed – a problem not dissimilar to the one that was being solved.

The RSA algorithm provides a solution but at the cost of additional computing resources. Complementary public and private keys are created and the private key kept out of circulation. Confidential messages are encrypted with a public key and decrypted by the only holder of the corresponding private key.

Digital envelopes offer a hybrid solution. The message is encrypted and the decryption key accompanies the message. To prevent this decryption key becoming widely available, it is itself encrypted with the public keys of the authorized recipients. Recipients decrypt the key to the encrypted message using their private keys and then can decrypt the confidential message intended for them.

4.2 Integrity

Confidentiality is not the only requirement. Sometimes it is unimportant whether or not people know the content of messages and sometimes it is even desirable that people are familiar with the content, but it is vital that messages remain unaltered when, for instance they traverse publicly accessible networks. Encryption is a feature of some techniques that offer assurance about the integrity of messages.

4.2.1 Encryption offers protection

Some security measures, such as putting documents in a safe, are not always primarily intended to offer privacy but to make the documents inaccessible to potential fraudsters who might profit by altering them. Encryption can, similarly, provide protection against meaningful unauthorized alterations. Although forgers can meddle with an accessible ciphertext, without cracking the encryption they cannot know what the effects of any alteration will be on the decrypted ciphertext. For instance, if Alice encrypts the sentence

IOWEYOUFIFTYPOUNDS

and the ciphertext is

UVCZSOBEIFAXTJVYJP

without the key it is not obvious to Freda the forger how to change the ciphertext to match a known effect on the plaintext, even if she knew the encryption method and the original message.[88] Of course, if Freda were able to discover the key then she could encrypt a modified plaintext and replace the resulting ciphertext. And if she just wanted to sabotage the message she could arbitrarily make changes to the ciphertext knowing it would have an effect but without knowing quite what that effect would be. Changing a single letter, the third letter in the ciphertext, arbitrarily from C to D, for example, would, when decrypted with the valid key, give the unintelligible message:

SKKJGYCPXKHZLADGEE

in place of the original

IOWEYOUFIFTYPOUNDS

Encryption, therefore, does not prevent people making changes that can be damaging, but it does make it difficult to make meaningful changes that might go undetected by an authorized recipient.

4.2.2 Cross-checking

Locking things up, or encrypting them, is not always practicable, particularly when the plaintext data or documents are regularly and legitimately referred to.

A deterrent to potential counterfeiters is to keep duplicates of important documents. Bob may, for example, lock away an original document in a strong box and circulate a duplicate as a working copy. If Alice suspects that an unauthorized change has been made to the document, she can ask Bob, the authorized keyholder, to open the strong box, retrieve the original and compare it with the working copy. Any discrepancy would suggest that someone had tampered with it. Of course, Alice would have to trust Bob to do the comparison honestly and to ensure the safekeeping of the original.

Alternatively, Bob could treat the original as plaintext, which he encrypts to produce a ciphertext. When Alice questions the authenticity of the plaintext document, she can ask Bob to decrypt the ciphertext. Any alterations to either the plaintext or the ciphertext would show up as a discrepancy between the freshly decrypted ciphertext and the plaintext.

Now Alice can have a copy of the original plaintext and a copy of the ciphertext. She does not have to rely on Bob to keep the ciphertext secure. He can send Alice both parts:

$B \rightarrow A : M, \{M\}_K$	Bob sends Alice a message and a copy of the message, which is encrypted with a key K

To check the integrity of the message Alice can return the plaintext and the ciphertext to Bob and ask him to decrypt it and compare the result with the plaintext. Alternatively, Alice might ask Bob to decrypt the ciphertext and ask him to return the decrypted version so that she can check it herself.

But the method will fail if messages can be intercepted; for instance, Freda might intercept the messages, meddle with them and fool Alice into believing that the documents from Bob are intact. Again, Bob sends Alice a message and a copy of the message that is encrypted with a key K but Freda intercepts it:

$B \rightarrow F : M, \{M\}_K$	Bob's message is intercepted by Freda

Freda modifies the message to give M' and sends it to Alice. The cross-check does not match, but Alice does not know this:

$F \rightarrow A : M', \{M\}_K$	Freda sends the modified message to Alice

Alice is suspicious of the message and returns the corrupted message and ciphertext to Bob for checking, but Freda intercepts it:

$A \rightarrow F : M', \{M\}_K$	Freda intercepts the message intended for Bob from Alice

Freda recognizes the altered message, corrects it and sends it to Bob:

$F \rightarrow B : M, \{M\}_K$	Bob receives his original message

Bob can carry out the check and will find nothing wrong with the message and the cross-check and he will, therefore, confirm the integrity of the message. Alice will then have been totally misled by Freda's intervention.

4.2.3   Give Alice the key

Alice could detect changes to the message if Bob lets her have the decryption key $\overline{K}$, so that she can do the decryption and perform the check herself. If she finds that the decrypted ciphertext and the original plaintext match then she can assume that the message is intact.

Of course, it is possible for Freda to alter both the plaintext and the corresponding ciphertext but, with a robust encryption scheme, unless the encrypted version is decrypted, altered and encrypted again, it is infeasible for Freda to make alterations to the ciphertext that mirror her modification of the plaintext.

To demonstrate the difficulties that a forger would have I will use larger numbers than my earlier examples and assume encryption is performed using exponentiation. With larger numbers I can encrypt larger groups of letters using the same principles as outlined in the discussion about digraphs in subsection 2.2.3. For instance, the text 'CEASE', when treated as a single block of five letters, can be coded by the number[89] 984728. Bob can encrypt this code using modulo 11881379 exponentiation, chosen because it is a prime number that can accommodate coded strings of five letters.[90] With a valid key of 6661611 the encryption operation is described by the daunting expression:

$$984728^{6661611} \bmod 11881379$$

Using a computer, the encrypted result turns out to be 991359 or converted back to a string of characters is 'CEKNF'. Putting the legitimate message and Bob's ciphertext for the message together gives

CEASE CEKNF

Obviously decrypting the ciphertext portion with the decryption key gives the original plaintext – 'CEASE'– and the cross-check confirms the integrity of the message. Now, suppose Freda altered the message saying 'CEASE' by changing one letter to give the message 'CHASE'. It is easy to see how to alter the plaintext to get the modified result but, without the key, it is not obvious how the ciphertext portion of the legitimate message 'CEKNF' should be altered to ensure that the plaintext and the ciphertext match Freda's corrupted version.

Freda, having changed the second letter of the plaintext to give the adulterated word 'CHASE', might be tempted to change the second letter of the ciphertext in the same way – from 'CEKNF' to 'CHKNF'. She would then send:

CHASE CHKNF

Unfortunately for Freda, when this altered ciphertext is decrypted by someone who knows the key that created the cross-check, the result is 'SVURM' which bears little resemblance to the plaintext word 'CHASE' and the cross-check fails. The obvious difference would suggest that unauthorized changes have been made to the message, the ciphertext or both.

If Freda's modified plaintext was encrypted using Bob's key, the ciphertext, as it happens, would be 'TWEWY'. To ensure consistency and prevent the discovery of the alteration, Freda would need to create the altered message and its corresponding ciphertext, which would have to be:

CHASE TWEWY

Without the key, Freda cannot know this.

4.2.4 Coerced keyholders

In the scheme for checking the integrity of a message, only a *keyholder* stands much of a chance of maintaining consistency between the altered plaintext and an accompanying ciphertext. If, however, alterations are suspected that manage to maintain consistency between the message and its encrypted version then the honesty of a keyholder is called into question. Bearing in mind the darker side of human behaviour, it is conceivable that a keyholder, Bob, was honest but that he was coerced into making alterations by threats from Vince, a vicious third party, and his gang.

To detect malpractices involving an honest or dishonest keyholder a second ciphertext can be created with a *new* key by another keyholder who does not know Bob's key. For instance Diane might encrypt the plaintext 'CEASE' with a key of 9486471 to create the ciphertext 'BLLUY'. The original plaintext and the two encrypted versions from Bob and Diane can be assembled in a sequence:

CEASE CEKNF BLLUY

This sequence offers Alice two possible checks on the original data. An outsider wanting to make changes that were undetectable would now have to intimidate two keyholders rather than one – a less likely prospect.

4.2.5   Public / Private

Bob may be trusted, and is therefore asked to append encrypted cross-checks to documents. He would encrypt using an encryption key, but there may be several people, such as Alice, Tom and Rachel, who wish to be able to check the documents for themselves. They will each need decryption keys to decrypt the cross-check. This widespread distribution of keys makes it more likely that someone will slip up and reveal a key to a determined forger. If any of these keyholders was careless and Freda got hold of the key then she could forge modified plaintexts and their corresponding ciphertexts at will. Her forgeries would be undetectable.

Public / private key techniques allow Bob to encrypt with his private key and to distribute only his corresponding public key. This does not reveal information that could, in practice, lead to the exposure of his private encryption key. At first glance this may not seem promising. If Bob were to encrypt a message with his private key then anyone could decrypt the message with the readily available public key and the message would not remain confidential. But confidentiality may not be important. A ciphertext that can be decrypted using Bob's public key and that renders an intelligible message must have been created by Bob and could only have been modified by him since his public key decrypts ciphertext created using his privately held key, and he should be the only person holding it. Encryption with a private key, therefore, makes documents readily available, but gives assurance about their integrity.

Documents are not always immediately intelligible. For instance, Bob may want to send a computer program to Alice, but she may be unfamiliar with the coding that Bob has used. He could encrypt the program with his public key, but Alice would not be able to tell whether the decrypted version was unintelligible because, for instance, Freda might have interfered with it or because Alice did not understand the coding. Alice might be able to find out by running the program, but that would be risky if it had been tampered with. Alice could be sure that she had the right message if Bob sent the message encrypted with his private key alongside the plaintext message.

$B \rightarrow A : M, \{M\}_{\overline{K}_B}$	Bob sends Alice a message and a version encrypted with his private key

Alice could then check the integrity of Bob's plaintext message by decrypting the ciphertext with his widely available public key. No one could forge the encrypted cross-check because they do not have Bob's private key and cannot work it out from the available public key.

4.2.6 Compact checks

The integrity checks described so far require the plaintext message to be transmitted and, additionally, the whole plaintext has to be encrypted and the encrypted version sent. In some circumstances people may be discouraged from adding secure cross-checks because of the overheads demanded, firstly by the encryption of the lengthy message and secondly by the transmission of the encrypted duplicate. Some economies are possible. Instead of using the complete verbatim message, the cross-check can be derived from a compactly expressed characteristic of the message. To take a simple example, Alice could use the number of vowels or consonants as a check. If the message she was sending to Bob was

MEETMEATJIMSPLACEATFIVETOMORROW

she could count the number of vowels to get the number 13, which she could encrypt. Suppose she and Bob anticipated up to twenty vowels in their messages, then Alice could encrypt using modulo 23 multiplication (chosen because it is the first prime number that comes after twenty). With a secret key of 9, the encryption of the number of vowels in the example involves finding out the result of $13 \times 9 \bmod 23$, which is 2. This encrypted check can be encoded as the letter C, the third letter of the alphabet, and appended to the message:

MEETMEATJIMSPLACEATFIVETOMORROWC

An alteration of the message that changes the number of vowels will make the appended characteristic inconsistent with the message and it should be detectable. Suppose Freda intercepted the message and altered it to say:

MEETMEATALISPLACEATFIVETOMORROWC

When Bob received the message, he would discover that the number of vowels in the body of the message was now 14. Encrypting 14 using the secret key of 9 produces the encrypted result of $14 \times 9 \bmod 23 \equiv 11$, which does not correspond to the letter C in the cross-check. It is therefore evident that someone tampered with the message.

However, suppose instead Freda altered the message to say:

MEETMEATJIMSPLACEATFOURTOMORROWC

Because the number of vowels remains the same, the calculated and encrypted cross-check will be consistent with the modified message and the forgery will not be detectable.

The price Alice and Bob pay for using compact cross-checks is that some kinds of alteration will be undetectable. Using one letter there are at most twenty-six possible values for the cross-check while there may be many thousands of possible messages. Each value of the cross-check will therefore be potentially compatible with thousands of messages, so there are many ways of altering a message while maintaining consistency between the message and the encrypted cross-check. Broadly, the longer the cross-check, the more likely it is that alterations will be detected, but shorter cross-checks are more economical in their use of communication, storage and processing resources.

4.2.7 Hashing

Take a slightly more involved example using the message:

MEETMEUNDERTHEELEPHANTATELEVEN

The message can be divided into groups of five letters:

MEETM EUNDE RTHEE LEPHA NTATE LEVEN

Each of these groups can be encoded as a number:[91]

5557226 2188294 8107376 5107362 6275130 5111353

Taking these numbers and adding them up using a suitable modulus will generate a characteristic of the message. For instance, 11881379 is a prime number, which was used earlier in this chapter as a modulus for the encryption of five-letter blocks, and the sum of the above sequence of numbers modulo 11881379 turns out to be 8583983. This number can be converted back into a block of five letters and the result happens to be 'SUKFF'. This five-letter sequence then has been derived from the thirty-letter sequence of the original message.

This same operation could be applied to messages of any length that are broken into five-letter chunks; the result would always be a five-letter group. An operation, like this, which takes data strings of any length and reduces them all to a data string of the same length, and which depends on all of the original data, is called a *hash function*. The outcome of applying the hash function to a message is called *message digest*.

The five-letter message digest that has been derived can now be encrypted. Encrypting 'SUKFF' using its numerical equivalent 8583983, exponentiation with a modulus of 11881379 and a key of, for instance 5452805, gives, using a computer to do the calculations, the ciphertext 'GTTRW'. The original message and the encrypted digest can be put together:

MEETMEUNDERTHE ELEPHANTATELEVEN GTTRW

A keyholder can check whether the message has been modified or not, by recreating the message digest from the message. This new digest is encrypted and the result compared with the encrypted digest appended to the message. Some assurance about the integrity of the message is provided when the original encrypted digest and the encrypted recalculated digest are the same.

4.2.8   Collision resistance

Again, because more than one message can create the same digest, there is a danger that a message can be altered in such a way that the digest does not change. Such an alteration could, therefore, not be detected. Suppose the message was:

AFTERSEVENPAYCHARLIETHREEHUNDREDWITHUSEDNOTES

Divided into groups of five letters this becomes:

AFTER SEVEN PAYCH ARLIE THREE HUNDR EDWIT HUSED NOTES

Encoding the groups as numbers gives:

100845 8310185 6870923 306440 8817176 3559235 1895731 3562627 6199718

These numbers would be summed to give the message digest. Notice that, in the groups of five letters, the words 'SEVEN' and 'THREE' are in groups on their own. Interchanging these words would substantially change the message, but it would not change the encoding of the groups of five letters – it would only change their order. The same numbers would be added up to get the message digest and the result would be the same for the corrupted message as it was for the original message. An alteration that involved interchanging a group of letters would therefore not be detected by comparing the message digest of the original message with the message digest of the modified message.

It is desirable, therefore, for hash functions to have what are known as *collision-resistant properties*. A hash function is collision-free if any procedure for finding two messages with the same message digest is computationally infeasible. This prevents someone finding out ways in which they could alter messages that would leave the message digest intact. When the hash function is collision-free forgers have no way of knowing whether an alteration will affect the message digest or not. The only sensible assumption they can make is that the old encrypted digest will, most likely, not be consistent with an altered message and so an alteration would be detectable. The hope would then be that forgers would be deterred from making alterations. The examples that I have given would not, in practice, be particularly secure because they clearly do not have collision-resistant properties.

4.2.9 One-way hash

There are a host of potential hash functions and some of them effectively form the digest and encrypt at the same time. A calculation for working out the message digest for a message M can be indicated by the expression $H(M)$ where H stands for the hash function. In the calculation I performed in the previous section, I first found the value of the hash function and then encrypted the result before appending it to the message. This can be described by the expression:

$$M, \{H(M)\}_K$$

In some instances, the hash function works as though it included encryption but the information that would be needed to find the decryption key has been thrown away. Such hash functions are called *one-way* hash functions. For a one-way hash function that is collision-resistant:

1   It is straightforward to calculate the hash value from the message.

2   It is computationally infeasible to work out from the encrypted message digest which messages would generate the digest.

3   It is computationally infeasible to find two messages that have the same digest.

With these strange functions, even when you know the function, it is impracticable to predict what the result of applying the function to a particular message will be. The one-way hash function effectively creates an encrypted message digest. Everyone can use the same hash function, say $H(M)$. Alice could send Bob the message and its digest:

$A \rightarrow B : M, H(M)$	Alice sends a message and a message digest

When Bob receives the message, he can apply the widely known hash function $H(M)$ to the message and reconstruct the digest to see whether or not it matches the digest that Alice sent him. If it does match he can assume that the message is intact. The weakness of such a scheme is that Freda could masquerade as Alice, concoct an alternative message, send it to Bob, and with the widely available hash function create a new consistent cross-check.

4.2.10 Summary

Integrity is to do with making sure data and communicated messages are intact and not sabotaged. Encryption makes it impossible for anyone but the keyholders to know what the effect of altering a message would be. It therefore prevents meaningful modifications being made, but it does not prevent uninformed alterations which generate unintelligible plaintext.

A document or message can be copied and the copy and original compared if there is a suspicion that a change has been made to either one. Encrypting the copy would make it infeasible for someone without the key to make a change in the ciphertext that matched an alteration in the original plaintext. Encrypting with a private key would also eliminate the need to distribute keys that should be kept secret.

A message can, therefore, be sent accompanied by a copy encrypted with a private key. To check for alterations the encrypted copy can be decrypted with the appropriate public key and the result compared with the plaintext message. A discrepancy would suggest that the message had been altered.

To reduce the computational effort a message digest can be created, encrypted and appended to a copy of the message. Processing a message using a hash function creates a message digest. Recreating the message digest from the copy of the message then provides a check on the integrity of the message. Some assurance is given when the newly created digest matches the digest derived from the original message.

To prevent forgery hash functions should ideally be collision-free so that it is not feasible to work out which messages correspond to a particular digest. Hash functions often effectively create an encrypted message digest and digests created with one-way hash functions cannot, feasibly, be decrypted.

4.3   Binding

Messages can relate two or more items of data. When such a message, just like any other message, is encrypted it becomes impossible to change the ciphertext and know what effect it will have on the plaintext. For a message that describes a relationship this implies that it is unlikely that a forger can tamper with the message to promote an intelligible change in the recorded relationship. Encryption thus binds data together so that it is practically impossible to destroy relationships described in messages. Because a ciphertext depends on both the original message and the key, encryption also secures the relationship between the key and the message. If the key or an item of data in the message is associated with an individual, then encryption indirectly *binds* that individual with the data and the relationships described within the message.

4.3.1   Securing a relationship

Take the example where Ian, an intruder, intercepts a message between Bob and Alice, which relates the time T and place P where they are to meet.

Suppose Ian has access to the public network that Bob and Alice use and that Ian can intercept, modify and forward messages. Ian can substitute a new location P', perhaps obtained from another intercepted message, and fool Alice.

$B \rightarrow I : T, P$	Bob sends Alice a time and place which Ian intercepts
$I \rightarrow A : T, P'$	Ian forwards Bob's message to Alice after altering the location

Bob could encrypt the time and place, using an encryption key K, for which he believes Alice has the decryption key. Ian will not then be able to make sense of the parts of the message and he will not know when and where Bob and Alice are to meet. However, he can still disrupt Bob and Alice's rendezvous. First, he records an earlier message:

$B \rightarrow I : \{T\}_K, \{P\}_K$	Bob sends Alice a message identifying a time and place which Ian intercepts
$I \rightarrow A : \{T\}_K, \{P\}_K$	Ian records and forwards Bob's message to Alice

Ian, without having the decryption key, can construct combinations of parts of recent and old messages that will be intelligible when decrypted, and which might deceive Alice:

$B \rightarrow I : \{T'\}_K, \{P'\}_K$	Bob sends Alice a message about another meeting, giving a new time and place, which Ian intercepts
$I \rightarrow A : \{T'\}_K, \{P\}_K$	Ian forwards Bob's message after replacing Bob's new encrypted location $\{P'\}_K$ with the old one $\{P\}_K$

Because of the encryption, Ian will not know what the content of the messages is, but if he knows the format of the message he can forestall Alice and Bob's tryst.[92] If Bob is to prevent Ian making alterations that are intelligible but misleading for Alice then he must secure the relationship between the time and the place. Encrypting the *combination* of time and place can do this:

$B \rightarrow A : \{T, P\}_K$	Bob sends Alice an encrypted time and place

To Ian, without knowledge of the key K, the message would be garbled, he would not be able to pick out the time and place and it would be improbable that he could make a modification that would produce an intelligible plaintext.

The effect of the encryption is therefore to securely bind the time and the place together. For his scheme to be effective, Bob has to choose an encryption scheme that treats the combination of time and place as a single block and thoroughly mixes them up. Encrypting the relationship between time and place does not prevent Ian from sabotaging the message, but at least when Alice receives a corrupted message she will most likely see something unintelligible when she decrypts it. Alice would therefore not act on the directions provided by the altered message.

It is sometimes desirable to announce relationships publicly – for instance, the time and place of a public event. At the same time, people might want to be reassured that the announcement has not been altered. Encryption of the combination of name of the event, the time and the place with a private key would allow anyone to find out the relationship using a public key, but it would make it infeasible for anyone other than the private keyholder to make an acceptable alteration.

$B \rightarrow A, I, E, D : \{T, P, G\}_{\overline{K_B}}$	Bob announces to his colleagues the time, place and name of a gig and makes it publicly accessible by encrypting it with his private key.

4.3.2 A simple failure

At one time, a bank provided customers with cards for withdrawing cash that each had two items of data recorded on it – the account number and the PIN (personal identification number). The PIN was encrypted and only the bank knew the key. Anyone reading the encrypted PIN and who did not hold the key would be unable to deduce the PIN. The interaction between the customers with their cards and the cash machine or teller T consisted of two parts: reading the card and entering the PIN. Supposing Charlie wanted to withdraw money:

$C \rightarrow T : Ac, \{PINc\}_K$	Charlie provides a card carrying an account number, Ac, and his PIN, $PINc$, encrypted
$C \rightarrow T : PINc$	Charlie provides a PIN

The cash machine had access to the decryption key and could automatically check that the encrypted PIN on the card corresponded to the PIN that Charlie typed. This gave some assurance that the person who offered the card was the authorized cardholder, Charlie. The cash machine then delivered the requested cash and debited Charlie's account identified by the number given on the card, Ac. Anyone getting hold of Charlie's card could not find out his PIN because it was encrypted. They could therefore not use the card to withdraw money. The account number was not encrypted, but nothing secret was being divulged because account numbers are used openly in other kinds of transactions.

But because the account number was not encrypted, it could be altered with suitable machinery. A fraudster, Freda, could therefore use her *own* legitimately owned card and PIN but could change the account number, perhaps, to pinpoint Charlie's account. When she presented her card and typed her PIN, it would be accepted because it corresponded to the encrypted PIN on the card, the cash would be delivered but Charlie's account would be debited.[93]

$F \rightarrow T : Ac, \{PINf\}_K$	Freda provides a card carrying Charlie's account number, Ac, and Freda's PIN, $PINf$, encrypted
$F \rightarrow T : PINf$	Freda provides her PIN

The major weakness in this protocol was that although the account number and the PIN were bound together by being on the same card, this binding was not secure since the two pieces of data on the card could be altered independently. The encrypted PIN could be retained and the account number altered.

One solution might have been to encrypt the PIN together with the account number, $\{Ac, PIN\}_K$, not with the intention of hiding the account number but to securely bind the account number to a specific PIN.

4.3.3   Summary

Messages often carry items of data that are strongly related. Such messages provide forgers with the opportunity to alter relationships. Encrypting individual items of data does not prevent forgers from generating illicit but intelligible relationships that might contribute to significant and potentially undetectable fraud. Encryption of the combination of items of data can bind the separate items together and make it infeasible to construct messages outlining new and intelligible relationships.

4.4   Conclusion

The encryption of messages provides the means of keeping messages secret. Secrecy is maintained if the encryption and decryption keys are kept secret. The problem of keeping messages secret is replaced by the problem of distributing keys and keeping them secret. The public/private key techniques eliminate the need to distribute the private key and are not compromised when the public key is distributed. Encryption with a public key hides messages from everyone but the holder of the corresponding private key.

Encryption can provide confidentiality; it can make meaningful alterations to messages detectable and secure relationships. In some instances, where the computational effort is excessive, encryption can be applied to message digests and still offer adequate guarantees about the integrity of the message and the relationships it describes. Encryption is therefore not solely used to keep things secret.

Chapter Five

Protocols

The transmitting of a message securely is always part of a wider activity such as making a purchase, watching Pay TV or conducting a battle. Such activities involve the interchange of sequences of messages often according to some rough preconceived pattern. An exchange might involve first the building of trust between the communicating partners, then an exchange that specifies the nature of their business, the execution of their transaction and, finally, a way of signalling that everything has been completed. In purchasing something a shopper might first send a message specifying the goods, then the vendor replies by naming the price. The shopper then specifies the quantity and the vendor responds by confirming that he or she has the goods in stock. Their interaction would continue as the order was placed, payment offered and confirmed, and delivery arrangements made. Often where information technology is involved such a sequence of messages is rigidly defined so that at least some of procedures can be performed by computers. An exchange of messages following a strict set of rules like this is called a *protocol*.

The relationships between the messages in a protocol can provide additional information to eavesdroppers, which helps them to subvert transactions or discover secrets. An analysis that aims to assess the security surrounding a protocol, therefore, must examine the combination of encryption method and the sequences of messages defined by the protocol.

5.1 A simple protocol

It is not essential to issue keys in order to exchange information in secret. There is a simple protocol, which I will refer to as the *double locking protocol*, for exchanging a message in secret but without the need to distribute any keys. The transfer of the secret is conducted in three stages and each stage requires a message in a specific form. Hence, the exchange is conducted using a protocol.

5.1.1 Analogy

It is helpful, sometimes, to describe a protocol in terms of an analogy. One common analogy is the locked box. Instead of talking or writing about encryption it is assumed that messages are placed in boxes and can be locked and unlocked with a key. Locking is analogous to encryption and unlocking to decryption. A simple transaction, where Alice sends Bob an encrypted message that Bob can decrypt with a copy of Alice's key, might be described in terms of the analogy as follows:

> 'Alice takes her secret message and places it in a box. She locks the box with her key and sends the box to Bob. Bob has a copy of the key that Alice used and is able to unlock the box, take out the message and read it.'

The double locking protocol can also be described in terms of locked boxes. Bob and Alice have their own locks and keys. Bob wishes to send Alice a message but does not want to risk copying his key. Alice, too, does not want to let her key out of her sight.

> Bob places his message in a box and padlocks it. It can then be sent securely to Alice.

On receipt of the box:

> Alice locks the box again with her padlock. She returns the doubly locked box to Bob.

Bob can unlock his padlock and remove it leaving the box securely locked with Alice's padlock.

> The locked box can be sent again to Alice secured by Alice's padlock.

Alice receives the box and is able to unlock it with her key, remove the message and read it. An eavesdropper might intercept one of the boxes but at each stage the box is locked. He or she cannot read the message (except perhaps by using brute force to open the box and exposing his or her intervention).

This protocol has a direct analogy in terms of encryption processes.

$B \rightarrow A : \{M\}_{K_B}$	Bob sends Alice a message encrypted using his secret key
$A \rightarrow B : \{\{M\}_{K_B}\}_{K_A}$	Alice encrypts Bob's message using her secret key and sends it back to Bob
	Bob decrypts the message using his decryption key $\overline{K}_B$ derived from his encryption key
$B \rightarrow A : \{M\}_{K_A}$	Once decrypted with his key, Bob sends the result to Alice

Finally, Alice decrypts the message she received using her decryption key to uncover the message.

5.1.2   Protocol requirements

The double locking protocol may not work. It relies on certain properties of the encryption and decryption calculations. In some instances, the analogy with the locked box may break down, or, at least, a different analogy is needed. The whole process would fail, for example, if Bob locked the secret in a box and then Alice locked the box *inside* another box and returned it to Bob. Bob would be stumped because his box was locked inside Alice's and Alice had the key.

For the protocol to work, the order in which Bob and Alice lock and unlock things should not affect the outcome. When the protocol is interpreted as a sequence of encryptions and decryptions this means that Bob should be able to undo the effects of his encryption although Alice had added her layer of encryption.

Suppose the first letter of the secret message that Bob wishes to send is 'C', encoded as a 2. Using the Caesar code and Bob's secret key, 12, the encrypted version will be given by:

$$2 + \underline{12} \bmod 26$$

I have underlined Bob's key. Bob sends this to Alice who encodes it again using her key, 19, by working out:

$$2 + \underline{12} + 19 \bmod 26$$

This result is returned to Bob who then decrypts the result using his decryption key, 14. Without doing the arithmetic Bob's new message is given by:

$$2 + \underline{12} + 19 + \underline{14} \bmod 26$$

Bob's decryption key has also been underlined. For the protocol to work, it turns out that I must be able to swap Bob's and Alice's keys in this calculation so that Bob's decryption undoes the effect of Bob's encryption. This is equivalent to saying Bob can unlock his padlock even when the box is locked with Alice's. Now, it is usually taken for granted that it does not matter what order addition is performed. So to work out the result I can swap the 12 and the 19:

$$2 + \overset{\overset{\text{swap}}{\longleftrightarrow}}{\underline{12} + 19} + \underline{14} \equiv 2 + 19 + \underline{12} + \underline{14} \bmod 26$$

Then I can continue the calculation using the properties of modulo 26 addition:

$$2 + 19 + \underline{12} + \underline{14} \equiv 2 + 19 + \underline{26} \equiv 2 + 19 \bmod 26$$

which shows that the message that Bob has prepared is equivalent to the original message but encrypted now by Alice's key rather than his. Decryption with Alice's decryption key, 7, will reconstruct Bob's original code to reveal his secret to Alice:

$$2 + 19 + 7 \equiv 2 + 26 \equiv 2 \bmod 26$$

The demonstration of this result required me to say that $12 + 19 \equiv 19 + 12 \bmod 26$. This works for addition, but for some mathematical operations, changing the order of the numbers does matter. This requirement for the encryption and decryption operations for the double locking protocol can be written as:

$$a \circ b \equiv b \circ a$$

where a and b are values taken from the Group being encrypted and $\circ$ is the operation to be performed on a and b. This is the mathematical equivalent of saying Alice and Bob can lock and unlock boxes in any order. In the case of modulo 26 addition it is certainly correct to write:

$$a + b \equiv b + a \bmod 26$$

This also works for multiplication for any modulus since

$$a \times b \equiv b \times a \bmod n$$

Technical names are given to operations and Groups that allow the exchange of terms. An operation that gives a result that is insensitive to the order of the things it is operating on is called *commutative* and a Group with a commutative operation is named after a mathematician named Abel, and hence called an *Abelian Group*. The double locking protocol relies on this property and therefore only works when the encryption operation is commutative.

5.1.3 Protocol failures

People who want to undermine the security of a transaction are unlikely to be bound by any rules that the principals set out, and protocols can sometimes be subverted by using the interactions that take place in a transaction in a different way to that described in the protocol. Take, for example, the double locking protocol using the Caesar code where Bob has the encryption key K_B and Alice has the encryption key K_A. Suppose Bob wants to send the message M to Alice in secret. Three messages are transmitted. Bob sends Alice the encrypted message $M + K_B \bmod 26$. She encrypts this with her key and sends the result $M + K_B + K_A \bmod 26$ back to Bob. He decrypts this and effectively sends Alice $M + K_A \bmod 26$, which she can decrypt.

Eve may be able to pick up these messages but since they are each encrypted, she will not be able to find out the content of the message and without an explicit transfer of keys she will not have the opportunity to intercept a key.

However, because the transfer of a secret is a protocol, Eve knows that several related messages will be transmitted and she may be able to make use of the relationships. Eve could carry out some calculations; for instance by subtracting the first message from the second one Eve would get:

$$\left(M + K_B + K_A\right) - \left(M + K_B\right) \equiv M + K_B + K_A - M - K_B$$
$$\equiv K_A \bmod 26$$

and hence Eve would discover Alice's key. Similarly, Eve could subtract the third message from the second one to get Bob's key and with either key could decrypt the first or the third message and find out the original plaintext M. Notice that in this process Eve has not had to crack any codes but has performed calculations similar to those used by the principals, Alice and Bob, to encrypt the message. Eve has also only had to perform calculations on this one transaction to discover Alice's and Bob's keys. Eve therefore performed roughly the same number and kind of operations as the principals so if they could find the computational resources to execute the protocol it is likely that she could find the computational resources to subvert it.

The individual interactions between Alice and Bob were made secure by encryption. It is the combination of messages, the protocol in combination with the type of encryption operation, that makes the interactions insecure. The ease of finding the keys suggests that this is a protocol failure.

While a protocol may demand particular kinds of calculation, crackers would use a different calculation to break-in. They have a myriad potential calculations that they could try, and this makes it impossible to guarantee that a protocol is safe from interference or subversion. Unfortunately, there is no universal method for detecting all the kinds of weaknesses in the combinations of protocols and encryption methods and it is widely accepted that the best defence is to publish protocols and let other security specialists analyse and criticize security techniques, and then adopt those that have stood the test of time, or better, those that have had both extensive use and received thorough analysis.

5.1.4 Making things difficult for Eve

The weakness in the double locked box protocol arises in part because of the properties of the encryption operation. The commutative property of addition that ensured the protocol worked also made it easy for Eve to subvert it. The exponentiation operation has properties similar to but not quite the same as the commutative property. For a message M and a key K encryption is performed by the operation denoted as:

$$M^K \bmod n$$

Clearly the exponentiation algorithm is not commutative since, except perhaps in a few special cases, M^K is not the same as K^M. A simple example shows this: $3^4 = 81$ is not, in general[94], the same as $4^3 = 64$. However, if I apply the exponentiation algorithm twice, that is I encrypt with Alice's key and then with Bob's key, then I get:

$$\left(M^{K_A}\right)^{K_B} \bmod n$$

which is the same as

$$M^{K_A K_B} \bmod n$$

Now, because of the properties of multiplication I can swap K_A and K_B

$$M^{K_A K_B} \bmod n \equiv M^{K_B K_A} \bmod n$$

and this can be written as

$$\left(M^{K_B}\right)^{K_A} \bmod n$$

So, for a *given* message I can form a group of all the possible ways of encrypting this particular message and in this group the operation of encrypting with one key and then another is commutative. I can therefore change the order in which encryption and decryption are done and get the same result. This property enables the double padlocked box protocol to work with encryption using exponentiation but makes it more difficult for an eavesdropper to subvert it. Now, Bob sends Alice $M^{K_B} \bmod n$, Alice sends Bob $\left(M^{K_B}\right)^{K_A} \bmod n$ which, because of the commutative property, gives the same result as $\left(M^{K_A}\right)^{K_B} \bmod n$. Bob then creates $\left(\left(M^{K_A}\right)^{K_B}\right)^{\overline{K_B}} \equiv M^{K_A} \bmod n$, which Alice can decrypt to find out his message.

Previously, Eve was able to perform an operation on the first and the second messages to find out Alice's key, but now there is no immediately obvious way of doing this except by trial and error. A part of Eve's problem is that she cannot know which group Alice and Bob are working with unless she can find out the message. And encryption sets out to hide that message from Eve.

5.1.5 Summary

The double locking procedure is an example of a protocol because it requires messages to follow a specified pattern. The protocol can be described using an analogy. Sometimes, explanations using locked boxes can offer a clearer account than a description in terms of encryption and decryption. On the other hand, as with other analogies, the analogy can, occasionally, be misleading or become over-complicated.

The protocol only works if the encryption scheme has the mathematical properties of an *Abelian Group*. In an Abelian Group the operation is commutative, which means the things being operated on can be swapped about. Addition, multiplication and exponentiation have the required property.

The protocol fails when encryption is performed using the Caesar code. An eavesdropper can combine the related messages to discover the encryption keys, although exponentiation can overcome the failure.

5.2 Threats

In practice, the threats that can undermine security are less to do with the strength of encryption schemes. They are more to do with the management of secure systems, the carelessness of the users of the secure system and the failure of protocols.

5.2.1 Encryption is not enough

In secure communications the messages following a protocol will often be encrypted in order to prevent eavesdroppers from discovering the content of the messages. However, sometimes eavesdroppers can deduce things from the message sequence without decrypting them. Each message that is sent can reveal something about the nature of the communications and by piecing together these scraps of information, ingenious eavesdroppers can sometimes deduce things that are supposed to remain undisclosed. For instance, the numbers of messages that pass between two companies might be an indication, to an industrial spy, of the level of business that the companies are engaged in. Where this kind of deduction might have serious consequences, sending dummy messages when there is nothing else to send can thwart the analysis. Provided encrypted dummy messages are indistinguishable from genuine messages, an eavesdropper will be misled about the message traffic.

A flurry of messages, therefore, introduces new kinds of risks even though the contents may be securely encrypted. People might, for instance, record messages and play them back later in a sequence of interactions to cause confusion or trigger mistakes that work to their advantage. An elementary example would be an interchange where one person with authority ordered someone to pay me some money. If I intercepted the message, recorded and replayed it after a judiciously chosen interval, then I might get paid twice.

Encryption alone, therefore, is not enough to ensure that infiltrators are kept in the dark or that transactions are conducted with security. Some care has to be taken over the sequences in which messages are sent.

5.2.2 Effectiveness

The effectiveness of a protocol to attain a security goal depends on the difficulty of cracking the encryption but it appears that it is a misconception that 'a clever opponent will "break" the cryptographic algorithm'[95] – the cracking of codes appears to be rare. As Ross Anderson noted:

> 'Designers focussed on what could go wrong, rather on what was likely to; and many of their products are so complicated and tricky to use that they are rarely used properly. … As a result, most security failures are due to implementation and management errors'. [96]

Roger Needham and Martin Abadi who studied a range of protocols wrote that:

> 'Cryptographic protocols … are prone to design errors of every kind.' [97]

Indeed, Roger Needham with Schroeder designed a protocol that was subsequently and unexpectedly found to contain vulnerabilities,[98] which brought home their own message that such protocols 'are prone to extremely subtle errors that are unlikely to be detected in normal operations'.[99]

It is not uncommon for the designers of protocols to be confused about the role of encryption in their protocols and to therefore make claims that their protocols cannot fulfil. Goldwasser and Bellare reported that 'confusion between data encryption and data authentication' caused, they claim, by 'a lack of specification of what exactly is the problem that [the designer] is trying to solve'.[100] They also warned that 'it is easy to come up with concrete proposals which are logically correct but which are blatantly insecure'.

5.2.3 Assumptions

There are elaborate mathematical analyses that provide assessments of the level of security provided by different encryption schemes. These assessments guide people in choosing suitable encryption algorithms for their applications and in choosing things like the length of the key. They are based on how easy it is for the legitimate partners to perform encryption and decryption compared with how difficult it would be for someone trying to crack the code. This ease, or difficulty, is related to the available mathematical procedures for dealing with a method of encryption and to the capability of computers for performing these mathematically derived procedures.

As computer technology and mathematics evolve so too does the relative cryptographic strength of different methods of encryption. To avoid becoming tangled up in these deeply mathematical matters, the descriptions of the ways in which messages are exchanged to fulfil various security requirements usually rely on a number of assumptions. For a full analysis, it would be necessary to confirm that, for the proposed encryption methods, these assumptions are valid.

Often they are not, but practical systems can be created that meet the requirements demanded by theoretical analysis closely enough to give adequate levels of security. The kinds of assumptions that are made are:

- A cracker cannot find out the key given a sequence of messages encrypted with that key.

- A cracker cannot find out the key given both the plaintext and the ciphertext.

- It is not possible to work out how to change the ciphertext to match a particular alteration in the plaintext and hence forge a plaintext without the need to decrypt the ciphertext.

Analyses also make assumptions about how intruders will try to subvert a security scheme. For instance, they may try to find out the content of messages or they may try to forge messages – unintelligible ones that just waste people's time or intelligible ones that mislead the recipients.

Even if designers are explicit about the assumptions they made when designing a protocol, the users are often unaware of the assumptions made about who is to be trusted and about the capabilities of intruders or eavesdroppers. Users of protocols, out of ignorance or through carelessness, will often open up opportunities for intruders. Security protocols, therefore, on occasions fail to provide the protection that their users anticipated.

5.2.4 Summary

Analysis of protocols must examine the information that an eavesdropper can glean from the sequence of related messages in the protocol. Creating strong encryption schemes is not enough. Secure systems are often subverted because of carelessness or lapses in management.

People who threaten security do not have to abide by the rules of a protocol and a great deal of imagination is needed to envisage how eavesdroppers and forgers can undermine security. Ultimately, it is not feasible to investigate every conceivable threat, and analyses have to be limited by a set of credible assumptions.

5.3 Conclusion

In many situations, passing a single message does not complete a transaction and, in some cases, the sequence of interactions has to follow certain rules. The set of rules that describe the interactions and their sequence is called a protocol. Different assumptions are likely to lead to different answers to apparently similar security questions. There is, therefore, a proliferation of security protocols – many ways of doing apparently the same thing, but as yet there is no method for selecting a security protocol.

Protocols specify sequences of messages and the relationships between those messages give crackers new opportunities. In practice, codes are rarely cracked and security breaches are more likely to be a result of carelessness or the exploitation of an unforeseen relationship between the component messages in a protocol.

Relying on established protocols is not always a good guide. Some long-established protocols have been shown to have weaknesses and, of course, when weaknesses are discovered in protocols in operational systems, their operators are unlikely to advertise the fact. Assessing the security of a system is, therefore, a matter of assessment of risk and of choosing methods that offer acceptable risks. With the possibility of a security breach always present, a comprehensive security system needs systems for monitoring, policing and reporting, and contingency plans for when things go seriously wrong.

Chapter Six

Authentication

A common application of security protocols is in confirming the identity of the principals in a transaction. Assurance about the authenticity of a document can come from knowing who supplied the document and knowing that it has not been altered since the original sender dispatched it. A process called, in security circles, *authentication* gives the first kind of warranty. Authentication identifies the source of documents. Integrity, as mentioned earlier, is the term used to talk about guarantees of documents being intact. One way of making people feel insecure is to pass them credible but erroneous information. Authentication helps to undermine such deceptions by linking documents with trusted sources.

Authentication involves securely identifying a relationship between messages and an identity. Ultimately, one goal in secure protocols is to provide information that binds messages and new relationships to trustworthy sources that can be relied upon to vouch for the authenticity of those messages and relationships.

6.1 Signatures

Transactions spawn promises and commitments. Fraud often involves the exchange of promises where one partner in the deal honours his or her commitment and the other does not. It becomes impossible for the injured partner to withdraw because he or she is implicated and identified with a binding deal whereas the fraudster's identity is either untraceable or ambiguous. Troublemakers, too, meddle with their identity so that their damaging actions get attributed to someone else. To remove the anxiety of becoming a victim of a fraud or of an impersonation, elements are added to messages to confirm the identity of participants and to provide accounts of their actions.

6.1.1 Identification

Alice can send Bob a message encrypted with a secret key that they both hold:

$$A \rightarrow B : \{M\}_K \qquad \text{Alice sends an encrypted message } M \text{ to Bob}$$

If Bob receives ciphertext that when decrypted on the assumption that it was encrypted using the key K generates an unfamiliar but intelligible message, then he can deduce that the message originally came from Alice who has the only other copy of the key. Provided encryption keys are managed with care, encryption can keep messages secret and also securely associate messages with their keyholders. Encryption and subsequent decryption, therefore, helps to authenticate the source of a message.

Of course, neither Bob nor Alice can be quite sure that the other partner has not given away the key, so even if Bob is scrupulously careful with his key he cannot be totally confident that the message originated with Alice. And Alice, similarly, cannot be sure that Bob will be convinced about the source of the message, especially if he has knowingly been careless with his copy of the key.

6.1.2 Signing

The use of public and private keys can give a little more confidence because the private key does not have to be communicated to anyone. Alice can encrypt her message with her private key. This does not make the message private since the corresponding public key should be readily available and anyone can decrypt it.

$A \rightarrow B : \{M\}_{\overline{K}_A}$	Alice sends a message to Bob encrypted with her private key

Because the message can be decrypted with Alice's public key, Alice must have encrypted it with her private key. One key decrypts what the other encrypts. The encrypted message is inextricably bound up with the private key, which would not normally be distributed, so the encryption with a private key binds Alice's identity to a message. The operation of encryption with a private key is, therefore, sometimes referred to as *signing*.

Receiving an encrypted message is like receiving a locked box and not knowing which of many keys will open it. It is helpful, to save Bob from the effort of trying all his keys, for Alice to include data about her identity A in what she sends him. This will let him know he has to use Alice's public key to decrypt the message. The letter A in the description of a message can represent the data that identifies Alice.

$A \rightarrow B : A, \{M\}_{\overline{K}_A}$	A complete signed message from Alice incorporating her identity

If Bob did not know that the message had come from Alice then he would recognize her identity in the message and try her public key. Clearly, the identity in the message could easily be altered so adding it to the communication is a courtesy rather than a security measure. When Bob can readily identify the source of the message the identity adds nothing. I will assume that in most instances it is not necessary to add data to identify the senders of messages.

If Alice has looked after her private key then she can be assured that no third party can use her key to deceive Bob. Bob on the other hand still has to have faith in Alice's care of her private key.

6.1.3   Signatures

When a message itself is obscure, possibly consisting of strings of numerical data, it can be hard to say whether the decrypted message is sensible and is indeed what was intended. When Bob decrypts a message using Alice's public key and gets an unintelligible result, it could mean that either the original was not encrypted using her private key or that she sent an unintelligible message. No conclusion can be drawn about the identity of the originator.

As with the integrity check in subsection 4.2.5, a composite message can be formed from the original message and a version encrypted with the author's private key. Because it is intended to identify the author of the message, the encrypted addition is called a *signature*.

$$A \rightarrow B : M, \{M\}_{\overline{K_A}}$$ Alice sends a message and a signature to Bob

Bob can check the signature by decrypting it with Alice's public key to see if it matches the original message M. When Bob carries out such a check he does not have to supply any special information himself, everything that he needs is publicly available. Anybody, then, can check that Alice endorsed this message.

Since this identity check is similar to the arrangement for checking the integrity of messages, a signature may serve both purposes. By using a private key, the message is associated with a particular keyholder. When the decrypted message fails to match the plaintext, and there is no anticipated threat to the integrity of transmissions, then the discrepancy must be treated as a case of mistaken identity and attributed to the failure of the chosen decryption key to decrypt the signature correctly. The choice of public key was, therefore, incorrect and the identity of the author is not confirmed. If, however, there are threats to the integrity of messages then the failure could be due to an alteration, a misidentification or both.

6.1.4   Using a hash

Just as with an integrity check, it is not necessary, in many applications, to encrypt all of the message to form a signature. An adequate signature can be formed by first creating a message digest. Alice can then encrypt the message digest with her private key and append the result to the message. She generates the message digest, using a well known hash function H, encrypts it with her *private* key and appends the encrypted message digest – the signature – to the original message:

$A \rightarrow B : M, \{H(M)\}_{\overline{K_A}}$	Alice sends Bob an encrypted, hashed message appended to the complete plaintext message

To check that it is Alice's signature, Bob first creates a fresh message digest from the copy of the message he receives using the hash function H. Secondly, he decrypts the signature using Alice's public key to obtain the copy of the message digest that Alice has generated, signed and dispatched with the message. Finally, he compares the copy of the message digest he generated with the encrypted one that accompanied the message. If they are the same, Bob will most likely conclude that Alice has signed the document.

It is sometimes useful to have a notation for identifying a signature. I will use the Greek letter σ (a lower case 'sigma') to denote a signature formed from an encrypted message digest and I will add a suffix to identify the signatory. A message M, signed by Alice and sent to Bob, will be written as:

$A \rightarrow B : M, \sigma_A(M)$	A complete signed message from Alice incorporating her identity

6.1.5 Taking the blame

The study of security involves thinking the worst of people who you might have to deal with. People could, for instance, when shown their signature on a document, deny that they had signed it and thus deny responsibility for the effects of the message. The term used to describe a denial of responsibility for an action in the face of, possibly dubious, evidence is repudiation. Components of messages, such as signatures, are added to provide evidence that makes it impossible to repudiate a claim. A digital signature provides evidence that a signatory has endorsed the message by deploying his or her private key. Signed messages are therefore said to offer the ugly-sounding property of '*non-repudiation*'.

Strictly speaking, in the schemes that use a message digest to form a signature, Alice only encrypted the digest. She could claim that she was tricked into encrypting it and that someone later appended it to the message. The digest is a jumbled and condensed version of the message that, on its own, probably makes little sense. Alice could claim that although the digest had been signed, she had not read the message. Whether or not Alice's denial is accepted will depend upon other evidence and the rules that people are expected to follow when creating a digital signature in her particular situation. If Alice had signed the complete message rather than the digest, her denial would be less plausible.

6.1.6 Taking credit

Messages serve as a record of events. These records deter misconduct because from records it is possible to trace sequences of events that lead to security breaches and to identify both the actions that trigger the misdeeds and the people involved. Where people know that such evidence is being collected, they are more likely to be cautious and the result might be a higher level of security.

Accounts of sequences of actions help in attributing blame, but they also help in assigning credit, where credit is due.

Now, suppose Alice has been known to make brilliant suggestions for the development of Bob's business and he has always rewarded her well for her good tips. Vince might decide that he wants to profit from Alice's work so when she sends a message to Bob, Vince intercepts it:

$A \rightarrow V : M, \{H(M)\}_{\overline{K}_A}$	Alice, unknowingly, sends her signed message to Vince

Vince can read the message, see that it has come from Alice and he can decrypt Alice's signature using her public key to get the message digest $H(M)$. He can, if he thinks Alice has a good idea, replace her identity with his own and encrypt the message digest with his private key and forward it all to Bob:

$V \rightarrow B : M, \{H(M)\}_{\overline{K}_V}$	Vince sends Alice's message to Bob with Vince's signature attached

Thus Vince does not have to recreate the message digest or know how it was created to construct a message that will fool Bob into believing that Alice's good idea came from Vince.

Vince's digital signature on the document therefore shows that he endorsed the document, but it does not prove that the message originated with him. He may persuade Bob that he should be rewarded for an idea that originated with Alice. On the other hand, if things were to go wrong then Vince's signature is evidence that he agreed with the content of the message and in spite of his protests, he would either have to take the blame for the content of the message or confess to his forgery.

6.1.7 Summary

Because encryption keys are kept secret, they are associated with only a few people. Encryption with a particular key therefore identifies the plaintext with the members of the group holding that key. Since a private key may be held by only one person, a message that can be decrypted with the corresponding public key is almost certainly associated with that individual private keyholder.

Complete assurance cannot be given, since people can be careless and fraudsters ruthless and ingenious, allowing private keys to become exposed.

Computational effort can be reduced by encrypting a message digest. A message digest encrypted with a private key offers evidence that the keyholder encrypted the digest. It does not prove conclusively that he or she read the message. Encrypting a message or a message digest provides what is known as a signature. A message accompanied by a signature gives the assurance that the signatory endorsed the message, but it does not guarantee that he or she is the author or that they sent it. Anyone can sign a copy of a message. Signatures are useful for attributing blame but may not offer adequate proof when rewards are being handed out.

6.2 Challenges

A closer relationship between messages and individuals can be created by issuing *challenges* that anticipate a response from a trusted partner. When the response is not what was anticipated there are grounds for suspicion. An anticipated response, however, gives some assurance about the correspondent. It is clear that because a challenge requires a request and a response that it forms a sequence of messages and hence is an example of a protocol.

6.2.1 Ask a question

Bob wants to be sure that he is dealing with Alice and not some rogue, such as Vince masquerading as her. Bob could challenge Alice and ask 'Who am I communicating with?', and Alice could respond with the message 'It's me. Alice':

$B \rightarrow A : Q$	Bob questions Alice
$A \rightarrow B : A$	Alice responds to the question with her identity A

An impostor, Ian, could send the very same reply as Alice, and Bob might be fooled or come to the conclusion that he still does not know who he is dealing with.

$B \rightarrow I : Q$	Bob thinks he is questioning Alice but the message is intercepted by Ian
$I \rightarrow B : A$	Ian responds to the question by sending Alice's identity A

To be sure he is dealing with Alice, Bob needs her to tell him something that only she can know and that he can check. Bob might ask 'Tell me our little secret', but if Alice replied 'We both love gherkins' then the secret would be revealed to an eavesdropper, such as Eve:

$B \rightarrow A : Q$	Bob questions Alice about a secret
$A \rightarrow B, E : R$	Alice responds to Bob, but also reveals the secret to Eve in her response R

In a subsequent challenge, Alice could not use the same response, as it was no longer a secret. Eve could generate an identical response to Alice and Bob would not know, on subsequent occasions, who had produced the response 'We both love gherkins'. To hide the secret in the first instance, Alice could encrypt it using a key that only she and Bob shared, K, then Bob would be able to check the secret but, without the key, Eve would not be able to find out what the secret was.

$B \rightarrow A : Q$	Bob questions Alice
$A \rightarrow B : \{R\}_K$	Alice responds to the question

Eve would not be able to find out the secret, but she could record Alice's response. Later Eve could masquerade as Alice. When Bob next asked the question, 'Tell me our little secret', although Eve does not know the secret or the encryption key, she can reply with her recording of Alice's encrypted answer:

$B \rightarrow A : Q$	Bob questions Alice
$A \rightarrow B : \{R\}_K$	Alice encrypts her response to the question
	Eve records Alice's response $\{R\}_K$. In a subsequent interchange Eve masquerades as Alice
$B \rightarrow E : Q$	Bob thinks he is questioning Alice about her secret, but Eve intercepts the message
$E \rightarrow B : \{R\}_K$	Eve responds to the question using her recording of Alice's earlier response

Bob will receive Eve's response, which answers his question and is encrypted with a key that only he and Alice know. He might be fooled into believing that he is dealing with Alice.

There are two clues that seem to confirm Alice's involvement. Firstly, the response incorporated a secret that, apart from Bob, only she could have known. Secondly, the response could be decrypted by assuming that it was encrypted using a key that only Bob and Alice shared. These clues imply that the message originated with Alice, but it does not guarantee that the copy Bob received came from her. In the interchange there is no evidence about whether her response was freshly prepared or a recording.

6.2.2 Freshness

In protocols, *freshness* can be indicated in a number of different ways. Alice could add the time to her response:

$B \rightarrow A : Q$	Bob questions Alice
$A \rightarrow B : \{R, T\}_K$	Alice responds with her secret and the time both were encrypted

The part of a message that carries the time is often referred to as a *time-stamp*. Bob gains some assurance about the freshness or the currency of the reply from the time embedded in Alice's response. He can be assured that the response came from Alice because it is effectively signed with the secret key that they share. The secret response R is not strictly necessary; encryption with the secret key is sufficient to identify the message with Alice. The response R is not needed; it could be omitted but could also be replaced by a message M that Alice wishes to convey to Bob. Alice could also use her private key and then Bob, or anyone else, could decrypt her response with her public key to see the message:

$B \rightarrow A : Q$	Bob questions Alice
$A \rightarrow B : A, \{M, T\}_{\overline{K}_A}$	Alice responds with a message bound to the time and signed with her private key

Since the message could be decrypted with Alice's public key, Bob gets confirmation that the message originated with her. The encryption also binds the time-stamp to the message and shows how current it is. If Eve tried to record Alice's response and replay it later, then Bob should detect the attempted deception because the time recorded in the message would indicate that the message was stale.

Of course, in a transaction across a network between Alice and Bob there will be a delay between Alice adding the time to a message and Bob's check, so Bob's clock will not match Alice's time-stamp exactly. If Bob offers little leeway, he may reject some of Alice's genuine but delayed responses. On the other hand if he is lax, he gives eavesdroppers time to exploit their recordings of Alice's response.

Alice and Bob carry out four tasks to provide the check on the freshness of the message:

1   They pick a freshness identifier: when Alice uses time-stamps, her clock effectively provides the freshness identifier.

2   The freshness identifier is bound to a secret that identifies the respondent: Alice, for instance, bound the time to her identity by encrypting the time with her secret key.

3   The identity of the respondent is substantiated: Bob confirms Alice's identity by obtaining an intelligible and plausible time after decrypting the message and by assuming that she had encrypted it with a key that only she knew.

4   They verify that the message is fresh: Bob confirms the message is fresh by making a judgement about the difference in time shown on his clock and the time recorded in the message.

6.2.3   Serial numbers

Another approach uses *serial numbers* as freshness identifiers instead of the time. Alice, for example, might keep a count of the messages she has sent Bob and append the serial number of the message n to the message M before encrypting and sending the result to him:

$B \rightarrow A : Q$	Bob questions Alice
$A \rightarrow B : \{M, n\}_{\overline{K_A}}$	Alice responds with a message bound to the serial number and signed with her private key

The primary purpose of the encryption in this protocol is not to keep things secret, but to bind the message, the serial number and Alice's identity using her private or secret key. Encryption with Alice's secret key identifies the plaintext with her. Decrypting the ciphertext with a key associated with Alice provides a check on the link between the message, the sequence number and her identity.

This time Eve cannot use a recording of Alice's missive to mislead Bob because he will be checking that responses from Alice have consecutive serial numbers. Eve's recording would duplicate a serial number that Bob had probably already seen.

Unfortunately, in some communication systems, messages can take different routes and do not necessarily arrive in the order in which they are sent. If Bob receives messages that appear to be out of sequence, he cannot know if it is due to fluctuating delays in the communications system, delays introduced by a saboteur or because Alice has numbered the messages incorrectly. To cast blame on Bob or 'the system', Alice, for instance, might deliberately muddle up the serial numbers of the messages so that Bob's account, which relies on message numbers, does not match the order in which she actually did things.

6.2.4 Nonces

If Bob is especially mistrustful then he may want to choose the freshness identifier himself, and to thwart any attempt by Alice to mislead him about the order of things he needs freshness identifiers that she cannot predict. The systematic way in which the time changes, or serial numbers change allows Alice and others to guess acceptable future and past values of time or sequence numbers, and to forge messages that deceive Bob. Bob might instead pick a number N at random, and such a number incorporated in a message is known as a *nonce*.

$B \rightarrow A : N$	Bob challenges Alice with a nonce
$A \rightarrow B : \{M, N\}_{\overline{K}_A}$	Alice responds with a message bound to the nonce and signed with her private key

In this case, Bob is firmly in command:

1   Bob picks the freshness identifier, a nonce.

2   Alice binds the message and the freshness identifier to her identity using her private key.

3   Bob confirms the identity of the respondent using Alice's public key.

4   Bob confirms that the message is fresh by checking that the value of the nonce is the one he recently issued.

With this protocol Bob may feel quite secure about who he is dealing with.

6.2.5 Summary

A challenge is effectively a request for someone to confirm their identity. It can be a simple question and answer. When the response is encrypted, and the decryption process generates an intelligible result, the decryption key identifies the encryption key and thus associates the response with particular keyholders. When encryption is performed using a private key, the response can be identified with an individual. To prevent eavesdroppers fooling the questioner by replaying a recording of an earlier response, freshness identifiers are incorporated in the encrypted reply. Nonces, time-stamps and serial numbers are examples of freshness identifiers.

6.3   Accountability

Challenges and responses offer the principals assurances about who they are dealing with. They can then communicate confident of the sources and destinations of their messages. If things go wrong, honest as well as dishonest people can be accused of misdeeds and will find that to escape conviction they will need to persuade other people who were not involved in a transaction. Insecurity is fuelled by the knowledge that the transcripts of transactions do not provide adequate evidence to prove the identity of the communicating partners.

6.3.1 Encrypt with a public key

Suppose Bob, in his work, has to deal with a villain, Vince. During the course of their dealings, something goes wrong, Bob and Vince are investigated and the investigators are seeking evidence. Vince denies that he was involved in the suspect transactions but Bob has kept a record of his transactions and he reveals a fragment of a transcript of his dealings.

$B \rightarrow V : \{N\}_{K_V}$	Bob challenges Vince with a nonce encrypted with Vince's public key
$V \rightarrow B : N$	Vince responds with the nonce

Bob claims that Vince must have been involved as he is the only person with the private key that could decrypt the nonce. Vince, though, says 'Someone has fabricated the transcript'. There is nothing in the sequence of messages that is secret and Bob cannot substantiate the sequence of events. After the alleged events, the transcript is just a record of a nonce that anyone could pick, and the same nonce encrypted with Vince's public key, which is accessible to everyone. There is no evidence that Vince saw these messages. The investigators find they cannot pin the blame on Vince or Bob, but aware of this weakness they propose that the protocol be altered so that the evidence shows that Vince is involved in the transactions.

6.3.2 Encrypt with a private key

Again, something goes wrong and Vince and Bob are under investigation. Bob knows that he has issued a challenge and that Vince has signed it with his private key. The record shows this:

$B \rightarrow V : N$	Bob challenges Vince with a nonce
$V \rightarrow B : \{N\}_{\overline{K_V}}$	Vince responds with the nonce signed with his private key

Bob is certain Vince is involved because only Vince could have signed the nonce.

Vince's defence is that Bob has meddled with the record. He claims that anyone, even Bob perhaps, could have taken some arbitrary message M and said it was Vince's ciphertext:

$$M = \{N\}_{\overline{K}_V}$$

Bob could then have decrypted the arbitrary message with Vince's *public* key:

$$\{M\}_{K_V} = \left\{\{N\}_{\overline{K}_V}\right\}_{K_V} = N$$

and taken the result, whatever it was, and called it the nonce that Vince was alleged to have received.

What is presented in evidence by Bob, if Bob is accused of cheating is:

1   a nonce

2   a garbled message alleged by Bob to be a nonce encrypted by Vince's private key. Now Bob could create an arbitrary message without using any keys and claim it was the encrypted nonce. If Bob were cheating Vince would not be involved in doing this. Bob could then decrypt the arbitrary message using Vince's public key and claim that the decrypted result was the nonce he sent in the first place. Using the bogus nonce and the arbitrary message Bob could create a transcript that contained a nonce and the encrypted nonce that appeared to come from Vince. Indeed, anyone could have faked the portion of the transcript that was supposed to prove Vince's involvement.

6.3.3   Add a one-way hash

The frustrated investigators, who have inadequate evidence to discover who is lying, propose a new scheme. They need a protocol that will prevent Bob from fabricating a nonce that corresponds to a piece of Vince's ciphertext. They incorporate *one-way hash* functions in the new protocol.

$B \rightarrow V : N$	Bob challenges Vince with a nonce
$V \rightarrow B : \{H(N)\}_{\overline{K}_V}$	Vince responds with the nonce hashed with a known one-way hash function and then encrypted

After Vince has sent his message, Bob confirms that he is dealing with Vince by forming a one-way hash value of a copy of the nonce he sent to Vince and then comparing it with the decrypted version of Vince's response, which should also be the hashed nonce. The response in this protocol:

1   must have come from Vince since it is signed with his private key

2   cannot be forged by Bob because he does not have Vince's private key

3   prevents anyone calculating the nonce from Vince's message because the hash functions are chosen to make it practically impossible for the original message, the nonce, to be calculated from the message digest sent by Vince.

The hash function has provided proof about the order of events. Since it is a one-way hash function, nobody can construct the nonce N from the hash $H(N)$. The nonce must therefore have existed before the hash was created.

6.3.4   Summary

This protocol prevents Bob from cheating,[101] however he was the honest partner in the transactions. Nevertheless, in order to point the finger at Vince a protocol was required that absolved Bob from blame. If there was any *possibility* that Bob could cheat convincingly, even if he had no intention of doing so, then Vince could always find a way to accuse him of the security breach that he could not rebuff. Most of the protocols in this section would convince Bob that he was dealing with Vince, but only the last one would create adequate evidence for him to convince the investigators that he had communicated with Vince or one of his accomplices. For the earlier protocols, Vince could repudiate the claim that he was involved. As the example shows, a protocol that has the property of non-repudiation has to prevent both the dishonest and the honest principals from cheating, and has to offer evidence that would convince an outsider.

Resourceful Vince might still claim that Bob obtained the record from a recording of another transaction with him. The investigators would then have to invent more elaborate protocols.

6.4   Time services

Where the communicating partners have an insecure relationship, they might prefer to use a well-known and trusted third party to provide their freshness identifiers. Alice might send a message to Bob, for example, that incorporated a time-stamp provided by a time-stamping service that they both trusted. The time-stamping service would append the time to Alice's message (or a digest of her message) and then encrypt the result with its private key before sending it back to Alice, who could retain a copy of the time service's response and forward another copy to Bob.

6.4.1   A simple service

Trustworthy people who certify the time when documents are shown to them are called *notaries*. Suppose trustworthy notary, Simon, runs a time-stamping service.

$A \rightarrow S : M$	Alice sends her message to Simon's time service
$S \rightarrow A : \{M,T\}_{\overline{K}_S}$	Simon returns Alice's message bound to a time-stamp and encrypted with his private key
$A \rightarrow B : \{M,T\}_{\overline{K}_S}$	Alice sends the timed, encrypted message to Bob

Alice may be worried that someone might tamper with her message on its way to Simon; however, when he returns the message she can decrypt it with his public key and check that it is intact before forwarding it to Bob. When Bob receives the message, he can decrypt it with Simon's public key and be assured, because he trusts Simon, that the message was in existence at the time given by the time-stamp. Simon's encryption does three things; it:

1   prevents anyone, including Alice, making an intelligible alteration to the message or time-stamp after it has been endorsed by Simon

2   binds the message to the time-stamp so that it is known that that particular message was associated with that particular time.

3   assures the recipient that trustworthy Simon inserted the time and bound the two items together.

The whole process could be streamlined if Simon dealt with hash values for documents:

$A \rightarrow S : H(M)$	Alice sends the message's hash value to Simon's time service
$S \rightarrow A : \{H(M),T\}_{\overline{K}_S}$	Simon returns to Alice the message's hash value bound to a time-stamp and encrypted with his private key
$A \rightarrow B : M, \{H(M),T\}_{\overline{K}_S}$	Alice sends the original message with the timed encrypted hash value to Bob

The message Simon returns to Alice certifies that the message M existed at the time given by his response. In the message Bob receives, the time is bound to the message digest through Simon's encryption and the message digest is bound to the message because the digest can be derived from the message. Indirectly, the time is bound with the message.

6.4.2   Order, not time

Sometimes, the exact time that a document is issued is not important, but what does matter is the order in which things have been issued. Recording the time that documents are issued helps to reconstruct a sequence of events, but there is an alternative.

One-way hash functions help to define the order in which particular events occur. Because a document cannot be derived from its digest, it must have existed before the message digest. The progressive use of hash functions can therefore help to fix where documents are in a sequence.

One possible scheme assumes that Simon, in a new revised time service, records a list of hash values that he openly publishes. Suppose Simon has a hash value, which is currently h.

$S \rightarrow Everyone : h$	Simon publishes his hash
$A \rightarrow S : M_A$	Alice sends a message M_A to Simon
	Simon appends his current hash value h to Alice's document to get M_A,h and then he calculates a new hash value using the combination to get $H(M_A,h)$
$S \rightarrow A : h, H(M_A,h)$	Simon sends his old hash value h with the newly calculated hash value to Alice
$S \rightarrow Everyone : h'$	Simon gives the calculated hash value derived from Alice's message $H(M_A,h)$ the name h', publishes it and uses it in place of h
$A \rightarrow B : M_A, h, H(M_A,h)$	Alice sends Bob the document M_A, the old hash value and the newly calculated hash

Bob can recalculate the hash value using the message M_A and the value of h, which Alice sent him. He can then confirm that the hash value that Alice sent him was, in all probability, derived from the message M_A and h. Bob can also look up h and h' in Simon's list of published hash values and deduce that it was Alice's document that led to the change in Simon's published values from h to $H(M_A,h)$, or h'.

If Alice is worried that Simon is dishonest she can check the hash value for herself, and she can check the published data.

Suppose, now, Charlie sends another message M_C to Simon and Simon follows his normal procedure:

$C \rightarrow S : M_C$	Charlie sends a message M_C to Simon
	Simon appends the hash value h' to Charlie's document and calculates the hash value of the combination M_C,h' to get $H(M_C,h')$
$S \rightarrow C : h', H(M_C,h')$	Simon sends the hash value h' with the newly

	calculated hash value to Charlie
$S \rightarrow Everyone : h''$	Simon gives the calculated hash value the name h'', publishes it and uses it in place of h'

The hash value associated with Charlie's message depends on the content of his message and upon h', which in turn depended upon the content of Alice's message. The sequence of hash values, therefore, reflects the order in which documents are sent. Because nobody can know the content of all the messages that will be sent to Simon from his clients or the order in which he will receive them, the hash values form an unpredictable sequence and effectively provide a succession of nonces, which is related to the sequence in which he receives the messages. The sequence of nonces reveals the order in which a document is published relative to other published documents. The hash values are also bound to particular documents.

An advantage of such schemes is that no encryption is required. Assurances come, paradoxically, from publication rather than secrecy. Without the need for keys, the sequence of documents is not called into question when keys are compromised. Simon's primary role is to be a trustworthy creator, keeper and publisher of the hash sequences. More elaborate and more practical schemes but similar to Simon's revised scheme have been installed and are known as *digital notary services*.[102]

6.4.3 Summary

Trusted third parties can provide services that give reassurances about the time a document is issued. The time-stamp can indicate how fresh a message is and can also provide proof of when the existence of a document was first acknowledged. As a freshness identifier it may help to prevent attacks that attempt to replay messages. A certified time-stamp can also help to detect attempts at plagiarism when a copy of an old document is presented as an original contribution from a new author.

6.5   Digital certificates

Messages can be sent in confidence, from for instance Alice to Diane, without distributing secret keys. Alice can encrypt a message with Diane's public key that only Diane can decrypt since, Alice would assume, Diane is the only one in possession of the private key. Alice's assumption may be mistaken. In a moment of uncertainty, Alice might imagine that Eve is perhaps masquerading as Diane. Eve could have advertised her public key but associated it with Diane's name. Alice might then encrypt a message with Eve's public key in the mistaken belief that the message was only intelligible to Diane. Eve could then intercept Alice's message, decrypt it with her corresponding private key and dishonestly read the confidential content of Alice's note.

One way of reducing this threat is to get a trusted third party to provide assurances about the association between the key and an individual. *Digital certificates* are intended to provide these assurances.

6.5.1 Certification authorities

To send messages in confidence to Diane, Alice needs Diane's public key, K_D. If Alice has not dealt with Diane before, she will not have a copy of her key and will need to get it from somewhere. Digital certificates are publicly available digital documents that bind together public keys with data that identifies the holder of the corresponding private key.

If D is data that identifies Diane (perhaps her name) then the certificate would provide the combination D, K_D. Alice might be wary of using such a certificate because the identification data and the key are not securely bound together. Eve can easily forge a certificate that incorporates her public key and Diane's identity D, K_E. If Alice used the key in this certificate to send a message to Diane, she would, inadvertently, be encrypting confidential data with Eve's key. Diane would not be able to decrypt it as Alice had hoped, but Eve could. It would be a profitable scam to issue bogus certificates and keys. People unknowingly obtaining forged certificates would encrypt messages that impostors could decrypt. Alice needs to be assured that the certificate is not a forgery, comes from someone she can trust and has not been altered.

One possibility is to use an established *Certification Authority*. Certification Authorities (sometimes called Certificate Authorities or CAs) are expected to be trustworthy and, obviously, issue certificates. Suppose Tahira runs a trusted Certification Authority. To associate a certificate with her CA, she can encrypt it with her private key $\overline{K_T}$. Diane's certificate can then be described by the expression $\{D, K_D\}_{\overline{K_T}}$. Alice, or anyone else, can decrypt the certificate with Tahira's public key to confirm that someone identified by the data D has the public key K_D. The encryption by the trusted authority does not make the certificate secret but it does:

1. demonstrate that it was provided by an agency that held the Certification Authority's private key

2. bind together the identity of the keyholder with his or her key. Without encryption either the identity or the public key can be altered independently

3. show that the certificate has not been tampered with. A counterfeiter would, ultimately, have to encrypt forged data with the private key of the Certification Authority. The counterfeiter should not have this private key and so cannot create a plausible certificate.

6.5.2 The protocol

Encryption keys are often issued for a limited period or for a limited set of transactions. There are, therefore, restrictions on the valid uses for a key. Certificates can include data such as an expiry date, a date when the key became valid or a description of the rights that the private keyholder has. These restrictions are related to the key and the keyholder and should be bound to the public key and the keyholder's identity. If X_D denotes data about the restrictions on the use of Diane's key then Diane's completed certificate is described by the expression $\{D, K_D, X_D\}_{\overline{K_T}}$. Encryption of the three items together securely binds them and prevents a forger replacing any one component by copying it from another certificate.

For Alice to send a confidential message M to Diane she might engage in the following protocol:

$A \rightarrow T : A, D$	Alice requests Diane's certificate from Tahira, who runs the trusted authority, by giving her own, Alice's, and Diane's identities
$T \rightarrow A : \{D, K_D, X_D\}_{\overline{K_T}}$	Tahira sends Diane's certificate to Alice
	Alice can decrypt the certificate to find out Diane's public key
$A \rightarrow D : \{M\}_{K_D}$	Alice sends the confidential message encrypted with Diane's public key

Diane, on receipt of the message, can decrypt it with her private key and read its content. Alice can be assured that the message has been kept confidential because she obtained the public key from Tahira, who she trusts.

Of course, there must be an additional protocol that allows people like Diane and Alice to register their public keys with Tahira, and that protocol will have to confirm for Tahira which of her trusted clients she is dealing with.

6.5.3 Reaching out

Certification provides assurances about the legitimacy of public keys. But, as described so far, the assurances can only be given for keys that the trusted authority holds. Suppose Bob, after a family bereavement, tracks down a long lost uncle who is to receive a part of the inheritance. Bob wants to tell his uncle, Ron, the news and manages to track him down on the other side of the world. Bob, who is not sure what his uncle looks like after so many years, wants to encrypt the message to him so that an eavesdropper cannot pick it up, impersonate his uncle and collect his share of the legacy. Bob tries to find his uncle's public key by contacting Tahira at his own trusted Certification

Authority. Uncle Ron is not listed. Bob tries other Certification Authorities and obtains a certificate from a Certification Authority run by Quentin. The certificate can be denoted by $\{R, K_R, X_R\}_{\overline{K_Q}}$ where R identifies Uncle Ron, who has a public key K_R with restrictions denoted by X_R. Bob is uneasy because he does not know much about Quentin's Certification Authority and does not know whether it can be trusted. The certificate Bob receives is also encrypted with Quentin's private key $\overline{K_Q}$. Bob needs Quentin's public key before he can make sense of the certificate from the remote authority.

Bob can request from Tahira, who runs his trusted Certification Authority, a certificate for the questionable authority run by Quentin who provided him with his uncle's certificate. Bob thus obtains the mistrusted authority's public key from his own trusted authority. Hopefully, with this implicit endorsement from Tahira, Bob will now be able to trust what was once an unfamiliar authority, decrypt his uncle's certificate and obtain his public key. Bob then can send confidently an encrypted message to his uncle:

$B \rightarrow Q : R$	Bob requests his Uncle Ron's certificate from the unfamiliar authority, Quentin
$Q \rightarrow B : \{R, K_R, X_R\}_{\overline{K_Q}}$	The unfamiliar authority sends a certificate
$B \rightarrow T : Q$	Bob requests a certificate for the unfamiliar authority from his trusted authority
$T \rightarrow B : \{Q, K_Q, X_Q\}_{\overline{K_T}}$	Tahira, the trusted authority, sends Quentin's certificate to Bob
	Bob decrypts the certificate and finds Quentin's public key K_Q
	Bob decrypts the certificate from Quentin's authority to find his Uncle Ron's key K_R
$B \rightarrow R : \{M\}_{K_R}$	As Bob now trusts Quentin's authority he can send a confidential, encrypted message to his uncle

Luckily for Bob, Tahira had a copy of Quentin's certificate. But if she had not she might have known of some other Certification Authorities that she trusted. She could ask each of them for a certificate for Quentin's authority, and if they could not help, maybe they could relay the request to authorities that they trusted. Provided Tahira, Bob's trusted Certification Authority, holds certificates for at least some other trusted Certification Authorities then she can reach out across chains of authorities to find certificates for individuals. No centralized organization is needed. Of course, there has to be a limit otherwise requests for certificates might go around in circles. So, even if Tahira did not have Quentin's certificate, she might still have been able to get one for Bob. If Tahira failed to find a certificate or gave up her search, then Bob would have been without a certificate for Quentin and would have been unable to decrypt the certificate purported to be for his Uncle Ron.

6.5.4 Revocation

From time to time there will be breaches of security:

1 People are not always careful with their private keys and misplace them or inadvertently issue copies.

2 Because keys protect valuable data and documents, crooks find ways of breaking in and duplicating keys.

3 People change their roles and responsibilities. When they do, as well as relinquishing responsibility, they lose the authority to do certain things but their passwords, encryption and decryption keys may still be effective.

4 Some people may prove to be untrustworthy keyholders.

For all these reasons passwords, keys and thus certificates are changed frequently. When a suitably authorized request is made to a Certification Authority it will withdraw a certificate and in some instances replace it with a new one.

Continued use of a key extracted from a withdrawn certificate cannot guarantee continuing security. For instance, if Alice realized that Vince had tricked her into copying her private key she would probably generate a new private key and a corresponding public key. She would then tell Tahira of the trusted Certification Authority who would revoke her old key by issuing a new certificate containing her new public key. Bob may not know that Alice's key has changed and he may continue to use a copy of her digital certificate that he got from Tahira earlier. His use of Alice's revoked public key, though, allows Vince to intercept and read Bob's confidential correspondence to Alice.

People need to be warned about certificates that have been withdrawn, but because public keys are freely available there can be no organized record of who has a copy. Certification Authorities might keep a record of the requests made to them, but there is nothing stopping, for instance, Bob passing on a copy of Alice's certificate to Eve or anyone else. Certification Authorities, therefore, publish lists of *revoked certificates* and the responsibility for checking them rests with anyone embarking on a sensitive transaction that involves the use of the data recorded in a certificate.

Certificates commonly have expiry dates, and it is risky to use a certificate outside its period of validity, unless something is known about what a certified individual or organization does to protect its outdated private keys. It would seem that before the data on a certificate is used, some checks need to be made.

6.5.5　Timing

When a message is received, it is not always clear when it was sent, but if it is part of a transaction that involves a public key, then its timing might be significant. Messages encrypted or decrypted with a private key whose corresponding public key has expired or been revoked must be treated with suspicion.

For instance, imagine a situation where Anthea, a careless administrator, accidentally reveals Bob's private key. She reacts quickly and gets the Certification Authority to revoke Bob's public key certificate. Eve, however, notices that Bob's private key has been exposed and takes a copy. Quickly, she masquerades as Bob and sends an order to the florist, Fred, for a magnificent bouquet for herself. On the order she poses as Bob and also falsifies the record of the time, making it appear that the order was sent earlier than the instant of the security breach.

Eve encrypts the order with Bob's exposed private key. The dutiful florist checks the revocation list of his Certification Authority and finds that Bob's key has been revoked, but that the order appears to have been sent before the revocation came into force. Instead of confirming with Bob that the order is genuine, Fred delivers the bouquet. Eve collects the flowers and Bob eventually pays up, after protesting, only because Fred appears to have incontrovertible evidence that Bob had placed the order.

6.5.6　Summary

Digital certificates bind together data about someone's identity with his or her authorized public key. Certification Authorities have been established which issue certificates on behalf of their keyholders. To be effective, they have to be built up as trusted institutions. They encrypt keyholders' certificates with their own private keys, which identifies their certificates and securely binds the certified keyholders' identities to their public keys. Certification Authorities can also hold certificates of other trusted authorities and this allows one authority to form trusted links with other authorities in order to track down certificates for keys that it itself does not hold.

Complications can arise when keys are mislaid, or copied accidentally or illicitly. Certificates have to be revoked and new ones issued. Users of certificates need, therefore, to be cautious about the validity of the certificates that they use.

6.6 Conclusion

Trust is an ingredient of security. Dealing with people who are unknown is not easy when most communications traverse an IT network. It is relatively straightforward for determined fraudsters to masquerade as trusted individuals. Protocols, therefore, need to include measures that help to secure the identity of communicating partners.

The simplest method is to rely on encryption. Messages encrypted with keys that trusted people have gives some assurances provided the keys are not widely distributed. Private keys are especially useful because they do not have to be circulated. However, the computational effort to perform an encryption may prove to be too severe. An alternative is to append a digital signature to a message. First, applying a hash function to a message and then encrypting the compact message digest with a private key reduces the computational effort. Comparing a new message digest, formed from the message, with the decrypted message digest accompanying the message checks the signature. Because to be successfully decrypted the signature must have been encrypted with a private key, it gives assurance that the document was endorsed by the sole keyholder. It does not, however, offer proof that the message originated with the signatory. To give some immediacy to a check on identity some protocols initiate challenges and anticipate valid responses. They offer some protection against attacks that involve the recording and replaying of messages. Challenges and responses offer an illustration of the different standards of evidence needed when tracking down security breaches.

One way of providing additional and trustworthy evidence is to involve institutions that act as trusted third parties. There are timing and notary services that validate the timing of the existence of a document and there are Certification Authorities that distribute public keys with assurances about the identity of a keyholder.

Chapter Seven

Key management

Encryption schemes are at the heart of many security measures in digital systems. An essential feature of most encryption schemes is a secret key and, therefore, measures to distribute keys while keeping them secret have received widespread attention. Although the primary task is to get secret keys to trusted individuals there is a surprising variety of protocols and no obviously correct way of proceeding. Certain techniques, such as the public/private key systems, avoid the need for the distribution of keys. There are also approaches that permit key exchanges in secret and some methods involve trusted third parties that not only distribute keys in secret, but also provide assurances about the reliability of the holders of the complementary keys. The wide variety of published key distribution systems makes key distribution a valuable vehicle for illustrating how protocols are constructed.

Published work on key management includes descriptions of a number of protocol failures. Some of these are protocols that were devised by and commented on by reputable experts in the field and were deployed for some time before the failings were discovered. The failure of such well-reviewed protocols is a reminder that reasoning about security schemes is problematical.

7.1 Session keys

Encryption and decryption eat into computing resources. There is, in most encryption schemes, a trade-off between the likelihood that a code will be cracked and the time and computer power needed to carry out cryptographic operations. While long keys give greater security, the computation involved in encryption and decryption is prolonged. In some secure systems, different keys are used for different purposes. For instance, a short key, called a *session key*, is used to encrypt only a small batch of messages before a new session key is issued. The session keys themselves, though, may be distributed using a more robust encryption scheme employing longer keys.

7.1.1 The trade-offs

It might seem that as computers become more powerful the time to perform encryption and decryption operations would get less. However, the crackers' computers get faster too and they are able to crack codes quicker. To keep pace with the faster technology that the crackers own and to retain the same degree of security demands encryption with longer keys. Improvements in computer technology, therefore, do not substantially reduce the overheads imposed by encryption and decryption.

Access to a large amount of ciphertext makes the work of the cryptanalysts, the people who crack codes, easier, so greater security is to be expected if few messages are sent using any particular key. Hence, rather than use the same key continuously, keys are set up for a session of interactions. What constitutes a session will depend on the situation but, for example, a session key might be retained while a customer completes a purchase and discarded once the purchase is completed. Alternatively, a session key might be retained for a fixed period – for an hour or for a month. When a new session starts with a new key a cryptanalyst must discard most of his or her previous efforts and begin again.

The session key has a further advantage. If a key is compromised, because a code is cracked or because someone manages to steal the key, then the breach of security is limited to the session when the key was active. Also, if it is commonplace to change keys regularly and it is discovered that a key has been compromised then starting a new session is a matter of routine and special measures do not have to be invented and enacted to overcome the failure.

The obvious disadvantage of a system using session keys is that a succession of keys has to be created. It is, of course, desirable that a key cannot be predicted from earlier keys that may have been unmasked. Digital computers driven by programs do generate consistent and predictable results even when calculating sequences of random numbers. Some procedures do make it more difficult to make predictions and some exploit events outside the computer when creating keys. The generation of completely random keys is, therefore, a subject of study on its own, and the importance of key generators should not be underrated.

Public key encryption techniques, asymmetric key systems, avoid the need to distribute keys in secret; however, the overheads associated with public key systems have proven to be greater than systems that allow the decryption process to be derived from the encryption key – the so-called symmetric key systems. With symmetric key systems there are no public keys, all keys must be kept secret and any change of key implies the communication of secret information. The exchange of information about secret keys has to be handled particularly sensitively because revealing secrets about a secret key jeopardizes all the transactions carried out using that key. Reducing the number of secret key transfers reduces the possibility that a key will be uncovered; on the other hand sessions are then longer and more ciphertext is available to crackers. A compromise is possible where a lengthy, highly secure encryption operation is used occasionally to exchange short session keys used in symmetric key encryption, and those short keys are used for a limited period and impose relatively small computational demands. Protocols are therefore required for exchanging the secret session keys.

7.1.2 A simple key distribution protocol

Perhaps the simplest protocol that Bob and Alice can use to set up a new session involves one of them, Alice perhaps, selecting a new session key k. Alice then sends this new key to Bob encrypted with another key K that they use for setting up new sessions:

$A \rightarrow B : \{k\}_K$	Alice sends Bob an encrypted session key

Obviously, Alice and Bob need to be able to trust one another and must have, somehow, traded a copy of the key K beforehand.

7.1.3 Threats

While this protocol gets a key to Bob and should ensure secrecy, Alice does not know that Bob has received it, but worse still Bob cannot be sure that the message came from Alice. There are three possibilities:

1   The message did come from Alice.

2   An intruder, Ian, has sent an arbitrary message hoping that Bob will treat it as an encrypted key, decrypt it, get a bogus key and waste time in trying to use it to communicate with Alice.

3   Eve has reissued an old key by sending a message from Alice that Eve recorded earlier.

Eve's plan might have been to record a message carrying an encrypted session key that Alice sent to Bob. Eve then hoped to intercept all the messages encrypted with that session key and could then analyse the ciphertext to find out the relatively short session key. Since it would involve a lot of hard work, Eve might have thought it would be long after the session had been completed before she discovered the session key. By then, Bob and Alice would be using a different key. Eve can, however, once she has cracked the earlier session key, replay the encrypted key distribution message she recorded earlier and send it to Bob and Alice, who might be tricked into treating it as the new encrypted session key from his or her trusted partner. They might then use this resurrected key, which Eve has cracked, to converse with one another. Eve could then decrypt and read their correspondence or butt in and masquerade as either of them.

7.1.4 Remedies

The key that Bob and Alice share, K, provides authentication. If they trust one another to keep the key safe and one of them obtains an intelligible message, after he or she has decrypted ciphertext by assuming it was encrypted with K, then he or she can be sure that the ciphertext came from the trusted partner. Of course, to get an intelligible result, an intelligible text must have been encrypted in the first place. Encrypting the session key does not provide an intelligible result. The session key will work out, after decryption, to be some randomly chosen number. Something meaningful needs to be added to the original plaintext, which would prevent Ian from duping Bob with an arbitrary message.

Bob and Alice can thwart Ian and prevent Eve from deceiving them with replayed messages by adding a nonce to their protocols:

$B \rightarrow A : N$	Bob sends a nonce to Alice
$A \rightarrow B : \{k, N\}_K$	Alice chooses a session key. She sends Bob the session key and his nonce encrypted with their shared key K
$B \rightarrow A : \{M\}_k$	Bob sends Alice an intelligible message encrypted with the session key

Bob is the only person, apart from Alice, who can decrypt the session key in her message. When he decrypts it, he will discover the key and the nonce. The nonce tells Bob two things: firstly, it means that the message is a response to his recent message and is not a recording made earlier; secondly, because he recognizes his nonce the decrypted message is intelligible and must have been encrypted by Alice who holds the encryption key K. Bob can then use the session key k with confidence.

7.1.5 Summary

Session keys are chosen to speed up encryption and decryption operations. The implication is that messages encrypted with session keys are easier to crack. To restore adequate levels of security, session keys are used for limited numbers of messages and then they are replaced. This gives crackers less time to discover the key and reduces the amount of ciphertext that they have to work on. Session keys themselves have to be distributed. The protocols that are employed must reassure the principals that the session key that they receive has been kept confidential, is not a duplicate of an earlier session key and that it comes from an authorized source.

7.2 Diffie–Hellman

The double locking protocol described in Section 5.1 might be used by Bob to send Alice a secret key, which they could subsequently use in a simple encryption scheme as a shared key. There is a related classic protocol that enables Bob and Alice to agree on a key for encrypting subsequent messages, which does not require them to explicitly send the key. This protocol is named after Whitfield Diffie and Martin Hellman, who worked on it with Ralph

Merkle. Their particular protocol revolutionized the design of security systems since up until the time it was published it was assumed that keys had to be exchanged in the open before a series of secure interactions could begin.

7.2.1 Diffie–Hellman process

In the *Diffie–Hellman key exchange protocol*,[103] Bob and Alice agree on a message M and a modulus n. Neither M nor n has to be kept secret. They then send encrypted messages to one another using their own secret keys and using an encryption technique that has the properties of the exponentiation algorithm. They invent their own temporary keys k_A and k_B to do this encryption and keep the keys to themselves:

$A \rightarrow B : \{M\}_{k_A}$	Alice sends an encrypted message to Bob, which gives Bob $M^{k_A} \bmod n$
$B \rightarrow A : \{M\}_{k_B}$	Bob* sends Alice an encrypted message, which gives Alice $M^{k_B} \bmod n$

* It does not matter who sends their message first.

After the exchange, Alice encrypts the message Bob has sent her with her secret key and creates $\left(M^{k_B}\right)^{k_A} \equiv M^{k_B k_A} \bmod n$, and Bob encrypts the message that Alice sent and, since the commutative properties of exponentiation of a given message allow the exponents to be swapped without changing the answer, Bob creates exactly the same result:

$$\left(M^{k_A}\right)^{k_B} \equiv M^{k_A k_B} \equiv M^{k_B k_A} \bmod n$$

Therefore, Alice's calculation gives the same result as Bob's. This number is derived from a known message but, for an eavesdropper, unknown keys. The eavesdropper cannot work out Bob and Alice's result, which could be used itself as a key when they come to send further messages to one another.

7.2.2 An example

As an example, suppose Bob and Alice agree to work in modulo 23 and also agree to send the encrypted message 20 to one another. Alice chooses the valid key 9 and Bob chooses the valid key 17. The exponentiation algorithm they use involves raising the message to a power given by their key. Powers of 20 modulo 23 are shown in Table 21.

Table 21　Powers of 20 modulo 23

n	1	2	3	4	5	6	7	8	9	10	11	12	13	14	15	16	17	18	19	20	21	22
20^n	20	9	19	12	10	16	21	6	5	8	22	3	14	4	11	13	7	2	17	18	15	1

Alice encrypts the message with her key to get:

$$20^9 \equiv 5 \bmod 23$$

and sends it to Bob. Bob encrypts the same message as Alice but with his key he gets:

$$20^{17} \equiv 7 \bmod 23$$

Bob sends his encrypted message to Alice who encrypts it with her key:

$$7^9 \equiv 7^8 \times 7^1 \equiv (7^2)^4 \times 7^1 \equiv 49^4 \times 7^1 \bmod 23$$
$$\equiv 3^4 \times 7 \equiv (3^2)^2 \times 7 \equiv 9^2 \times 7 \equiv 81 \times 7 \bmod 23$$
$$\equiv 12 \times 7 \equiv 15 \bmod 23$$

Alice gets the number 15 as a result. Bob encrypts what he receives from Alice, the number 5, with his key:

$$5^{17} \equiv 5^{16} \times 5^1 \equiv (5^2)^8 \times 5^1 \equiv 25^8 \times 5 \bmod 23$$
$$\equiv 2^8 \times 5 \equiv (2^2)^4 \equiv 4^4 \times 5 \equiv 16^2 \times 5 \equiv 256 \times 5 \bmod 23$$
$$\equiv 3 \times 5 \equiv 15 \bmod 23$$

Bob, too, gets the number 15. They both obtain the same result, which they can then use as a shared encryption key. Eve may have recorded the messages that Bob and Alice exchanged but, surprisingly, she cannot work out, except by trial and error, what Alice and Bob's secret is. Obviously, in practice, much larger numbers would be used to make a trial and error search impossible for Eve.

7.2.3 Threats

In practice, the Diffie–Hellman scheme is not used alone. Eve could pretend to be Alice and contact Bob. Eve may know the message M that Bob and Alice commonly use to create keys. They may not have attempted to keep it secret. Eve can follow the procedure that Alice should use and there is nothing in the sequence of messages that reveals to Bob that he is dealing with Eve. Having created a secret key Bob might use it to send confidential messages to Alice, but Eve could intercept them, decrypt them and find out their confidential content. Bob and Alice must take additional precautions to authenticate who they are dealing with.

7.2.4 Summary

The Diffie–Hellman protocol demonstrates that the distribution of secret keys does not require people to find a way of communicating in secret. Encryption schemes with suitable properties allow two principals to construct the same secret without giving away data that allows an eavesdropper to discover their secret.

7.3 Third parties

Key distribution protocols should include data that confirms the identity of the communicating partners. Starting from scratch, especially if Alice and Bob are not acquainted, is fraught. Only if they share some secret can they confirm that they are dealing with one another. To allow strangers to establish session keys, a number of protocols introduce a *trusted third party*, who runs an *authentication service*.

There are two possible starting points for distributing authenticated session keys:

1   Alice and Bob do not know one another but Sarah, who runs an authentication service, trusts them both. Alice and Bob each have a key that allows them to communicate in secret with Sarah.

2   Alice and Bob have private keys and a Certification Authority holds their public keys.

7.3.1   Private keys

Bob and Alice can fetch digital certificates from a Certification Authority, perhaps Tahira's, and use the certificate's public key to encrypt the session key. They can also prevent Eve from deceiving them with replayed messages by adding nonces to their protocols.

$A \rightarrow B : N$	Alice sends a nonce to Bob
$B \rightarrow T : A$	Bob asks Tahira for Alice's certificate
$T \rightarrow B : \{A, K_A, X_A\}_{\overline{K_T}}$	Tahira returns Alice's certificate
$B \rightarrow A : \{\{k\}_{K_A}, N\}_{\overline{K_B}}$	Bob chooses a session key and encrypts it with the public key from the decrypted certificate. He adds the nonce and binds it by encrypting with his private key. He then sends the result to Alice
$A \rightarrow T : B$	Alice asks Tahira for Bob's certificate
$T \rightarrow A : \{B, K_B, X_B\}_{\overline{K_T}}$	Tahira returns Bob's certificate to Alice
$A \rightarrow B : \{M\}_k$	Alice decrypts Bob's message to find the session key, then she sends Bob a message encrypted with the session key

The crucial message is the one that Bob sends to Alice. It must have come from Bob because when it is decrypted with his public key it reveals intelligible data – the nonce that Alice sent recently encrypted with Bob's private key. It also provides Alice with a version of the session key that she can decrypt with her private key. She can be sure that the public key she has corresponds to Bob's private key because Tahira, who Alice trusts, sent a certificate that related Bob's identity with the public key Alice is using.

Bob is assured that Alice is the only person who can decrypt the session key in his message because it has to be decrypted with the private key that corresponded with the public key he obtained in the certificate from Tahira. The certificates are themselves authenticated because they have been encrypted with Tahira's private key.

7.3.2   Closing a loophole

It is possible that Alice's private key could be compromised. Eve might discover Alice's private key, but if Alice knows it is no longer secure then she would revoke her compromised key and create a new set of keys. Because Alice has changed her keys, Eve is unable to find out the new session keys that she and Bob have created.

Suppose Eve, the inveterate eavesdropper, has recorded Bob and Alice's conversations and with Alice's exposed private key is able to find out what the earlier session keys were. Once Eve has those session keys she can decrypt the earlier messages between Alice and Bob and perhaps learn some of their secrets.

The weakness is that the secret session key is carried in the message from Bob, but this can be avoided if the session key is created using the Diffie–Hellman technique.[104] Alice and Bob choose a modulus n and an arbitrary message M. Alice picks a number N_A and keeps it secret. Bob chooses his own secret number N_B. Next, Alice forms $M^{N_A} \bmod n$, which I will abbreviate to M^{N_A}, and Bob calculates $M^{N_B} \bmod n$, which I will abbreviate to M^{N_B}.

$A \to B : M^{N_A}$	Alice sends the results of her calculation to Bob
$B \to A : \{M^{N_B}, M^{N_A}\}_{\overline{K_B}}$	Bob sends Alice the results of his and Alice's calculation encrypted with his private key
$A \to B : \{M^{N_B}\}_{\overline{K_A}}$	Alice decrypts Bob's message using his public key, and encrypts the result of his initial calculation with her private key

Using the Diffie–Hellman procedure to obtain a session key, Alice decrypts Bob's message to obtain M^{N_B} and calculates $\left(M^{N_B}\right)^{N_A}$. To get the same number as Alice, Bob takes the M^{N_A} that she sent him and calculates $\left(M^{N_A}\right)^{N_B}$.

Because the numbers N_A and N_B can be chosen at random, the value of M^{N_A} is unpredictable and therefore also fulfils the role of a nonce. Alice can check that the value of M^{N_A} in Bob's message is the same as the value she sent in her first message. This confirms both that Bob's message is fresh and that it decrypts to an intelligible message when decrypted with his public key. There is nothing in the first two messages that links them with Alice so she uses M^{N_B} as though it were a nonce, encrypts it with her private key and returns it to Bob. Bob can decrypt Alice's message with her public key. Bob will get the value of M^{N_B} that he sent and because it was discovered by decrypting with Alice's public key, it must have come from her and this confirms that Bob has been dealing with Alice.

Eve can easily find out M^{N_A} and M^{N_B} from the exchange of messages, but because she does not know N_A or N_B, she cannot work out the session keys that Alice and Bob calculate. Encryption in this protocol does not hide anything from Eve. It effectively binds the nonces to private keys and authenticates the sources of the messages.

7.3.3   Authentication services

When Alice is not acquainted with the people she wants to deal with but does not want to use a private key system, she might subscribe to a *trusted authentication service*. There are then three parties involved in a transaction: Alice and Bob who are to communicate and Sarah, the third party, who runs the authentication service. Sarah's role is to make sure that the keys get to the right people and to assure Bob and Alice that they can trust one another.

Suppose Alice initiates a session with Bob. She has a choice as to who she contacts first – Bob or Sarah. There is also a decision to be made about who should issue the key and once that is resolved there are decisions to be made about who sends the key to whom. For instance, the protocol could require that Alice asks Sarah for a key and Sarah issues it directly to Alice and then to Bob. Alternatively, Alice could contact Bob first, and then he asks Sarah for a key. Sarah then sends it to him, and he forwards it to Alice. There are a surprising number of variations, but particular protocols will fix the sequence of the messages.

Since key generation is not straightforward, it is common to leave this specialist task to an authentication service.

7.3.4   The authentication service issues the keys

Suppose Alice sees that Romano's pizzeria is offering exactly the pizza she would like, but she is cautious about placing an order because she has not bought anything from him before. Alice might be happy to trust Sarah, who runs an authentication service that keeps records of people's identities, and selects and distributes session keys to people that she has vetted. Sarah is particularly careful about issuing session keys; she only issues them to people she trusts and does not put duplicates into circulation.

Alice has a key K_{AS} that Sarah gave her when she registered with Sarah's service. This key allows Alice to communicate with Sarah privately. Romano has a different key K_{RS} that allows him to communicate with Sarah in confidence. Alice would like to share a new session key with Romano, but only if he can be trusted. She decides to use Sarah's service, which issues fresh session keys that allow named and trusted clients to communicate with one another.[105]

$A \rightarrow R : N$	Alice sends Romano a nonce
$R \rightarrow S : A, N, N'$	Romano immediately sends Alice's identity, Alice's nonce and a new nonce to Sarah
$S \rightarrow A : \{N, k\}_{K_{AS}}$	Sarah sends Alice the ciphertext compiled from the session key and Alice's nonce
$S \rightarrow R : \{N', k\}_{K_{RS}}$	Sarah sends Romano an encrypted combination of a session key and his nonce

Both Romano and Alice receive in their message from Sarah a copy of the session key that Sarah has chosen for them. She has encrypted the session key and the two nonces using a key that allows them individually to perform the decryption. When Alice, for instance, decrypts her message with the key she shares with Sarah she will discover her nonce as well as the session key. The encrypted nonce will offer proof to Alice that the message must have come from Sarah, that the key is associated with her transaction with Romano and that the key is fresh. When Romano and Alice communicate effectively, they can assume they both have the same genuine session key. Because his interactions with Alice work, and he obtained his operative session key by decrypting with the key he shares with Sarah, he can be satisfied that Sarah has endorsed the session. Because Sarah was willing to issue a session key, Alice knows that Sarah trusts Romano and therefore Alice can trust him. She can go ahead and order her pizza.

7.3.5 A simplified view of Kerberos

Possibly because the exchange of keys is a critical part of security operations, many schemes for key distribution have been proposed and a great deal of analysis has been done. To give an example of the kind of variations that are possible I will look at the *Kerberos service*.

Cerberus, or Kerberos, is the fabled three-headed dog that guarded the infernal regions.[106] Kerberos is also a commonly used authentication service[107] that issues session keys. The Kerberos specification allows a number of variations in the service that is provided. I will omit details of these variations and give only an outline of the protocols.

Suppose Sam runs a Kerberos authentication service. She has a secure database of keys she uses for communicating with her clients. She has one key for each client. Her clients, on the other hand, are wary about one another and do not share any keys. They rely on Sam, who they trust to choose session keys for them. She also issues certificates, called *tickets* that help to establish trust between her clients.

Suppose Alice is registered with Sam's service and wants to communicate with Bob, who is also one of Sam's clients. Alice initiates the protocol by asking Sam for a ticket and a session key. In her message to Sam Alice gives her own and Bob's identity. Sam chooses a session key and incorporates it in a ticket. The ticket includes Alice's identity A and a session key k encrypted with a key shared only by Bob and Sam, K_{BS}. A simplified version of Alice's ticket can be described by the expression $\{A,k\}_{K_{BS}}$. Sam, at the authentication service, sends a copy of the ticket and an encrypted session key to Alice. Next, Alice forwards the ticket to Bob. Because the ticket is encrypted with Bob and Sam's shared key, Alice cannot alter the ticket and Bob can decrypt it.

$A \rightarrow S : A, B$	Alice requests a ticket from Sam for communication between Alice and Bob
$S \rightarrow A : B, \underbrace{\{A,k\}_{K_{BS}}}_{\text{Ticket}}, \{k\}_{K_{AS}}$	Sam sends a ticket incorporating Alice's identity and a session key encrypted with a key that Sam and Bob share. Alice also receives a copy of the session key encrypted with a key she shares with Sam's identity
$A \rightarrow B : A, \underbrace{\{A,k\}_{K_{BS}}}_{\text{Ticket}}$	Alice sends her identity and the ticket to Bob

Alice decrypts a part of the message she gets from Sam to find out the session key, and Bob decrypts the ticket to find out the session key that is to be used in communicating with Alice.

This oversimplified view of the Kerberos protocol shows how Sam distributes session keys, but it has a number of security weaknesses. For instance, in the last message Bob does not know for sure that it has come from Alice. To cure this weakness Alice adds to the message and provides an authenticator. The authenticator is composed of her identity and a time-stamp both encrypted with the session key:

$$A \rightarrow B : \underbrace{\{A, k\}_{K_{BS}}}_{\text{Ticket}}, \underbrace{\{A, T\}_{k}}_{\text{Authenticator}}$$

Alice sends the ticket and an authenticator to Bob

With this modification, Bob can decrypt the ticket to find out the session key. Once he has the session key he can decrypt the authenticator. He can then reason like this:

1   The ticket originated with Sam, and she intended it for me because it is encrypted with the key that only Sam and I share.

2   In the ticket $\{A, k\}_{K_{BS}}$ Sam says that the key is to be used with Alice. I trust Sam but this ticket could be a copy of an old ticket.

3   Because Sam's ticket says Alice is to be my partner in using the session key k, she must have also sent this session key to Alice securely.

4   Only Alice, Sam or I could encrypt things with the session key k, but Sam does not do that sort of thing, and I would know if I had done it myself. Alice must have encrypted the authenticator because it can be decrypted using the session key k.

5   When I decrypt the authenticator using the session key I find Alice's identity and a *recent* time. By encrypting her own identity she has confirmed that the authenticator came from her.

6   The authenticator and the ticket are bound together through the use of the session key in the authenticator and its secured declaration in the ticket.

7   Alice must have sent the whole message recently.

The complete Kerberos protocol has other security devices. The first and second messages, for instance, use a nonce to protect against anyone copying and replaying the messages, a time-stamp accompanies the session key and data is added for calculating the expiry time for the key. Kerberos also has features that allow it to be used in systems with multiple authentication services.

7.3.6   Summary

Third-party protocols for the distribution of keys involve trusted services. If the communicating partners can get a key from the trusted services it is assumed that the keyholders are themselves trustworthy. The certification services that provide digital certificates are an example of an agency that offers keys and guarantees about the source of those keys. The public key itself can be used to encrypt a session key and transmitted in secret to the private keyholder.

Secrecy is not always enough; key distribution protocols often also need to offer proof of the identity of the communicating parties and evidence that the key is fresh. Techniques using nonces and binding using encryption augment the confidentiality mechanisms.

Some key distribution mechanisms rely on trusted authentication services. Usually, an authentication service selects session keys and distributes them in response to requests from its clients. When it issues a session key, it is effectively vouching for the client who receives the session key. Clients receiving keys from an authentication service need to be reassured that the key has not come from an impostor. Similarly, the authentication service has to be able to identify exactly who it is dealing with. Registration with an authentication service is bound to involve the generation of keys that identify the service and its new client.

7.4   Classic failures

Failures are often uncovered because someone dreams up a new way of meddling with the messages in a protocol. The design of a protocol may, therefore, have been checked against all anticipated threats and proved to be robust. Subsequently, an imaginative analyst or crook dreams up a new threat and well-established protocols become vulnerable. There is no way of preventing this and people who are responsible for security have to keep abreast of anticipated threats and be prepared to alter protocols, procedures and encryption methods when new threats emerge.

7.4.1   The wide-mouthed frog

Among the protocols proposed for key distribution there are some with notable faults. One such protocol is known as the *wide-mouthed frog*. This protocol can fail because it allows intruders to force an authentication service to extend the lifetime of a key. This might allow the intruder time to collect plenty of ciphertext, use it to uncover the encryption key and discover the plaintext of messages.

In this protocol, Alice chooses a session key k for communicating with Rajid, who sells clothes. Sally runs an authentication service and has individual keys for communicating with each of her clients. Alice knows that if Sally is prepared to forward the session key to Rajid then she can reckon that he is reliable. The protocol for issuing session keys includes time-stamps intended to show that a key is fresh:

$A \rightarrow S : \{T, R, k\}_{K_{AS}}$	Alice sends Sally an encrypted message containing the proposed session key for use with Rajid. Alice includes a time-stamp and Rajid's identity
$S \rightarrow R : \{T', A, k\}_{K_{RS}}$	Sally, who trusts Rajid and Alice, forwards Alice's key to Rajid in an encrypted message, containing Alice's identity and a new time-stamp

Rajid can decrypt the message from Sally, find out the session key and initiate a confidential conversation with Alice. Sometime after the time given by the time-stamps, Rajid and Alice will expect to replace their session key to avoid security breaches, which might otherwise, for instance, allow someone else to buy clothes using Alice's account.

Charlie might have realized that the two messages to and from Sally have an identical format. Charlie could record Sally's message to Rajid, and before the key is due to be replaced, Charlie could pretend to be Rajid and send the recorded message back to Sally.

$C \rightarrow S : \{T', A, k\}_{K_{RS}}$	Charlie, pretending to be Rajid, sends Sally's last message back to her
$S \rightarrow A : \{T'', R, k\}_{K_{AS}}$	Sally, who trusts Rajid and Alice, presumes Rajid is proposing a new session key for use with Alice and sends their old key back to Alice, with Rajid's identity and a new time-stamp

Charlie can repeat this trick using Sally's last message and this time she will assume the message came from Alice because it was encrypted with a key that she and Alice share:

$C \rightarrow S : \{T'', R, k\}_{K_{AS}}$	Charlie, pretending to be Alice, sends Sally's last message back to Sally
$S \rightarrow R : \{T''', A, k\}_{K_{RS}}$	Sally, who trusts Alice, presumes Alice is proposing a new session key and sends Alice's old key back to Rajid, with Alice's identity and another new time-stamp

Every time Charlie replays a message and sends it to Sally, she updates the time-stamp so if Charlie continues to copy and replay Sally's messages, Rajid and Alice will continue to receive messages that cause them to create new sessions with their same old key. Charlie may then have time to find out the key they are using and order clothes on Alice's account.

7.4.2 Denning–Sacco

A protocol proposed by Denning and Sacco[108] in 1982 provides a salutary lesson for those who wish to design security protocols. In 1994, twelve years[109] after its publication, the protocol was found to have a serious defect. Clearly, at a first glance the protocol looks robust. However, finding flaws in such protocols is not easy – it involves imagining ways in which an adversary might profit from an attack.

To see the failure of the *Denning–Sacco protocol* a cast of three characters is needed: Alice and Bob who are duped, and Vince who masquerades as Bob in dealings with Alice.

Bob innocently starts the proceedings by setting up a legitimate session with Vince. In the crucial part of the protocol Bob sends data about their identities and an encrypted, time-stamped session key k to Vince.

$B \rightarrow V : B, V, \{\{T,k\}_{\overline{K_B}}\}_{K_V}$	Bob sends an encrypted key to Vince

An inner layer of encryption with Bob's private key binds the time-stamp and the key together and verifies that the key originated with him. A second layer of encryption with Vince's public key ensures that the session key will remain confidential and that only Vince can extract it. All the proper assurances appear to be in place. Vince can find out the session key by decrypting the last part of the message with his private key and then with Bob's public key.

Later, however, Vince can use this message from Bob to deceive Alice. He takes the portion of his message that was encrypted with Bob's private key $\{T,k\}_{\overline{K_B}}$. Vince now has ciphertext that is signed by Bob. Vince encrypts it with Alice's public key, he adds Bob's and Alice's identity and sends it to Alice:

$V \rightarrow A : B, A, \{\{T,k\}_{\overline{K_B}}\}_{K_A}$	Vince sends an encrypted key to Alice

When Alice receives the message, she will most likely correctly assume that the inner part originated with Bob because it is encrypted with his private key. She extracts the session key and takes it for granted that the whole message came directly from Bob. Vince can then send messages encrypted with the session key to Alice, and she will presume they came from Bob. Vince may also intercept Alice's responses, pick up and decrypt her confidential replies intended for Bob but encrypted with the session key Vince sent her. Eventually, the time-stamp associated with the session key will invalidate the key and Vince's ruse will end.

7.4.3 Summary

Well-established and analysed protocols are vulnerable to newly discovered threats. The effectiveness of such threats do not necessarily involve cracking codes. But in many instances the threat exploits the combination of messages or the form of messages in a protocol. Any thorough analysis, therefore, needs to show an awareness of potential threats and needs to study both the protocol and the vulnerability of encryption schemes within the context of the protocol.

7.5 Conclusion

Key distribution is a process that has been widely studied and therefore provides a fund of illustrations of the variety of protocols, the techniques that are employed and the potential weaknesses. Private key systems obviate the need to distribute secret keys but can introduce an unwelcome computational overhead. To reduce the computational effort, it is common to use a multilevel system where relatively insecure but undemanding session keys encrypt routine secure messages. The session keys are used for a relatively short time to reduce the amount of data available to crackers and to limit the amount of ciphertext that is vulnerable if a key is compromised. Session keys are distributed using a more secure protocol, possibly using private key encryption.

An advantage of the private key system is that secret information does not have to be passed between possibly remotely sited correspondents. The Diffie–Hellman protocol exploits the properties of encryption using exponentiation and also offers a way of generating session keys without the need to explicitly exchange secret information.

When principals obtain keys, they want to be sure that the keys have not been exposed to eavesdroppers and that they originated with somebody they trust. Third-party protocols using established Certification Authorities or authentication services allow principals to capitalize on the trust they have built up with their agencies. The presumption is that the clients of trusted agencies can themselves be trusted. When a trusted agency issues a session key to Alice, so that she can communicate with Bob, it is implicitly saying that both Alice and Bob can be trusted.

Protocols are designed with a set of potential threats in mind. When circumstances change new threats may arise and a protocol may no longer provide the level of security demanded. These new circumstances may be a result of changes in the organization interested in secure communications or of someone suddenly imagining a new kind of threat and revealing new possibilities for infiltrators. There are, therefore, no long-term guarantees that may be attached to a protocol.

Chapter Eight

Applications

Encryption, authentication and key management are important processes in creating secure digital systems. These security techniques, however, are not incorporated for their own sakes. Security is a feature of digital systems because someone believes that something is at stake; identification of what is at stake and the choice of protection mechanisms are not just matters for security specialists. In some instances, the commonly established techniques for security will prove to be inadequate and new techniques may have to be invented, though clearly in matters of security established techniques may have a history that gives people faith in their effectiveness.

Proposals to replace traditional activities incorporating security measures with digital systems are not unusual – digital systems to replace cash and coinage, for instance. In some areas, though, the digital analogy cannot be pressed too far and there may not be feasible counterparts to traditional systems; in other applications novel techniques can help. This chapter looks at some applications and the security requirements that influence the choice of security mechanisms, and introduces a few specialized novel calculations but perhaps more significantly shows the extent to which common techniques can be adapted to specialized requirements.

The protocols in this chapter, like the protocols throughout this book, are simply outlines. It is likely that paying more attention to key distribution, integrity and authentication mechanisms would enhance security in most of the examples of this chapter.

8.1 Oblivious transfer

Oblivious transfers are a class of protocols in which the sender does not know whether the recipient can decrypt a message or not. The sender is, therefore, oblivious as to whether the recipient can gain anything of value from the plaintext or not. This protocol may not seem immediately useful but a number of applications have been proposed. Variants of the protocol do not use any out-of-the-ordinary encryption operations.

8.1.1 Checking a sample of goods

Suppose Alice wants to buy a collection of biscuit recipes that have been advertised by Vince. As a purchaser, she does not know whether the recipes are suitable or not. Worse, she may worry about being swindled; she might pay Vince and he may send her just a jumble of data that does not include any recipes, or he may send her lots of copies of the same recipe.

Vince, on the other hand, as a vendor does not want to hand over the goods until they have been paid for. He could send Alice the recipes and let her decide whether she wanted them or not, but Alice might then not pay, having found out what she wanted to know from her preview. She might even cheat Vince by secretly making a copy of the recipes and then refusing to pay. Vince could also send Alice a sample and she could check it and pay if she found the sample to be of a suitable quality. But Alice might suspect that Vince had chosen the sample to show his recipes in a good light.

Oblivious transfer provides another option – Vince divides all his data into sample-sized segments and encrypts each one with a different key. He might, for example, treat each recipe as a sample and encrypt each one with its own key. He then sends all the encrypted recipes to Alice. The oblivious transfer protocol then provides a way for Alice to obtain a single key that will decrypt just one of the recipes. She can look at the sample and then decide whether or not to purchase the keys to the remaining recipes. The protocol ensures that Vince cannot control which recipe Alice is able to decrypt. Alice can, therefore, be assured that Vince has not selected the sample that she looks at and Vince needs to ensure that all his samples are of a high standard, if he is to make a sale.

Vince generates a series of encryption keys $K_1, K_2, K_3, \ldots$ – one for each of his recipes. He mixes up the keys and sends them to Alice:

$V \to A : K_1, K_3, K_2, \ldots$	Vince jumbles the sequence of keys and sends them to Alice
$A \to V : \{k\}_{K_3}$	Alice picks a session key k, encrypts it with one of the keys Vince sends her, and sends the result to him

Alice has encrypted the session key k with one of the keys that Vince has sent her. She chose K_3, but Vince does not know this. He decrypts Alice's message with each of his keys. For instance, using the key K_1 gives the result

$$\left\{ \{k\}_{K_3} \right\}_{K_1}^{-1}$$

(recall the notation introduced in subsection 4.1.2 where the index -1 indicated that decryption should be carried out assuming that the encryption key was known and not the decryption key). I will call the result k_{31}. In this case, Vince's choice of key, K_1, does not match the key K_3 that Alice chose, and the result will not be the session key k that Alice sent. When Vince decrypts Alice's message with his second key K_2 he gets the result

$$\left\{\left\{k\right\}_{K_3}\right\}^{-1}_{K_2}$$

which I will call k_{32} and which again is not the session key k that Alice started with. But when Vince decrypts Alice's message with his key K_3, he gets her session key,

$$\left\{\left\{k\right\}_{K_3}\right\}^{-1}_{K_3} \equiv k$$

Vince cannot know that this result is Alice's session key since he does not know that she used K_3 for encryption. He continues to decrypt Alice's message with all his keys until he has a series of possible session keys $k_{31}, k_{32}, k, \ldots,$ only one of which is the session key Alice issued. Vince nevertheless encrypts successive recipes with this series of different possible session keys:

$V \rightarrow A : \left\{R_1\right\}_{k_{31}}, \left\{R_2\right\}_{k_{32}}, \left\{R_3\right\}_{k}, \ldots$	Vince sends Alice all the pieces encrypted with different keys

He sends all the encrypted recipes to Alice, and she attempts to decrypt them all with her key k, but only one recipe will produce an intelligible result. If Alice is happy with the intelligible recipe she might pay Vince and, in return, he can send her the remaining keys that he calculated, $k_{31}, k_{32}, \ldots$. Alice can then decrypt the other recipes.

If Alice and Vince are very suspicious of one another, then she can pay for one recipe at a time and they can repeat the oblivious transfer with the remaining recipes with Alice picking a new key from Vince's list after choosing a fresh session key.

8.1.2 Monitoring traffic

There are several ways of performing an oblivious transfer. In this subsection the protocol is based on the Diffie–Hellman key exchange and the application of oblivious transfer is in the monitoring of electronic traffic.

Suppose a suspicious authority wants to check the e-mails that Charlie is sending. It is conceivable that a law might allow them to check a certain proportion, but not all of them if the grounds for suspicion are weak.

Jason, a judge, issues a court order for the interception of Charlie's mail and Prunella, the police officer who is to monitor Charlie's correspondence, creates several keys with Charlie's cooperation using a Diffie–Hellman exchange. Of all the keys they create only one is known to Prunella.

As usual with the Diffie–Hellman exchange they agree on a message M and a modulus n, and they both choose keys that they keep secret. Prunella's secret key is k_P and Charlie's is k_C. To provide safeguards it is likely that Jason will be able to monitor Prunella's activities, but this is not shown in the following protocol description:

$P \rightarrow C : N_1, \{M\}_{k_P}, N_2, \ldots$	Prunella sends a message to Charlie, which includes $M^{k_P} \bmod n$ and a series of nonces in a randomly chosen order
$C \rightarrow P : \{M\}_{k_C}$	Charlie sends Prunella a message, which gives Prunella $M^{k_C} \bmod n$

Charlie encrypts the parts of the message Prunella has sent him with his secret key k_C and first uses N_1 to create $k_1 \equiv N_1^{k_C} \bmod n$, which he will use later as a session key. Then he encrypts the second part of Prunella's message with his secret key and creates

$$k \equiv \left(M^{k_P}\right)^{k_C} \equiv M^{k_P k_C} \bmod n$$

which is a second potential session key. He continues and calculates $k_2 \equiv N_2^{k_C} \bmod n$ and so on. He ends up with a series of potential session keys $k_1, k, k_2, \ldots$. Since Charlie does not have Prunella's secret key k_P, he cannot know which of his calculated keys was derived from the nonces or which key was derived from Prunella's encryption of the message M.

Prunella encrypts the message she receives from Charlie using her own secret key and creates $\left(M^{k_C}\right)^{k_P} \equiv M^{k_P k_C} \bmod n$ which is identical to the second key k created by Charlie. Prunella cannot recreate any of Charlie's other potential session keys derived from nonces because she does not know his secret key k_C.

However, Charlie is not supposed to be sending messages to Prunella. He is sending them to other people and Prunella is intercepting them. Suppose Charlie sends a message M_B to Bob. He should first choose one of the potential session keys and then encrypt his message with the chosen key, say k_1, to form a digital envelope that Bob can open using his public key:

$C \rightarrow B : \{M_B\}_{k_1}, \{k_1\}_{K_B}$	Charlie sends a message to Bob in a digital envelope

Prunella can intercept this message but she cannot decrypt it since she does not have the key k_1 or Bob's private key. However, if Charlie had chosen k, Prunella would be able to decrypt his message to Bob. Charlie does not know which key can be decrypted by Prunella. If he sticks with one key she may be able to decrypt all his messages, so he is likely to keep changing keys if he wants to be sure of retaining a degree of privacy. Prunella will then be able to decrypt only some of Charlie's messages – those encrypted with the key k.

8.1.3 Summary

In an oblivious transfer protocol, a number of keys are used to encrypt messages or samples issued by an originator. It ensures that a recipient has access to only one of the keys and so can only interpret a fraction of the encrypted messages or samples. The protocol also ensures that the originators cannot know which of the keys will generate the ciphertext that the recipient interprets. The protocol can be constructed from commonly available security operations.

8.2 Voting

Quite elaborate security applications can be dealt with using the standard security devices of encryption, signatures and private key encryption. This section looks at an application that benefits from an adaptation of existing techniques called *blinding*. Blinding combines encryption using exponentiation and multiplication. It has proved useful in a number of protocols where some aspects of a message are to be kept secret while other parts are exposed. The application described in this section is the outline of a secret voting system based on digital technologies.

Secret ballots are surrounded by a number of security requirements. Generally, the requirements are that:

1   How people vote is kept secret.

2   Only people who are on a voting register can vote.

3   Nobody can vote twice.

4   Nobody can forge someone else's vote.

5   The tally of votes is counted correctly and can be checked.

6   It should not be possible to coerce voters into revealing their vote.

7   Spoiled votes should not disrupt the process.

It is common to establish a number of broadly independent agencies to carry out the tasks needed to complete the election. For example, there may be separate agencies:

1   issuing the ballot forms

2   checking that voters are on the register

3   collecting the votes.

Most of these agencies have to be trusted, although if they are mistrusted parallel agencies with different personnel can provide cross-checks and thereby deter corrupt actions.

8.2.1 The voting form

The voter in this example, Vera, needs a ballot form. The ballot forms *Bf* are issued with a serial number *n*, and are signed by the Ballot Form Issuing Agency run by Fred. The ballot form will contain a list of candidates for an election or a list of questions if the ballot is part of a referendum.

Vera asks Fred for a ballot form:

$V \rightarrow F : R$	Vera requests a ballot form
$F \rightarrow V : \left\{ n, Bf, \sigma_F \left(n, Bf \right) \right\}_K, \left\{ \overline{K} \right\}_{K_V}$	Fred prepares a ballot form, adds a serial number and his signature, and puts it in a digital envelope for Vera

The ballot form is not confidential. However, the serial number identifies the form and if an eavesdropper saw the serial number and knew it was being sent to Vera he or she could later link Vera's vote on the form with her. The ballot paper is put in a digital envelope to hide the link between its serial number and Vera. Fred therefore sends the encrypted serial number, ballot paper and signature accompanied by the decryption key, itself encrypted with Vera's public key. Fred has to be trusted not to record the link between Vera and the serial number. I will assume he can be trusted.

8.2.2 Vera votes

Vera adds her vote X by indicating which candidate or issue she is voting for. She can then send this to the tellers to be added to the count. For a secret ballot this must be sent encrypted but must also be sent anonymously if Vera is not to be associated with the vote.

Anonymity is vital if Vera is worried about coercion after she has voted. Her potential bullies must be convinced that they cannot find out how she voted. If they do bully her and the vote is completely anonymous, she can give them the answer they want about her vote. They could not find out she was lying and return to exact their retribution.

To ensure anonymity Vera could send her vote to the tellers in a digital envelope:

$V \rightarrow T : \left\{ X, n, Bf, \sigma_F \left(n, Bf \right) \right\}_K, \left\{ \overline{K} \right\}_{K_T}$	Vera completes her ballot form and sends it to the tellers in a digital envelope

The completed vote encrypted with a key that is itself encrypted with the tellers' public key makes no reference to Vera's identity and can only be decrypted by the tellers. The serial number helps to detect duplicated votes. If someone copies Vera's encrypted vote, there will be two votes with the same serial number and the tellers should be able to detect this. Vera herself cannot alter the serial number without fear of detection since Fred signed the original ballot form with its serial number.

8.2.3   Registration

With the proposed scheme anyone can ask for a ballot form, vote and submit it to the tellers. Indeed, Vera could ask for a mountain of forms, complete them all and submit them. There is no check on who has voted. Vera's vote needs to be recorded against her name on the voting register. Once she has voted, new votes in her name should not be accepted. Of course, if her identity is not recorded in the register, her vote should be invalidated.

Let me suppose there is a registrar, Rosalind, who keeps the voters' register. During an election, Rosalind's job is to receive votes and to certify that they are from a certified voter and that that voter has not voted previously. The certified votes are submitted to the tellers for counting and they ignore votes that have not been certified by Rosalind.

To do her job, Rosalind needs proof that a vote has originated with a particular voter such as Vera. Vera can identify herself with her vote by encrypting it with her private key and then sending it to Rosalind:

$$V \rightarrow R : \{X, n, Bf, \sigma_F(n, Bf)\}_{\overline{K_V}} \qquad \text{Vera completes her ballot form, signs it and sends it to Rosalind}$$

Rosalind can decrypt this with Vera's public key. When Rosalind discovers the plaintext is a valid ballot form, she can be confident that Vera encrypted it and that she has voted.

This approach is unsatisfactory. Any unauthorized person, including Eve, could decrypt the completed form with Vera's public key to reveal how she has voted and since Eve could decrypt the vote with Vera's public key, this would confirm that Vera had completed that particular ballot form. Another layer of encryption using Rosalind's public key could hide the ballot from everyone except Rosalind. However, it is not necessary for Rosalind to know how Vera voted.

8.2.4   Blinding

An ingenious alternative is for Vera to blind her vote before sending it to Rosalind. Blinding is a way of getting a message signed without the signatory knowing the content of the message. It is like handing someone a message in a sealed envelope and asking them to sign the envelope firmly. Later, in their absence, the envelope can be opened and the impression of their signature is used as proof that they have validated the envelope and its content.

The process of blinding can be done using encryption by multiplication with a specially selected key. The first step involves working out the key. In the election process, Vera would choose a nonce N and encrypt it using exponentiation with Rosalind's public key. Recall that strictly a public key derived for the RSA algorithm has two parts, the key and the modulus for the encryption operation. Rosalind's key might be (K_R, n_R). Vera's nonce encrypted with Rosalind's public key generates a number that I will refer to as k, which will itself be used as an encryption key.

$$k \equiv N^{K_R} \bmod n_R$$

Vera keeps the nonce and the key k secret.

In the next step Vera encrypts her vote with the newly calculated key. Suppose Vera's completed and encoded ballot paper is represented by v, then it is encrypted by multiplication modulo n_R with the calculated key k to get $v \times k \bmod n_R$, which can be written as $\{v\}_k$. This result is the blinded message, which is part of what is sent by Vera to Rosalind. Because the blinded message has been encrypted using multiplication anybody who intercepts it cannot find out how Vera voted. She adds a signature to the blinded message to identify herself with the encrypted vote and sends it to Rosalind:

$V \to R : V, \{v\}_k, \sigma_V\left(\{v\}_k\right)$	Vera sends her blinded and signed message with an indication of her identity to Rosalind

In the third step, Rosalind checks that Vera endorsed her blinded message by checking the signature, but the blinded vote remains a secret. Rosalind cannot make sense of it because it is encrypted. After confirming Vera's identity, Rosalind checks that Vera is on the voting register, that she has not voted already, and marks the register to record her vote.

In the penultimate step, Rosalind encrypts the blinded message, with her private key $\left(\overline{K}_R, n_R\right)$ and this provides the proof that she, as a registrar, has certified the vote. Rosalind returns the endorsed vote to Vera:

$R \to V : R, \{\{v\}_k\}_{\overline{K}_R}$	Rosalind sends the newly encrypted, blinded message back to Vera

The process of blinding and then encrypting has some useful properties especially because the encryption key k that generated the blinded message is $N^{K_R} \bmod n_R$. The blinded encrypted vote is now $(v \times k)^{\overline{K}_R} \bmod n_R$ and this can be rearranged:

$$(v \times k)^{\overline{K}_R} \bmod n_R \equiv \left(v \times N^{K_R} \bmod n_R\right)^{\overline{K}_R} \bmod n_R$$

$$\equiv \left(v \times N^{K_R}\right)^{\overline{K}_R} \bmod n_R$$

$$\equiv v^{\overline{K}_R} \times N^{K_R \times \overline{K}_R} \bmod n_R$$

Rosalind's public and private keys are chosen, as usual, so that one decrypts what the other has encrypted and therefore for any value of N, $N^{K_R \times \overline{K}_R} \equiv N \bmod n_R$. So, the blinded message encrypted with Rosalind's private key that Vera receives is equivalent to:

$$v^{\overline{K}_R} \times N \bmod n_R$$

The overall effect of blinding and then encrypting with Rosalind's private key is, therefore, to form a new message, which can be interpreted as Vera's vote encrypted with Rosalind's private key and then multiplied by Vera's secret nonce N.

Finally, Vera can recover the vote. She is the only person who knows N and she can calculate a number $\overline{N}$ so that $N \times \overline{N} \equiv 1 \bmod n_R$. The procedure described in Section 3.4 and based on the Euler–Fermat Theorem provides the basis for calculating $\overline{N}$. Multiplying the message from Rosalind gives Vera the result:

$$v^{\overline{K}_R} \times N \times \overline{N} \bmod n_R$$

But, because $N \times \overline{N} \equiv 1 \bmod n_R$, the result is equivalent to:

$$v^{\overline{K}_R} \times 1 \bmod n_R \quad \text{or} \quad v^{\overline{K}_R} \bmod n_R$$

This is Vera's vote endorsed by Rosalind, $v^{\overline{K}_R} \bmod n_R$. Vera can check to see if Rosalind has meddled with her vote, by decrypting it with Rosalind's public key. The completed blinding process has therefore allowed Vera to submit her vote and to have it endorsed by the registrar without revealing how she voted.

8.2.5 Submitting the vote

When Vera is satisfied that the vote is correct, she can send the encrypted vote to the tellers in a digital envelope. The tellers can extract the encrypted vote from the envelope and then decrypt it with Rosalind's public key. They will be assured that Rosalind has certified the vote since no one else could have used her private key to encrypt Vera's vote.

$$V \rightarrow T : \left\{ \left\{ X, n, Bf, \sigma_F \left(n, Bf \right) \right\}_{\overline{K_R}} \right\}_K, \left\{ \overline{K} \right\}_{K_T}$$

> Vera extracts the vote signed by Rosalind and sends her certified vote to the tellers in a digital envelope

There is nothing in the completed ballot that identifies it with Vera, but it is certified by Rosalind to have come from a registered voter. Since it is a certified vote, the tellers can add Vera's vote to their count.

8.2.6 Summary

The balloting procedure described in this section offers a number of safeguards that have all been provided by common security operations. The operations that constitute the blinding process are themselves common encryption and decryption operations that allowed the registrar to endorse a vote without knowing the detailed content. Blinding exploits the combined properties of exponentiation and multiplication and therefore requires the ciphertext to be represented by mathematical objects that can be manipulated by these operations.

Blinding was the only special operation. Digital envelopes offered a way of submitting a vote without revealing the identity of the voter.

8.3   Sharing the burden

In pirate stories, the treasure seekers usually find that the pirates have divided the map that pinpoints the treasure. They have to find all the parts of the map before they can find the booty. The pirates, of course, have distributed the parts of the map, firstly, so that it is difficult to track down the treasure and, secondly, because no one pirate can locate the treasure with their piece of the map and grab it all for themselves.

There are situations where it is unwise to put the key to a secret in one person's hands. It might be that the secret could be dangerous in the wrong hands so that giving one person control over it is a source of anxiety for others who may become concerned about the sanity of the person responsible for the key or the possibility of he or she being coerced into revealing it. It could be that the circumstances for the revelation of the secret requires fine judgement and it might be reassuring to need the agreement of several people before the secret can be revealed. A system that needs the agreement of all the members of a group can also be risky. If anything should happen to one of the group, then the remainder would not be able to recover the secret.

This section outlines a technique for overcoming these difficulties and uses numerical examples to provide further illustrations of the operations of modular arithmetic. It is a demonstration of how, once objects that are to be secured are encoded as mathematical objects, further mathematical operations can create new and useful techniques.

8.3.1 Polynomials

The technique uses mathematical objects called *polynomials*. A polynomial is an algebraic object, for example:

$$3x^2 + 2x^1 + 5x^0$$

It is recognized as a polynomial because it is composed of a number of terms added together with each term consisting of two parts – a number, called a coefficient, and a power of a variable, x. Usually x^1 is written as x, and x^0, which always works out to be 1 whatever the value of x, is omitted. The example would therefore be abbreviated to:

$$3x^2 + 2x + 5$$

The highest power of x is called the order of the polynomial, and the highest power of x in the polynomial

$$10x^3 + 8x^2 + 13x + 9$$

is given in the term $10x^3$. The highest power of x is therefore 3, and the polynomial is referred to as a third-order polynomial. Polynomials can incorporate modular arithmetic as, for example, with the second-order polynomial:

$$2x^2 + 4x + 7 \bmod 11$$

A number can replace the variable x in a polynomial and the overall numerical value of the polynomial can be worked out. For example, in the previous example if x were replaced by 5 then the polynomial would work out to be:

$$\left[2x^2 + 4x + 7 \bmod 11\right]_{x=5} \equiv \left(2 \times 5^2\right) + \left(4 \times 5\right) + 7 \bmod 11$$
$$\equiv \left(2 \times 25\right) + 20 + 7 \bmod 11$$

Working to a modulus of 11 means that any terms greater than 11 can be reduced by repeatedly subtracting 11, so

$$\left(2 \times 25\right) + 20 + 7 \equiv 2 \times 3 + 9 + 7 \bmod 11$$
$$\equiv 6 + 9 + 7 \bmod 11$$
$$\equiv 22 \bmod 11$$
$$\equiv 0 \bmod 11$$

A polynomial can be used to construct pairs of numbers by combining the value substituted for x with the value of the polynomial with that substituted value of x. Sometimes a polynomial is written in a congruence such as:

$$y \equiv 2x^2 + 4x + 7 \bmod 11$$

In this case, with x replaced by 5, y is given by:

$$y \equiv 2 \times 5^2 + 4 \times 5 + 7 \equiv 0 \bmod 11$$

and this would make the pair (x,y) congruent with $(5,0)$.

8.3.2   Encoding the secret

In security applications a polynomial can be constructed with one of the coefficients, say the x term, representing a secret S. For example, if I chose a first-order polynomial modulo 23, the framework, or schema, for the polynomial is:

$$y \equiv Sx + N \bmod 23$$

The modulus has been chosen to be a prime number to guarantee that certain mathematical conditions hold. N is chosen at random. Suppose the secret S, perhaps the number of paces to the treasure, is 19 and the random choice for N is 17 then the polynomial would be:

$$y \equiv 19x + 17 \bmod 23$$

The secret is explicit in this polynomial; to encrypt it, values of x are chosen at random and paired with the corresponding value of the polynomial. These pairs are calculated and given to individuals:

	x	$y \equiv 19x + 17 \bmod 23$	Pair
Alice	3	$19 \times 3 + 17 \equiv 57 + 17 \bmod 23$ $\equiv 11 + 17 \equiv 28 \equiv 5 \bmod 23$	$(3,5)$
Bob	7	$19 \times 7 + 17 \equiv 133 + 17 \bmod 23$ $\equiv 18 + 17 \equiv 35 \equiv 12 \bmod 23$	$(7,12)$
Charlie	9	$19 \times 9 + 17 \equiv 171 + 17 \bmod 23$ $\equiv 10 + 17 \equiv 27 \equiv 4 \bmod 23$	$(9,4)$
Diane	16	$19 \times 16 + 17 \equiv 304 + 17 \bmod 23$ $\equiv 5 + 17 \equiv 22 \bmod 23$	$(16,22)$

The ciphertexts may be calculated by an authority who issues them without giving away the secret so that none of the keepers of the ciphertext know the data that is being protected.

Calculations using only some of the pairs that make up the encrypted data allow the secret to be uncovered. However, below a threshold number of pairs, it is not possible to work out the values of the coefficients. It is the order of the polynomial that determines how many pairs are needed. The example uses a first-order polynomial and from this it is known that there will be two coefficients in the original polynomial. With two coefficients to calculate, at least two different pairs will be needed to uncover the polynomial coefficients.

Alice, not knowing the secret, can, as one of the partners, take her pair of numbers (3,5) and insert it in the schema for the polynomial $y \equiv Sx + N \bmod 23$. Substituting for x and y she could write down:

$$5 \equiv S3 + N \bmod 23$$

Such expressions are customarily rearranged and written as:

$$3S + N \equiv 5 \bmod 23$$

This congruence does not allow Alice to work out the secret S. A second congruence is needed, and she will need to get the co-operation of a second ciphertext holder. She could ask her old comrade, Bob, who has the pair (7,12). Using this second ciphertext, Bob and Alice can write down a second congruence:

$$12 \equiv S7 + N \bmod 23 \quad \text{which is rewritten as} \quad 7S + N \equiv 12 \bmod 23$$

Given just these two congruences derived from the data that Bob and Alice held, there are various systematic ways of finding S. The crucial feature of this set of congruences is that the solver has two unknown things (S and N) and two congruences to help. The general rule is that if the number of unknowns equals the number of congruences then the unknowns can be determined. (There are, as with many general rules, exceptions). The processes for finding S are laborious but some approaches can easily be converted into computer programs.

8.3.3   Uncovering the secret

I will start by writing down the two congruences:

$$3S + N \equiv 5 \bmod 23$$

$$7S + N \equiv 12 \bmod 23$$

Congruences can be manipulated provided they are maintained between the left-hand side and the right-hand side. For instance, I can add $4S$ to the left-hand side of a congruence, provided $4S$ is also added to the right-hand side. Thus the first congruence, derived from Alice's numbers, can be rewritten as:

$$4S + 3S + N \equiv 4S + 5 \bmod 23$$

and this simplifies to:

$$7S + N \equiv 4S + 5 \bmod 23$$

so that the left-hand side of Alice's congruence is identical to the left-hand side of the congruence derived from Bob's numbers. In Alice's modified congruence $7S + N$ is congruent with $4S + 5 \bmod 23$ while Bob's congruence provides the extra information that means $7S + N$ is also congruent with $12 \bmod 23$. Putting these two pieces of information together implies that $4S + 5$ must be congruent to $12 \bmod 23$, so:

$$4S + 5 \equiv 7S + N \equiv 12 \bmod 23$$

Rearranging this congruence should reveal the secret S. To simplify the result and eliminate the 5 from the left-hand side I can first add 18 (18 because $5 + 18 \equiv 23 \equiv 0 \bmod 23$) to both sides of the congruence:

$$4S + 5 + 18 \equiv 12 + 18 \bmod 23$$

which becomes:

$$4S + 23 = 30 \bmod 23$$

Using the properties of the modulo 23 arithmetic the congruence derived from Alice's and Bob's ciphertext can be rewritten as:

$$4S \equiv 7 \bmod 23$$

More work is needed to find S. I can eliminate the number 4 on the right-hand side by exploiting the Euler–Fermat Theorem, which tells me that when working to a prime modulus like 23, I can write for any number, represented by r, and prime modulus n,

$$r^{n-1} \equiv 1 \bmod n$$

This means that if I choose r to be 4 and I work with a modulus of 23 so that n is 23 then the theorem tells me that:

$$4^{23-1} \equiv 4^{22} \equiv 1 \bmod 23$$

Returning to the congruence $4S \equiv 7 \bmod 23$ that is to reveal the secret, both sides of this congruence can be multiplied by 4^{21}. The congruence becomes:

$$4^{21} \times 4S \equiv 4^{21} \times 7 \bmod 23$$

and, crucially, the left-hand side is:

$$4^{21} \times 4S \equiv 4^{22} S \bmod 23$$

From the result of applying the Euler–Fermat Theorem I discover that $4^{22} \bmod 23$ can be replaced by 1 and the expression $4^{22} S \bmod 23$ is thus equivalent to $1 \times S \bmod 23$ or $S \bmod 23$. Putting this together shows that the secret is revealed as:

$$S \equiv 4^{21} \times 7 \bmod 23$$

Using the usual techniques for working out powers gives the final result for the secret:

$$S \equiv 4^{21} \times 7 \equiv 4^{16+4+1} \times 7 \bmod 23$$

Table 22 gives the result of calculating selected powers of 4 modulo 23.

Table 22   Selected powers of 4 modulo 23

$$4^2 \equiv 16 \bmod 23$$
$$4^4 \equiv \left(4^2\right)^2 \equiv 16^2 \equiv 256 \equiv (256 - 11 \times 23) \equiv 3 \bmod 23$$
$$4^8 \equiv \left(4^4\right)^2 \equiv 3^2 \equiv 9 \bmod 23$$
$$4^{16} \equiv \left(4^8\right)^2 \equiv 4^2 \equiv 81 \equiv (81 - 3 \times 23) \equiv 12 \bmod 23$$

Using the results in the table the calculation of the secret becomes:

$$S \equiv 4^{16} \times 4^4 \times 4^1 \times 7 \equiv 12 \times 3 \times 4 \times 7 \bmod 23$$
$$\equiv 36 \times 4 \times 7 \equiv (36 - 1 \times 23) \times 4 \times 7 \bmod 23$$
$$\equiv 13 \times 4 \times 7 \equiv 52 \times 7 \equiv (52 - 2 \times 23) \times 7 \bmod 23$$
$$\equiv 6 \times 7 \equiv 42 \equiv (42 - 1 \times 23) \bmod 23$$
$$\equiv 19 \bmod 23$$

The collaborators could do the calculation using any two pairs and should get the same result. Charlie and Diane with the pairs (9,4) and (16,22) can form the two congruences:

$$9S + N \equiv 4 \bmod 23$$

$$16S + N \equiv 22 \bmod 23$$

Adding $7S$ to the left-hand side of the first congruence produces:

$$7S + 9S + N \equiv 16S + N \bmod 23$$

This is the same as the left-hand side of the second congruence, which is itself congruent with 22. I can therefore use the right-hand side of the first congruence with $7S$ added to form a new congruence:

$$7S + 4 \equiv 16S + N \equiv 22 \bmod 23$$

Adding 19 to both sides gives the result:

$$7S + 4 + 19 \equiv 22 + 19 \bmod 23$$

which is simplified when the modulus is taken into account to give:

$$7S \equiv 41 \equiv 18 \bmod 23$$

The Euler–Fermat Theorem ensures that $7^{23-1} \equiv 7^{22} \equiv 1 \bmod 23$ so multiplying both sides of the congruence by 7^{21} generates for the left-hand side:

$$7^{21} \times 7S \equiv 7^{22}S \equiv 1 \times S \equiv S \bmod 23$$

and the right-hand side becomes:

$$7^{21} \times 18 \bmod 23$$

The secret is then given by the congruence:

$$S \equiv 7^{16+4+1} \times 18 \bmod 23$$

Table 23 gives the result of calculating selected powers of 7 modulo 23.

Table 23   Selected powers of 7 modulo 23

$$7^2 \equiv 49 \equiv 2 \times 23 + 3 \equiv 3 \bmod 23$$

$$7^4 \equiv \left(7^2\right)^2 \equiv 3^2 \equiv 9 \bmod 23$$

$$7^8 \equiv \left(7^4\right)^2 \equiv 9^2 \equiv 81 \equiv \left(81 - 3 \times 23\right) \equiv 12 \bmod 23$$

$$7^{16} \equiv \left(7^8\right)^2 \equiv 12^2 \equiv 144 \equiv \left(144 - 6 \times 23\right) \equiv 6 \bmod 23$$

Using the results in the table the calculation of the secret becomes:

$$7^{16} \times 7^4 \times 7^1 \times 18 \equiv 6 \times 9 \times 7 \times 18 \bmod 23$$
$$\equiv 54 \times 7 \times 18 \equiv \left(54 - 2 \times 23\right) \times 7 \times 18 \bmod 23$$
$$\equiv 8 \times 7 \times 18 \equiv 56 \times 18 \equiv \left(56 - 2 \times 23\right) \times 7 \times 18 \bmod 23$$
$$\equiv 10 \times 18 \equiv 180 \equiv \left(180 - 7 \times 23\right) \bmod 23$$
$$\equiv 19 \bmod 23$$

The result again is the secret number 19. The fact that the second calculation gives the same result as the first provides a check on the validity of the data that the collaborators have provided.

Any two pairs of numbers derived from the original congruence $y \equiv 19x + 17 \bmod 23$ should generate the secret number. If, however, an inconsistent result occurs then that implies that at least one of the pairs of numbers is incorrect. This could be because someone has made a mistake or that someone is deliberately trying to generate the wrong result.

8.3.4 Summary

Polynomials are algebraic objects, which have a number of components. One component can be treated as a secret and a series of paired numbers can provide clues to the secret. The people decrypting the secret need a number of pairs and if these have been allocated to different people, decryption will require their collaboration. The number of pairs required depends on the order of the polynomial and is one more than the order of the polynomial. If a larger number of pairs is available, then they can help to provide a check on the validity of the data that the partners have provided. In the illustration in this section, a first-order polynomial required two collaborators. Using higher-order polynomials forces the collaboration of more people. A third-order polynomial, for example, would require collaboration by four people before the secret could be uncovered.

The secret number that is conveyed in this scheme could be a coded or encrypted secret. Alternatively, the secret number could be a key, which allows the partners to decrypt other ciphertext. For instance, instead of providing the number of steps to the treasure, the secret could be a key to decrypt a complete encrypted map.

The scheme has three useful features. First, it divides the responsibility for keeping the ciphertext secret; second, it enforces collaboration between the partners when exposing secrets; and third, it enables checks to be made on the validity of the ciphertext.

It is possible to use polynomials when secrets are themselves encoded as numbers. It is a further demonstration of an advantage of transforming data into a mathematical form. Once a mathematical object represents data, there are ranges of operations that have been widely studied and that can be performed on the data. In some instances, these operations prove to have useful properties for security applications.

8.4 Digital cash

Some well-established traditional activities demand and provide a means to conduct transactions with a degree of security. One technology that we often take for granted is in the use of cash. Cash is so widely integrated into our social fabric that there is an expectation that *digital cash* will be an automatic and easy extension to monetary technology. Cash, though, is a potential application of digital technology that has proved to be far from straightforward. One reason, for example, that a system of cash tokens, such as coins and notes, works is because it is relatively difficult to reproduce them. It is possible to produce convincing forgeries, but the effort involved makes it unprofitable. The digital equivalents of notes and coins, however, are easy to copy. This section cannot, therefore, describe a complete and robust digital analogy for cash. The proposal here is incomplete but does provide a further example of the use of blinding to protect the anonymity of, in this case, a holder of a digital coin.

Various proposals have been made for simulating cash transactions on communication networks. Cash deals are a special kind of transaction because they do not involve the identities of the dealers and can be carried out anonymously. The requirements for a system like cash are:

1   The identity of a dealer is not needed for a transaction.

2   A single transaction involves only the dealers.

3   No cash is created in or lost from the system during a transaction.

4   Forgery of cash is not worthwhile.

5   Agencies, such as banks, that are willing to turn the cash into other kinds of assets such as bank accounts.

There are three kinds of protocols required:

1   cash issue –when people obtain their cash

2   payment – when people pass cash from one to another

3   cash deposit – when people deposit their cash.

8.4.1   A system for issuing cash

Here is the outline of a small part of a system that has been proposed.[110] Alice begins by obtaining a digital coin, which is to be endorsed by Bob, working at the bank. Bob issues a public key, which stands for the denomination of a coin, say one pound, $K_£$. He keeps the corresponding private key. Alice chooses a random number N_A, which she keeps secret. She encrypts it with the bank's public key:

$$N_A{}^{K_£} \bmod n$$

She then uses the result as a key to encrypt a text using multiplication.[111] The text that she encrypts is a description of the coin incorporating an identification number N that she picks at random. The message can be written as $M(N)$ and when encrypted Alice gets:

$$M(N) \times N_A{}^{K_£} \bmod n$$

Alice signs the whole bundle and sends it with her signature to Bob at the bank:

$A \to B : \{M(N)\}_{\{N_A\}_{K_£}}, \sigma_A\left(\{M(N)\}_{\{N_A\}_{K_£}}\right)$	Alice sends the signed, encrypted message to Bob

Bob checks the signature and, providing Alice's signature is valid, he deducts one pound (plus a handling charge, no doubt) from her account and encrypts her coin with the bank's private key used for endorsing coins worth one pound:

$B \to A : \left\{\{M(N)\}_{\{N_A\}_{K_£}}\right\}_{\overline{K}_£}$	Bob returns Alice's coin, which he has endorsed

The sequence of encryption operations partially nullify one another because N_A is effectively encrypted by Alice with Bob's public key and then decrypted by Bob with his private key.

$$\left(M(N) \times N_A{}^{K_£}\right)^{\overline{K}_£} \equiv M(N)^{\overline{K}_£} \times N_A{}^{K_£ \times \overline{K}_£} \bmod n$$
$$\equiv M(N)^{\overline{K}_£} \times N_A \bmod n$$

Implanted in this message is the digital coin $M(N)^{\overline{K}_£}$, which Alice has paid for. Bob does not have to encrypt what he sends back to Alice as it is effectively encrypted through multiplication by N_A. Alice has kept the number N_A secret so nobody except her can decrypt the digital coin (even Bob does not know how to do so).

Alice can use a result described in subsection 3.4.1 and derived from the Euler–Fermat Theorem to find a number $\overline{N}_A$ that generates the result $N_A \times \overline{N}_A \equiv 1 \bmod n$. Multiplying the message she received from Bob by $\overline{N}_A$ gives:

$$M(N)^{\overline{K}_£} \times N_A \times \overline{N}_A \equiv M(N)^{\overline{K}_£} \times 1 \equiv M(N)^{\overline{K}_£} \bmod n$$

Alice, therefore, decrypts the message from Bob to get $M(N)^{\overline{K}_£}$. This is the description of the coin, including its serial number, encrypted with the private key held by the bank specifically for endorsing one pound digital coins. She keeps the result in her electronic purse. When she wants to spend her coin, in for example, Steve's shop, she sends the coin to him:

$A \rightarrow S : \{M(N)\}_{\overline{K_£}}$	Alice sends the coin to Steve

Note that because the serial number is a part of the message encrypted with the bank's private key, anyone can decrypt it using the bank's public key to check it. Steve can check the coin, and because he can decrypt it with the bank's public key for one pound coins he can accept it and know what value to attribute to it.

Later, Steve might deposit the coin at Bob's bank:

$S \rightarrow B : \{M(N)\}_{\overline{K_£}}, \sigma_S(\{M(N)\}_{\overline{K_£}})$	Steve signs the coin and deposits it at the bank

The bank can check Steve's signature and credit his account. Provided Alice does not reveal that she put the serial number on the coin, her transaction with Steve is anonymous. Indeed Alice's coin can remain in circulation until someone decides to return it to the bank.

8.4.2 The weakness

A number of protocols have been proposed for digital cash systems, but they are all vulnerable as it is so easy to copy digital coins. An opportunist could withdraw digital coins from a bank and duplicate them before spending them. Or someone could duplicate coins before depositing the originals in the bank. Various solutions have been proposed. For example, as every item of cash is identified by a serial number then when a duplicate is made it will carry the identical serial number to the original. Checks can be made to see if a duplicate exists before the digital coin is accepted, but the question arises as to when this check should be carried out. If coins are only checked when they are deposited in the bank then forgeries can circulate undetected. If they are checked during the course of every transaction then substantial communication would be needed to maintain the register of coin owners and their coins. The bank would have to monitor every transaction, and the anonymity of cash would be lost.

In the protocol outlined above Alice chose the serial number of the coin, encrypted it and sent it to the bank. This retained her anonymity as blinding obscured the serial number and prevented the bank associating it with Alice and thus tracking down what she buys with her money. On the other hand, with everybody choosing their own serial numbers, occasionally there will be duplicates. If there are relatively few possible serial numbers, duplicates will occur more frequently, but allowing a wider range of serial numbers will make it less likely. This may be acceptable. Cash systems are never completely foolproof and there are always risks that a fraud will remain undetected. However, in this case, because the chosen system allows honest people to create duplicate coins, it can support false accusations of fraud. So although allowing a wider range of serial numbers can reduce the risk of false allegations, false accusations can still occur. This will increase the insecurity people might feel when using the system and also provide a credible defence for counterfeiters.

8.4.3 Summary

The technology of coins and notes has developed over centuries and has become integrated into many social practices. Because it is so widely deployed, it would be useful to incorporate cash systems into newer technological devices as they become available. Simulating coins and notes, though, has proved to be difficult. Part of the difficulty is that no cash systems are risk-free, or, in other words, none are totally secure. As the technology of money evolves so the kinds of risks change, but it is hard in advance to identify the risks and to imagine how people will react to those risks. Electronic cash is an example of where, at present, no suitable set of mathematical objects compatible with digital technology can provide the level of authenticity and anonymity that people will trust as much as they trust coins and notes.

8.5 Securing bindings

Many protocol failures occur because components of transactions that should be securely bound to one another are not. This section describes a protocol for conducting commercial transactions in which details of a payment, an order for goods and an individual identity must be *securely bound*. It illustrates how a binding can be assured using hash functions and signatures.

8.5.1 A simple example

Two or more items can be bound using encryption or hash functions. For instance, Alice could securely bind a message M and its time of issue T with her private key $\overline{K}_A$ to get $\{M, T\}_{\overline{K}_A}$. No one else could reconstruct this relationship between the message, the time and Alice's identity since they do not have her private key. However, in a protocol the elements of a relationship may appear in different components of an interaction. And an additional term may be required to make the binding explicit:

$A \rightarrow B : M$	Alice sends Bob a message
$\vdots$	There may be further communications here
$A \rightarrow B : T$	Later, Alice sends Bob a time that is not bound

$\vdots$	There may be further communications here
$A \rightarrow B : \{M, T\}_{\overline{K}_A}$	Alice explicitly binds the time and the message and sends it to Bob

In this example, the time and the message are effectively sent twice. A more economical way of binding components together is to use a hash function. $H(M,T)$ produces the message digest for a text made up of the original message and the time. Although this combined message may never be transmitted, it can be constructed from earlier interactions:

$A \rightarrow B : M$	Alice sends Bob a message
$\vdots$	There may be further communications here
$A \rightarrow B : T$	Later, Alice sends Bob a time that is not bound
$\vdots$	There may be further communications here
$A \rightarrow B : H(M,T)$	Alice binds the time and the message using a hash function and sends the result to Bob

Bob can, from the earlier messages, construct $H(M,T)$ and compare it with Alice's final message to confirm that she intended to bind the message and the time. Alice can secure the binding by encrypting the message digest with her private key. Effectively, she forms a signature of the combination of the message and the time and this binds the time, the message and Alice's identity in a compact form:

$A \rightarrow B : M$	Alice sends Bob a message
$\vdots$	There may be further communications here
$A \rightarrow B : T$	Later, Alice sends Bob a time that is not bound
$\vdots$	There may be further communications here
$A \rightarrow B : \sigma_A(M,T)$	Alice binds the time and the message and secures the binding by forming a signature of the combination

Bob can confirm the binding by checking that the signature is derived from a combination of M and T and is signed with Alice's private key. The binding cannot be altered by anyone but Alice since she has the private key for forming her signatures.

8.5.2 The SET protocol

The initials SET stand for *secure electronic transaction*, which is a specification for a collection of protocols to aid electronic commerce.[112] The assumption in SET is that there are customers, or cardholders, and merchants who wish to trade. The customers have credentials that are acceptable at payment gateways. If things go well, a cardholder offers his or her credentials to the merchant, which he relays to the payment gateway. The payment gateway signals to the merchant that the credentials are in order and that a financial transfer is under way. Finally, the merchant notifies the customer that the goods have been released and payment has been made. There have to be additional protocols, however, because things do not always go so smoothly and there are also protocols for users and merchants who have to register with the payment system initially.

I will examine the Purchase request. The protocol assumes that the cardholder has selected the goods and ordered them. The merchant is awaiting payment before proceeding with the despatch of the goods. First, the cardholder, Charlie, sends a message to the merchant, Magnus. Charlie's message B indicates the brand of card that he wants to use:

$C \rightarrow M : B$	Charlie notifies Magnus of the brand of payment card

Magnus replies by sending his public key certificate C_M and the public key certificate of the payment gateway that will accept Charlie's card, C_G. The certificates will give Charlie public keys for Magnus and the payment gateway. Magnus sends a brief response R, encrypted with his private key $\overline{K}_M$, to acknowledge the start of the transaction:

$M \rightarrow C : C_M, C_G, \{R\}_{\overline{K}_M}$	Magnus responds and sends Charlie two digital certificates

Charlie decrypts the certificates with the Certification Authority's public key to confirm their validity, extracts Magnus's public key and decrypts the message he has sent him. Next, Charlie assembles information about his order O and his payment P. Charlie forms a message digest of each one, puts them together and then creates a new message digest of the combination, which he encrypts with a private key he reserves for signatures to give $\{H(H(O), H(P))\}_{\overline{K}_C}$. The SET literature refers to this as a *double signature*. Note that this signature, which only Charlie can produce, binds the order, the payment information and his identity. I will write this double signature as $\sigma_C^2(O, P)$. Charlie now compiles an elaborate message. He picks a key K and uses it to form a digital envelope around the payment information and the dual signature. When encrypting the key K with Magnus's public key, Charlie takes the opportunity to add the details of his account, Ac. This digital envelope is appended to the order information and another copy of the double signature. Finally, Charlie adds his own digital certificate.

$$C \to M : O, \sigma_C^2(O,P), \underline{\{K, Ac\}_{K_M}, \{P, \sigma_C^2(O,P)\}_K}, C_C$$
$$\text{Digital Envelope}$$

In this message, the account information and the payment information is kept confidential by encryption with Magnus's public key or with the session key K. The double signature binds the payment and order information together, and the payment and account information are also bound together through their association with the key K. Magnus can use his private key to discover the key K. He can then extract the payment information P, combine it with the order and make sure that the double signature binds them together. Magnus can also check Charlie's digital certificate to make sure that he constructed the signatures. After completing his analysis of Charlie's message, Magnus should be satisfied that the payment information, the order and Charlie's identity are bound together.

An additional binding is made with the digital certificate, which binds data about Charlie's identity with his public key, while the double signatures are encrypted with his private key and can be decrypted with the corresponding public key. The contents of the signature are therefore bound to Charlie's public key and through the certificate with data about his identity.

Magnus uses the account and payment information to ask the payment gateway for authorization to proceed and sends a message S to Charlie to say that this is the status of the transaction. Magnus adds his signature and his digital certificate.

$M \to C : S, \sigma_M(S), C_M$	Magnus confirms that the payment is being processed

Charlie can read the message and check the signature to prove that it came from Magnus. The remaining interactions are out of his hands. Magnus interacts with the payment gateway and if it authorizes the payment he dispatches the goods.

8.5.3 Summary

Where the components of a relationship are built up during a succession of interactions, the binding between the components may be lost. An additional message or component of a message may be required to make the binding explicit. The additional data, though, contains redundant information when it includes the components of the relationship that had already been conveyed.

Some protocol designers have, therefore, been tempted to omit explicit declarations of the binding and this can make the protocol vulnerable to intruders.

A more economical arrangement is to send a compact message digest of the relationship and secure it encrypted with a private key. A signature can therefore be an adequate replacement for a full description of a relationship.

8.6 Committal

In commerce, people enter into contracts, which describe the commitments they are willing to enter into. For instance, Vince might promise to paint Bob's office and, in return, Bob would promise to pay Vince a sum of money. When Vince finishes the painting Bob will pay Vince. Of course, things do not always go smoothly. They might try to cheat one another. Vince might ask for a payment knowing that he has not done all the work that he has promised to do, or Bob might try to pay Vince less than they agreed.

A contract is an example of a commital or a promise. While security measures cannot ensure that people keep their promises or stick to their contracts, protocols can include elements that ensure the integrity of the contracts and that suitable evidence can be collected which will allow honest contractors to obtain redress when things go wrong.

8.6.1 Signing the contract

Written contracts are produced to help resolve disputes but they can be fraudulently amended. Vince, for instance, might ask Bob for more money and use a forged copy of the contract as proof that he should pay up. To prevent a forgery an integrity check can be added to the contract and the contract signed to show that Bob and Vince both endorsed its content:

$V \rightarrow B : M$	Vince sends Bob a draft contract
$B \rightarrow V : \sigma_B(M)$	If Bob thinks the contract is satisfactory, he sends Vince a signature to the contract
$V \rightarrow B : \sigma_V(M)$	Vince checks Bob's signature and sends his own signature to him

In the initial stages, Bob may find the contract unsatisfactory but will negotiate with Vince to formulate an agreeable deal. Once the final version is in place both Bob and Vince will endorse the contract by creating a digital signature, first by creating a message digest and then encrypting it with a private key. For each of them the contract will represent a commitment to complete a task. For instance, Vince might be committed to painting Bob's office while Bob might be committed to paying an agreed sum when the work is complete. The moment either one of them creates a signature, he endorses the contract and effectively enters into a commitment.

To provide a greater level of security they can deposit their signatures with a third party – Alice perhaps. Vince may be tempted to alter his copy of the contract, but if a dispute occurs afterwards Alice can ask for copies of the contract, and Vince will be found out because his signature will not match the modified contract he sent Alice. But Vince may be a little more cunning. He might send Bob one contract M to sign and then sign another version M' himself:

$V \rightarrow B : M$	Vince sends Bob a draft contract
$B \rightarrow V : \sigma_B(M)$	If Bob thinks the contract is satisfactory, he sends Vince a signature to the contract
$V \rightarrow B : \sigma_V(M')$	Vince checks Bob's signature and sends his own signature to a modified contract to Bob

Bob may not notice Vince's fraud until the work is complete or he may notice it straightaway but only after he has already made his commitment. In settling the dispute, Vince might capitulate, but then loses nothing. But if Bob's challenge fails or a compromise is reached, Bob will lose out. A dishonest Vince would be tempted to cheat.

Each signature binds an identity (via the private key) to a document. There is nothing in the protocol that binds Vince's first and second versions of the document and they can, therefore, be quite distinct. The two identities and a single document can be bound if Vince is required to encrypt Bob's signature. Bob forms his signature by encrypting a message digest of the contract with his private key. Vince can check that Bob is not cheating by finding the digest of the contract and comparing it with the message digest embedded in his signature. Vince cannot forge Bob's signature, since he does not have Bob's private key. When Vince is satisfied that Bob's signature is valid, he can endorse Bob's signature rather than the contract, by encrypting it with his private key to get $\{\{H(M)\}_{\overline{K_B}}\}_{\overline{K_V}}$. In doing so Vince binds his identity with the same document as Bob because the digest of the document is embedded in Bob's signature. Bob and the third party, Alice, can check Vince's commitment by decrypting the ciphertext using Vince's and Bob's public keys to uncover the digest of the contract. This can be compared with the digest of the versions of the contract that Bob and Vince claim is the correct one. The version that they both endorsed would then be apparent.

8.6.2 Placing a bet

Bets are a kind of contract, where someone promises that if a particular outcome occurs then they will pay up. The details of the contract are usually embedded in the rules of the gambling game but, in addition, someone has to name the outcome they are gambling on. For instance, Eve and Alice might gamble with a simulated dice remotely from one another. They agree a set of rules and start with ten tokens each. The rules say that they are to take turns in 'throwing' the dice and in guessing what the value will be after the throw. With an incorrect guess they have to put a token into the kitty, but if they guess correctly then they get the tokens in the kitty. The loser is the one who loses all his or her tokens and the winner cashes in the tokens that are on the table.

Before a throw the gambler, say Alice, tells Eve her guess. She cannot then change her mind. Once the simulated dice throw takes place she either wins or pays up. Neither Alice nor Eve should have an opportunity to cheat. If Eve, unseen by Alice, simulated the dice she could ignore the result if it meant that Alice would win and instead report a number that did not correspond to Alice's guess, and Alice would lose. If Alice threw then she could cheat by saying that the dice had showed her number.

An alternative way of simulating the dice would be to allow both to pick a number. Suppose Eve picks 32 and Alice picks 15, and their numbers are added in modulo 6:

$$32 + 15 = 47 = 5 \bmod 6$$

Then 1 is added to the result using ordinary arithmetic. For the current throw the result would be $5 + 1 = 6$. However, this method also presents opportunities for cheats. If Eve picks 32 and tells Alice first, then Alice will know what numbers to pick to ensure the result is in her favour. Similarly, if Alice picks first, Eve can work out what to say to make sure Alice loses. One solution is for the person who picks a number first to commit to it but then to hide it. For instance, when Eve picks the number 32, she can write it on a piece of paper, lock it in a box and send the box to Alice. Alice cannot open the box so does not know what Eve's number is, but because Alice has the box she knows Eve cannot change what has been written down. Alice then picks her number and sends it to Eve. Eve can work out the result of adding her own and Alice's numbers and hence the result of the simulated dice throw.

Next, Eve sends Alice the key to the box and Alice can find out the number that Eve chose. Alice can also work out the result confident that Eve cannot cheat. Eve cannot renege on her choice because Alice has a copy securely locked away. Alice cannot cheat because although she has a copy of Eve's number in the locked box she cannot open it.

Obviously, the analogy of the locked boxes can be translated into the processes of encryption and decryption:

$A \rightarrow E : N$	Alice bets Eve that the next number will be N
$E \rightarrow A : \{N_E\}_K$	To simulate the dice Eve picks a number, copies it, encrypts it and sends the encrypted version to Alice
$A \rightarrow E : N_A$	For her contribution to the simulation Alice picks another number and sends it to Eve
$E \rightarrow A : K$	Eve combines her choice with Alice's to work out the value shown on the simulated dice and simultaneously sends the decryption key to Alice

Alice receives the decryption key, decrypts Eve's encrypted number and works out for herself the result, $(N_A + N_E \bmod 6) + 1$, shown on the simulated dice.

When Eve sends the encrypted number $\{N_E\}_K$ to Alice, she commits herself to that number. For this reason, Eve's action of sending an encrypted number to Alice is referred to as a *committal*. Eve cannot change her mind without Alice knowing. For greater security, it could be in Eve's and Alice's interest to publish Eve's encrypted number so that, later, a third party could vouch for her commitment.

Obviously, Eve will need to choose a new key for every throw of the dice and Alice will need to be sure that the method of encryption does not allow Eve to predictably manipulate the result of the decryption by choosing the decryption key she sends her.

8.6.3   Tendering

In commerce, contracts are sometimes issued through a process of competitive tendering. A number of organizations are invited to offer contracts for an item of work. Bob, for instance, might ask for tenders for painting his office. He would probably set a deadline. When the deadline arrived, he would look at all the bids and choose the one that offered him the best deal. He would then notify the bidders of the result and enter into a contract with his preferred contractor. With a number of organizations involved there are hazards in the bidding process that are usually avoided by asking only for sealed bids. The concerns are usually about the fairness of the bidding process. After the deadline, the sealed bids are opened and a choice made.

A sealed bid binds an identity to a concealed document. In a digital network, a signature can fulfil the same function. When Bob asks for tenders for the work on his office, he can ask people to send commitments to Tahira, a trusted third party. Because the tenders are to be kept confidential the bidders, Vince, Diane and Eve, send only the signatures of their tenders to the trusted agent:

$V \rightarrow T : \sigma_V(M_V)$	Vince sends Tahira a signature for his tender
$D \rightarrow T : \sigma_D(M_D)$	Diane sends Tahira a signature for her tender
$E \rightarrow T : \sigma_E(M_E)$	Eve sends Tahira a signature for her tender

These signatures each represent a commitment to a different contract by different potential contractors. The shuffling, compression and encryption involved in forming the message digest embedded in the signature makes it impossible to work out the details of the contracts. The bids therefore remain confidential. After the deadline, the bidders send the plaintext of their contracts to Bob who picks his preferred bid. Perhaps he picks Eve's contract M_E. He then asks Tahira to check that Eve's signature corresponds to Eve's contract and that she has not cheated by making alterations after she has made her commitment. If Bob is satisfied then he can endorse Eve's offer by encrypting her signature with his private key. This whole procedure does not necessarily bring Bob any benefits, but it does reassure the losing bidders that the competition was fair.

8.6.4 Summary

Contracts are agreements between several partners. The contractors link their identity with the contract and provide an integrity check by signing the document with their unique signature. Integrity checks are required, because it can be enticing for a contractor to alter a contract after an agreement has been reached. Contractors need to protect themselves from the dishonesty of others by ensuring that everyone endorses the same document. This can be done by asking each contractor to endorse, not the contract, but the endorsements of the other contractors. The first contractor signs the contract and the other contractors encrypt that signature progressively with their private keys. Because the first signature is derived from the message digest of the contract, the identities of the contractors are then all bound to the contract.

Some contractual processes require people to make a commitment at a time when revealing the contractual details would disadvantageous. This introduces simultaneous concerns about integrity and confidentiality. Both can be dealt with by encryption. A confidential commitment can be made by circulating an encrypted pledge. At an appropriate time, the pledge can be revealed by providing the means for its decryption. An alternative is to use the encryption inherent in some hash functions. A pledge can be signed and the signature submitted as a token of a commitment. When the plaintext of the pledge is revealed, the signature confirms the integrity of the commitment and the identity of the guarantor.

The creation and operation of contracts gives rise to anxieties that can be dealt with by exploiting common security devices such as encryption, signatures and private keys. At the same time, making the processes and their outcomes public can enhance security because when disputes arise there will be witnesses that can resolve dishonestly concocted differences.

8.7   An auction

People are often happy to contribute to surveys and statistical studies as long as the data cannot be attributed to themselves as individuals. The requirement is for individuals to make contributions confidentially and for their individual contributions to be pooled to reveal something about the group. There are examples of protocols where this requirement can be met by exploiting simple mathematical relationships. A relationship between the keys held by the participants is translated into a relationship amongst the messages that they submit while their individual messages remain confidential. A field of application for these protocols is in on-line auctions. People sometimes go to some lengths to retain their anonymity in auctions and film makers have made a great deal of the secret gestures that people are supposed to use in signalling their bid to an auctioneer.

8.7.1   The secret bid

Suppose Alice, who at one time worked as an auctioneer, is given the job of establishing an on-line auction house. The procedure she wants to adopt starts with the auctioneer inviting bids. The bidders make a decision as to whether they want to bid or not. After someone bids, Alice moves to the next round by announcing a higher price. If nobody bids then that is the end of the auction and the person who bid in the previous round becomes the winner of the auction. He or she is expected to pay for the goods and collect them. If more than one person bid in the previous round then Alice will move to a more refined protocol.

On-line auctions[113] require variations, because not everyone who is bidding is necessarily on-line at the same time and they will need notification of a new round starting. The rounds can be timed so that the bidders are told when a round starts and when it finishes and they can then bid within that period. A bidder, though, might claim that he or she had made a bid but that it had not got through. One approach is to ask the bidders in each round to send a message indicating whether or not they are bidding.

To keep their bidding secret, the bidders can use variations on what has become known as a solution to the *Dining Cryptographers Problem*, which considers a fictitious occasion when a number of cryptographers had a meal together. The problem is that the meal has been paid for, and without being explicitly told the cryptographers set about finding out whether one of the diners has paid or if it was an anonymous benefactor. The solution can reveal that one of the cryptographers has paid, but not which one.

8.7.2 Choosing the keys

Before an auction starts, Alice establishes a modulus n that she, and the bidders, will use for their calculations. Suppose there is an auction with four bidders: Bob, Charlie, Diane and Eve. Before a round starts each bidder has to establish an encryption key. They do this in a special way that makes sure nobody else knows their keys, but also makes sure there is a special relationship between the keys.

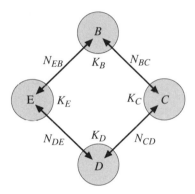

Figure 13   The distribution of numbers and keys

In pairs, they pick a random number, perhaps using the Diffie–Hellman technique. Once this has been done Bob shares a number with Charlie N_{BC}, Charlie shares a number with Diane N_{CD}, Diane shares a number with Eve N_{DE}, and Eve shares a number with Bob N_{EB}. Figure 13 illustrates how the numbers are distributed. They each then have two numbers, for instance, Diane shares numbers with both Eve and Charlie, N_{CD} and N_{DE}, but she does not know anything about the number that Bob and Charlie created, N_{BC}.

Next, they create their encryption keys from the two numbers that they have. They each create a key by subtracting one of their numbers from the other. Bob's key is:

$$K_B \equiv N_{BC} - N_{EB} \bmod n$$

Notice that although Charlie knows N_{BC}, he does not know N_{EB}, so he cannot work out Bob's key. Similarly, Eve knows N_{EB} but does not know N_{BC}. Diane knows neither of the numbers Bob has used to calculate his key, so Bob's key is his secret. In the same way Eve's, Diane's and Charlie's keys are secret. The four keys are:

1   Bob's key: $K_B \equiv N_{BC} - N_{EB} \bmod n$

2   Charlie's key: $K_C \equiv N_{CD} - N_{BC} \bmod n$

3   Diane's key $K_D \equiv N_{DE} - N_{CD} \bmod n$

4   Eve's key $K_E \equiv N_{EB} - N_{DE} \bmod n$

The important features of the keys calculated in this way are:

1   They are secrets that only the keyholders know.

2   They are related so that

$$
\begin{aligned}
K_B + K_C + K_D + K_E &\equiv \left(N_{BC} - N_{EB}\right) + \left(N_{CD} - N_{BC}\right) + \left(N_{DE} - N_{CD}\right) + \left(N_{EB} - N_{DE}\right) \bmod n \\
&\equiv N_{BC} - N_{BC} + N_{CD} - N_{CD} + N_{DE} - N_{DE} + N_{EB} - N_{EB} \bmod n \\
&\equiv 0
\end{aligned}
$$

8.7.3   Making the bid

The bidders encode their bidding intentions as a number. For instance, they could use a 1 to mean 'I am making a bid', and a 0 to mean 'I am abstaining in this round'. Bob encrypts his bid B_B by adding the key to it:

$B_B + K_B \bmod n$

Bob will send this to Alice. Alice, or an eavesdropper, cannot work out what Bob's bid is because they do not know his key. Charlie constructs his message for Alice by encrypting his bid B_C with his key to get:

$B_C + K_C \bmod n$

Diane's bid is B_D and encrypted this is:

$B_D + K_D \bmod n$

and, finally, Eve's bid is B_E and encrypted this creates:

$B_E + K_E \bmod n$

Alice, or an eavesdropper, cannot decrypt the individual bids because they do not know the encryption keys.

The bidders all send their bids to Alice. She performs a calculation on the data she receives from Bob, Charlie, Diane and Eve:

$$\underbrace{B_B + K_B}_{\text{From Bob}} + \underbrace{B_C + K_C}_{\text{From Charlie}} + \underbrace{B_D + K_D}_{\text{From Diane}} + \underbrace{B_E + K_E}_{\text{From Eve}} \bmod n$$

Because of the relationship between the keys this becomes:

$$B_B + B_C + B_D + B_E + K_B + K_C + K_D + K_E \equiv B_B + B_C + B_D + B_E \bmod n$$

The result is the sum of the bids, which will be zero when nobody bids, or one, two, three or four depending on how many people enter the bidding.

8.7.4 A numerical example

Suppose Alice has announced that bids will be encrypted using a modulus of 19 and bidding has started with Diane and Bob wanting to make a bid. Charlie and Eve are sitting it out thus:

$$B_B \equiv 1 \bmod n \quad B_C \equiv 0 \bmod n \quad B_D \equiv 1 \bmod n \quad B_E \equiv 0 \bmod n$$

They use the Diffie–Hellman procedure to create shared random numbers and get the following results:

1 Bob and Charlie – $N_{BC} \equiv 18 \bmod 19$

2 Charlie and Diane – $N_{CD} \equiv 3 \bmod 19$

3 Diane and Eve – $N_{DE} \equiv 17 \bmod 19$

4 Eve and Bob – $N_{EB} \equiv 8 \bmod 19$

Next, they compute their keys and use them to encrypt their bids:

1 Bob:
$$K_B \equiv N_{BC} - N_{EB} \equiv 18 - 8 \equiv 10 \bmod 19$$
$$B_B + K_B \equiv 1 + 10 \equiv 11 \bmod 19$$

2 Charlie:[114]
$$K_C \equiv N_{CD} - N_{BC} = 3 \quad 18 = 19 + 3 - 18 \equiv 4 \bmod 19$$
$$B_C + K_C \equiv 0 + 4 \equiv 4 \bmod 19$$

3 Diane:
$$K_D \equiv N_{DE} - N_{CD} \equiv 17 - 3 \equiv 14 \bmod 19$$
$$B_D + K_D \equiv 1 + 14 \equiv 15 \bmod 19$$

4 Eve:
$$K_E \equiv N_{EB} - N_{DE} \equiv 8 - 17 \equiv 19 + 8 - 17 \equiv 10 \bmod 19$$
$$B_E + K_E \equiv 0 + 10 \equiv 10 \bmod 19$$

Alice receives these encrypted bids and adds them up:

$$B_B + K_B + B_C + K_C + B_D + K_D + B_E + K_E \equiv 11 + 4 + 15 + 10 \equiv 40 \equiv 2 \bmod 19$$

Alice knows that two bids have been made and that she should continue with the next round of the auction, but she does not know who made the bids.

8.7.5 Summary

When a bidder is successful, Alice will need to complete the deal with that individual and his or her identity must be made known. An addition to the protocol would, therefore, have to record the commitments of the bidders and their identities but keep their commitments confidential until the bidding has been completed and it becomes necessary to identify the winning bidder. Once identified the successful bidder can be sent the bill and the goods that have been bid for.

In this application the procedure for choosing the keys made sure that there was a particular relationship between the keys. Everyone would know about that relationship but only the individual keyholders would know about their individual keys. Because of the relationship between the keys, the encrypted messages, together, encapsulated that relationship. By combining the encrypted messages in a particular way the effects of encryption could be neutralized; however, the outcome was not a specific piece of plaintext, but an aggregated plaintext that in this instance revealed a statistic about the bidding. Because the plaintext was encoded as a number of mathematical objects, in this case numbers, it was possible to exploit mathematical relationships in creating a solution to provide a degree of security to people who wished their actions to be kept anonymous.

8.8 Conclusion

Protocols can be devised for a surprising variety of activities where people need assurances about the honesty and integrity of their partners. Common encryption techniques play a vital role, and in many instances little more is needed. In some instances, though, further mathematical procedures are required and modular arithmetic provides a rich source of operations that can augment the encryption processes. The exploitation of modular arithmetic is only possible once the objects to be secured have been encoded as mathematical objects such as numbers or polynomials.

Often the inspiration for an application of digital techniques comes from a traditional activity built around a traditional technology. However, digital analogies are not always available, or when they are they sometimes fail in crucial respects.

Protocols for oblivious transfers need no special techniques and deal with situations where an exchange of valuable data takes place between people who do not fully trust one another. Secret ballots are activities where there is much at stake and electors need reassurances about the secrecy of their votes and protection from intimidation. In the election protocol described here the properties of modular arithmetic were exploited in the process of blinding that permitted the endorsement of the secret vote. Polynomials are another kind of mathematical object that fit within the framework of modular arithmetic and algebra and can make a contribution to protocols. In the example given here the polynomials allowed a secret to be shared and discovered only when several people cooperated.

It would be useful to find a digital analogy for cash that people would trust. Many proposals have been made, but the ease of copying digital coins means that simple analogies are not adequate. Not all traditional technologies, therefore, can be simply translated into digital editions.

A transaction involving money requires bindings between the partners, the goods and the payment. Encryption can bind items of data together and secure a description of a relationship; however, in a protocol the relationship may become distributed across a series of messages and connections lost. Protocol failures often arise because intruders exploit relationships that have not been explicitly secured. Signatures provide a way of preventing such failures by economically asserting and securing the description of a relationship.

During the course of a transaction people will enter into commitments. When the transaction involves a negotiation they may be unwilling to reveal their commitment. Publicly declared signatures can, on these occasions, represent a commitment while hiding its details. Subsequently, when the commitment is itself made public the signature provides a check that the underwriter has not reneged on his or her promise. A bid in an auction is a promise to buy goods should the bid be successful. Bidders sometimes like to keep their bidding secret and therefore an auction provides a scenario for a protocol where people, the bidders, submit information knowing that it will remain secret. Within such a protocol relationships can be established between keys that can be transferred to the data provided. Individual contributions remain secret but a statistic about the contributions can be computed, which, in the case of the auction, was the number of bids.

None of the protocols described in this section are complete and should not be treated as prototypes for creating secure systems. The descriptions have been abbreviated to reveal the varying requirements of security systems, the extent to which common security techniques can offer solutions, the potential for integrating further mathematical operations and the fact that in some instances satisfactory solutions may not yet be available.

Chapter Nine

Conclusions

Few people can say that they feel completely secure. There always seems to be uncertainties. Technologies of all kinds are built to ameliorate risks, and the technology associated with the topic of 'security' attempts to protect things of value and in digital systems things of value are always reducible to collections of bits. This is convenient because it allows security techniques to be built on long-established and thoroughly explored mathematical results. These mathematical results can give assurances about how difficult it is to thwart the techniques and provide clues for new applications.

Mathematics, though, is a developing subject. New results are continually emerging and hence the conclusions that can be drawn about specific techniques will change. There is always a risk that a mathematical discovery will invalidate an existing technique and new procedures will have to be adopted. But mathematics is only a component and developments elsewhere also pose threats to the security of digital systems. Certainly, as the capability of computational technology has improved, the feasibility of breaking into once secure installations has emerged. Security specialists must therefore respond and exploit the improved performance of computer technology to provide tougher challenges to those threatening security.

As more and more valuable data is stored and communicated, so the temptations to breach security grow. This is bound to attract more effort to the subversion of computer systems and this effort is likely to expose new kinds of weaknesses and pose new kinds of threats. Security techniques, therefore, have to also respond to evolving threats.

Security in digital systems brings an overhead. Encryption involves performing computations, which can slow down communications as additional data is communicated to demonstrate the integrity and authenticity of data. Computers relay messages confirming the identity of communicating partners. All these measures absorb communication and computational resources and, perhaps, reduce the resources available for other computations and communications.

Security techniques are deployed in a climate of evolving technology, mathematics and threats. And a response requires the expenditure of effort and finance that will, no doubt, need to be justified at some time or another. Beyond the technical details of encryption calculations and the design of robust protocols there is a need to assess threats and the cost of countering them and also to weigh up the relative severity of quite different kinds of security breaches and quite different kinds of security measures.

The technical details of encryption and the intricacies of protocols described in this book should be looked at in a wider perspective. Ultimately, the aim is make people feel more secure and limit the infringement of one another's rights.

The likelihood that providing one group with security will undermine the security of another implies that there may be no satisfactory resolution, and that issues of security will always be a part of a controversy. And in such controversies persuasive powers are often more effective than technical devices.

References and Notes

1   Schneier, B. (1995) *Applied Cryptography*, New York, Wiley, is an extensive treatise on computer security and contains copious references.

2   von Clausewitz, C. (1968) *On War* (*Vom Kriege*), Harmondsworth, England, Penguin, Rapoport, Anatol (ed.), Book III, Chapter IX, p. 270. First published in 1832, edited originally by Col. F.N. Maude, Pelican edition translated by Col. J.J. Graham.

3   *Ibid.*, Book III, Chapter IX, p.269.

4   *Ibid.*, Book III, Chapter IX, p.269.

5   *Ibid.*, Book III, Chapter X, p.274.

6   *Ibid.*, Book I, Chapter VI, p.162.

7   *Ibid.*, Book I, Chapter VI, p.162.

8   Shannon, C.E. (1949) 'Communication theory of secrecy systems', *Bell Systems Technical Journal*, pp.656–715.

9   Vernam, G.S. (1926) 'Cipher printing telegraph systems for secret wire and radio telegraphic communications', *Journal of the American Institute of Electrical Engineers*, February, pp.109–115.

10 *Ibid.*

11 *Ibid.*

12 Kahn, D. (1977) *The Codebreakers*, New York, Scribner, p.82.

13 *Ibid.*

14 *Ibid.*, pp.775–776.

15 Lewis Carroll, for instance, created an alphabet cipher in 1868 that is reproduced in Carroll, L. (1939) *The Complete Works of Lewis Carroll*, London, Nonesuch Library, pp.1156–1157.

16 Robert Harris, for example, wrote an exciting fictionalized account of events surrounding codebreaking in Britain in the Second World War. It is published in Harris, R. (1996) *Enigma*, London, Arrow.

17 Kerckhoffs was given the name Jean Guillaume-Hubert-Victor-François-Alexandre-Auguste Kerckhoffs; mercifully for us he shortened it to Auguste Kerckhoffs.

18 Kahn, p.235.

19   Tapscott, D. (1996) *The Digital Economy, Promise and Peril in the Age of Networked Intelligence*, New York, McGraw Hill, p.11.

20   Floridi, L. (1999) *Philosophy and Computing*, London, Routledge, p.4.

21   Gates, W.H. (1999) *Business@the Speed of Thought*, London, Penguin, p.154.

22   Williams, F. (1999) 'WIPO takes up the challenge', *Financial Times*, 17 September 1999, p.7.

23   Floridi, p.1.

24   Gates, p.xvi.

25   Glynn, M. (2000) 'Strong e-arm of the law', *Financial Times*, 29 June 2000, p.22.

26   Stefik, M. (1997) 'Trusted systems', *Scientific American*, vol. 276, no. 3, March, pp.87–81.

27   Nichols, K. (1999) 'The age of software patents', *IEEE Computer*, April, pp.25–31.

28   Gates, p.363.

29   Morris, R.H. and Thompson, K. (1979) 'Password security: a case history', *Communications of the ACM*, 22(11), November, pp.594–597.

30   Affadavit by D. Whalley, 'McConville & others v. Barclays Bank & others' (1992) High Court of Justice, Queen's Bench Division, ORB no. 812, reported in Andersen, R. (1993) 'Why cryptosystems fail', *Proceedings of the 1st Conference on Computer and Communications Security*, ACM.

31   Security systems have significance in war and in peacetime. What counts as justice is liable to be different in different political circumstances.

32   Meredith, M. (2000) *San Francisco Chronicle*, 15 June 2000, p.A26.

33   *Boston Globe*, 9 March 2000.

34   *Boston Globe*, 10 March 2000.

35   Kahn, pp.631–632.

36   Regina v. Stone and Hider (July 1991) Winchester Crown Court, reported in Andersen, R. (1993) 'Why cryptosystems fail', *Proceedings of the 1st Conference on Computer and Communications Security*, ACM.

37   Spafford, E.H. (1989) 'The Internet worm: crisis and aftermath', *Commuications of the ACM*, vol. 32, no. 6, pp.678–687.

38   *Ibid.*

39 *Ibid.*

40 Grampp, F.T. and Morris, R.H. (1984) 'UNIX operating system security', *AT&T Bell Laboratories Technical Journal*, vol. 63, no. 8, October, part 2, pp. 1649–1672.

41 *Ibid.*

42 Klein, D.V. (1990) 'Foiling the cracker: a survey of, and improvements to, password security', *Proceedings of the USENIX Second Security Workshop Program.*

43 Stoll, C. (1991) *The Cuckoo's Egg*, Pan, London, p.30

44 *Ibid.*, p.29.

45 *Ibid.*, p.30.

46 Some systems which allow several users to have separate accounts, have a special protected account known as 'root'. In such systems a nefarious user defeating the security measures and gaining access to the 'root' account can manipulate any files on the computer.

47 Cheswick, W. and Bellovin, S. (1994) *Firewalls and Internet Security: Repelling the wily hacker*, Addison-Wesley, Reading, Massachusetts, Chapter 10 An evening with Berferd.

48 Howard, J.D. (1997) *An Analysis of Security Incidents on the Internet 1989–1995*, Doctor of Philosophy Dissertation, 7 April 1997, Carnegie Mellon University, Section 8.4.

49 *Ibid.*, subsection 14.2.1.

50 Stoll, p.100.

51 *Ibid.*, p.103.

52 *Ibid.*, p.15.

53 *Ibid.*, p.31.

54 Morris, R.H. and Thompson, K.

55 Wilkes, M.V. (1968) *Time-Sharing Computer Systems*, New York American Elsevier, p.91.

56 Stoll, p.32.

57 *Ibid.*, p.47.

58 *Ibid.*, p.47.

59 *Ibid.*, pp.159–160.

60 *Ibid.*, pp.159–160.

61 *Ibid.*, p.272.

62 *Ibid.*, p.222.

63 *Ibid.*, p.223.

64 *Ibid.*, p.107.

65 *Ibid.*, p.122.

66 *Ibid.*, p.271.

67 *Ibid.*, p.216.

68 *Ibid.*, p.47.

69 *Ibid.*, p.225.

70 *Ibid.*, p.229.

71 *Ibid.*, pp.55–56.

72 Kahn, p.235.

73 Vernam.

74 Stoll.

75 Cyriax, R.J. (1947) 'The Collinson cryptograms' in *The Times*, Notes & Queries, CXCII, 20 July 1947, pp.322–323.

76 Collinson, R. (1889) *Journal of H.M.S. Enterprise*, London, p.337.

77 Klein.

78 Katzenbeisser, S. and Petitcolas, F.A.P. (eds) (2000) *Information Hiding Techniques for Steganography and Digital Watermarking*, Norwood Massachusetts, Artech House/Horizon, a book dedicated to the topic of steganography.

79 Kahn, p.763.

80 For example $(3 + 2) + 5$ is $5 + 5$ or 10, and $3 + (2 + 5)$ is $3 + 7$, which is also 10. However, division does not have this property: for example $(16/4)/2$ is $4/2$ or 2, but $16/(4/2)$ is $16/2$ or 8.

81 Shelley, M.W. (1912) *Frankenstein, or, the Modern Prometheus*, London, J.M. Dent and Son.

82 The decryption key is 23 and the message is, again forlornly, 'Why do you cot come or write for me? Such grief and adxiery! Oh! Love Love'. Again there are one or two typographical errors. This time 'e' is not the most frequent letter, but 'o' is.

83 The first line in the picture of Figure 11 was derived from the original sequence 0,0,3,31,16,0,0,0 … The numbers in this sequence encrypted using a key of 22 and a modulus of 32 produce the following results

$$0 + 22 \equiv 22 \bmod 32$$
$$3 + 22 \equiv 25 \bmod 32$$
$$31 + 22 \equiv 53 \equiv 53 - 32 \equiv 21 \bmod 32$$
$$16 + 22 \equiv 38 \equiv 38 - 32 \equiv 6 \bmod 32$$

The first row of the encrypted coded picture is given by the sequence

$$22, 22, 25, 21, 6, 22, 22, 22, \ldots$$

Which is next converted to 0s and 1s. Each number is treated as though it were composed of the sum of numbers taken from 16, 8, 4, 2 and 1. 22 can be written as 16+4+2. Or using the convention that a 1 in the leftmost position stands for 16, a 1 in the next position stands for 8 and so on I get 10110. Then using black for 1 and white for zero I get the sequence black, white, black, black, white which is in the top left hand corner of Figure 11. The other cells are coded in a similar fashion.

25 is 16+8+1 becomes 11001 or black, black, white, white, black
21 is 16+4+1 becomes 10101 or black, white, black, white, black
16 is 4+2 which becomes 00110 or white, white, black, black, white

84 Strictly the Euler–Fermat Theorem states that $x^{\phi(n)} \equiv 1 \bmod n$, provided n and x are coprime.

85 Singh, S. (1999) *The Code Book*, London, Fourth Estate, pp.279–292, gives an account of the British efforts.

86 Anon. (1854) *Quarterly Review*, XCV, June, pp.118–164.

87 Abadi, M. and Needham, R. (1994) 'Prudent engineering practice for cryptographic protocols', *SRC Research Report 125*, 1 June 1994, Systems Research Center, 130 Lytton Avenue, Palo Alto, California.

88 This text has been encoded as a number, encrypted using exponentiation with a modulus of 30658690608014475618985033 and using the key 98795864114076633705209 then recoded in letters.

89 Coding each letter by its position in the alphabet gives the sequence:

$$2, 4, 0, 18, 4$$

This is then coded into a single number by multiplying each item by a power of 26 and adding up the result. The calculation is of the form:

$$2 \times 26^4 + 4 \times 26^3 + 0 \times 26^2 + 18 \times 26 + 4$$

Clearly, a calculation best done using a computer!

90 The largest number created by a five-letter group is generated by the string *ZZZZZ* which yields the code:

$$25 \times 26^4 + 25 \times 26^3 + 25 \times 26^2 + 25 \times 26 + 25 = 11881375$$

91   Again, each letter is coded by its position in the alphabet. The first group for example, MEETM, yields the sequence:

$$12, 4, 4, 19, 12$$

This is then coded into a single number by multiplying each item by a power of 26 and adding up the result. The calculation is of the form:

$$12 \times 26^4 + 4 \times 26^3 + 4 \times 26^2 + 19 \times 26 + 12 = 5557226$$

92   Actually, from what can be gleaned from most of the security literature, Alice and Bob's relationship is probably purely platonic. Ian, though, could still be jealous of their close relationship.

93   Lewis, B. (1993) 'How to rob a bank the cash card way', *Sunday Telegraph*, 25 April 1993, p.5.

94   Modulo 17 it is!

95   Anderson, R. and Needham, R. (1995) 'Programming Satan's computer', in J. van Leeuwen (ed.) *Computer Science Today – Recent Trends and Developments*, Springer LNCS, v 1000, pp 426–440.

96   Anderson, R. (1993) 'Why cryptosystems fail', *Proceedings of the 1st Conference on Computer and Communications Security*, ACM.

97   Abadi. M. and Needham, R. (1994) 'Prudent engineering practice for cryptographic protocols', *SRC Research Report 125*, Systems Research Center, 130 Lytton Avenue, Palo Alto, California, 1 June 1994, p.1.

98   Burrows, M., Abadi, M. and Needham, R.M. (1989) 'A logic of authentication', *Proceedings of the Royal Society of London*, A, vol. 426, pp.233–271. A further vulnerability was pointed out in Lowe, G. (1995) 'An attack on the Needham–Schroeder public-key authentication protocol', *Information Processing Letters*, vol. 56, no. 3, pp.131–133.

99   Needham, R.M. and Schroeder, M.D. (1978) 'Using encryption for authentication in large networks of computers', *Communications of the ACM*, vol. 21, no. 12, December, pp.993–999.

100   Goldwasser, S. and Bellare, M. (1996) Lecture notes in cryptography, MIT summer course on cryptography, July, p.123.

101   At least in the ways I have described. Vince and his gang may have found a lucrative niche and will be working at ways of shifting the blame with this new protocol. In the meantime, when Vince gets caught he might quickly revoke his private key and claim that he thought someone had stolen it and then forged the transcript.

102 Haber, S. and Scott Stornetta, W. (1991) 'How to time-stamp a digital document', *Journal of Cryptography*, vol. 3, no. 2, pp.99–111. Also, Bayer, D., Haber, S. and Scott Stornetta, W. (1993) 'Improving the efficiency and reliability of digital time-stamping', in Capocelli, R.M., De Santis, A. and Vaccaro (eds) *Sequences II: Methods in Communication, Security, and Computer Science*, New York, Springer, pp.329–334.

103 Diffie, W. and Hellman, M.E. (1976) 'New directions in cryptography', *IEEE Transactions on Information Theory*, vol. IT22, November, pp.644–654.

104 This protocol is derived from Diffie, W., VanOorschot, P. and Wiener, M. (1992) *Authentication and Authenticated Key Exchanges, Designs Codes and Cryptography*, vol. 2, no. 2, June, pp.107–125.

105 This has been derived from the protocol described in Bellare, M. and Rogaway, P. (1995) 'Provably secure session key distribution – the three party case protection', *Proceedings, 27th Symposium of the Theory of Computing, Las Vegas, Association for Computing Machinery, 1995*, pp.57–66.

106 Perhaps it is not a cause for concern, but it is said that Orpheus lulled Cerberus to sleep by playing his lyre and, on another occasion, a Sybil doped Cerberus with a cake made with poppies and honey.

107 Kohl, J. and Neuman, C. (1993) 'The Kerberos Network Authentication Service (V5)', RFC 1510, September 1993.

108 Denning, D. and Sacco, G. (1981) 'Time-stamps in key distribution protocols', *Communications of the ACM*, vol. 24, no. 8, August, pp.533–536.

109 Reported in Anderson, R. and Needham, R. (1995) 'Programming Satan's computer', in J. van Leeuwen (ed.) *Computer Science Today*, Springer-Verlag. Martin Abadi found the flaw.

110 Chaum, D., Fiat, A. and Naor, M. (1990) 'Untraceable electronic cash', in: *Advances in Cryptology – Crypto '88 Proceedings*, Berlin , Springer-Verlag, pp.319–327.

111 This is called blinding and is also described in subsection 8.2.4.

112 The SET protocols are specified by a company, Secure Electronic Transaction LLC set up by major credit card organizations. The protocol presented here was inspired by the SET protocols but is simplified.

113 Many of the issues are spelled out in Stajano, F. and Anderson, R. (1999) 'The cocaine auction protocol: on the power of anonymous broadcast', in Pfitzmann, A. (ed.) *Proceedings of Information Hiding Workshop, Dresden, 1999*, Berlin, Springer-Verlag.

114 To perform the arithmetic on $3 - 18$ it first looks as though the result requires a larger number to be subtracted from a smaller one. But with modular arithmetic I can always add the modulus, which in this case is 19, and the result will be congruent with the original expression. So I can change the calculation to $19 + 3 - 18$ without affecting the result. This is $22 - 18$, and the final result is 4.

Index